INK-STAINED AMAZONS
AND
CINEMATIC WARRIORS

"Female heroes abound in literature, film and all walks of life, although most people don't know that they do. Not surprising given how much they challenge the gender roles in which women and girls have historically been confined. This wonderful book shows female heroes breaking out of gender boxes left and right and illuminates new possibilities for the indomitable hero in all of us."

—Kathleen Noble, Ph.D., author of *The Sound of the Silver Horn: Reclaiming the heroism in contemporary women's lives*

"Once upon a time—only a few years ago, actually—women could turn on their TV sets and glory in the adventures of Buffy, Xena, Sydney Bristow, Dana Scully, and many more strong, ass-kicking women. Today there is not one show on the small screen that stars a female action hero. What happened? Comics are not much better. Aside from the occasional exception (for which we are grateful) like *Birds of Prey*, and women writers like Ivory Madison (*The Huntress*) and Gail Simone's newly feminist interpretation of Wonder Woman, most comic book action heroines continue to be male-written and drawn creations whose breasts are bigger than their personalities.

Now along comes Jennifer Stuller, with her very entertaining book, *Ink-stained Amazons and Cinematic Warriors*, to explore the whys and wherefores of pop culture super women, and perhaps jolt us all into demanding more and stronger women characters. Thank you, Jennifer. We need those role models!"

—Trina Robbins, author of *The Great American Superheroines*

INK-STAINED AMAZONS
AND
CINEMATIC WARRIORS

Superwomen in Modern Mythology

Jennifer K. Stuller

I.B. TAURIS
LONDON · NEW YORK

Published in 2010 by I.B.Tauris & Co Ltd
6 Salem Road, London W2 4BU
175 Fifth Avenue, New York NY 10010
www.ibtauris.com

Distributed in the United States and Canada Exclusively by Palgrave Macmillan
175 Fifth Avenue, New York NY 10010

ISBN: 978 1 84511 965 2

A full CIP record for this book is available from the British Library
A full CIP record is available from the Library of Congress

Library of Congress Catalog Card Number: available

Typeset in AGaramond by Macmillan Publishing Solutions
Printed and bound in India by Thomson Press India Ltd

For Ryan
You are the Superman to my Superwoman

Contents

Foreword

A lot of people disapprove of female superheroes.

I am not just talking about other characters in the fictional worlds in which they exist—policemen who regard them as lawless vigilantes or headmasters who think they neglect their studies or parents who would rather they stopped. I am thinking about critics who worry that they are just an escapist way to avoid acknowledging female oppression in the real world, or a way for middle-aged men to fetishize young fit female bodies—and that's just people on the side of progress and justice. Back in the 1950s, Frederic Wertham disapproved most strongly of the only female superhero he knew about. He saw Wonder Woman's strength and independence as unhealthy and her friendship with women aviators as coded propaganda for lesbianism—and assumed that this was a bad thing.

One of the reasons why people want heroes is that they feel—often with good reason—that they are powerless in their daily lives; being able to dream of people for whom that condition is absent or different is a first step to taking steps to improve your own reality. Wonder Woman's creator William Moulton Marston saw her, quite specifically, as a way of encouraging young women to think about their own autonomy and ambitions, and the rise of second wave feminism has been paralleled at every turn by the creation of inspirational women characters in film, television, and comics. Jennifer Stuller's study documents their irresistible rise, but also defends them passionately as subjects for critical attention.

She is as eloquent about the classic leather jump-suited heroines of the pop 1960s as she is about more recent figures—there is a line of descent here from Honor Blackman's Cathy Gale and Diana Rigg's Emma Peel through to more recent characters like Jennifer Garner's Sydney Bristow in *Alias*. She is excellent on a selection of female superheroes from comics—Wonder Women in her various incarnations, in particular.

Like a lot of people, I was drawn to this area of the study of popular culture by Joss Whedon's Buffy and by his other strong female characters like Faith, Willow, and Cordelia; Faith's reference to herself and Buffy as "hot

x

chicks with superpowers" could almost have been a subtitle to *Ink-stained Amazons*. (I first encountered parts of this book in a presentation that Stuller did at the Slayage Buffy Studies conference in Barnesville, Georgia, and was instantly struck by the usefulness of her discussion.) Here she provides the study of Buffy, Xena, Ripley, and the other most-studied female superheroes with a historical and cultural context; this is an invaluable overview to the way modern women have been provided with this particularly empowering set of dreams.

—*Roz Kaveney*

Acknowledgments

When I first started this book, my friend Holly reminded me that it wasn't something I'd go through alone. "Haven't you ever seen the Acknowledgments page of a book?" she asked, adding, "A published book is ultimately the accomplishment of many people."

How true.

So many thanks are in order to the people who believed in me, encouraged me, took a chance on me, and have helped make this very personal project a reality. Thanks initially to Amy Peloff and Dr. Katherine Noble who almost simultaneously encouraged me to write a proposal for a book on female heroes. And thanks again to Amy for being my co-Slayer-in-Training and for bringing me Sophia and hugs—you make sure I never have to fight the forces of darkness alone.

Thanks to my Daddy, who also wrote a book over the past two years, for his support both commiserative and pragmatic.

Thanks to Roz Kaveney and Philippa Brewster for taking a chance on me. I'm grateful for Roz's input and Foreword, but most of all for her friendship. My gratitude also extends to Philippa's editorial advice and for her help in pushing me to shape this book into a thoughtful piece of work.

Thanks to Trina Robbins, who has taught me the meaning of "sisterhood," and to Anne Timmons and Margot Kidder for their generous time (also to Orion for his generous offer).

My gratitude extends again to Kate Noble, as well as to Phillip Thurtle and Ruby Blondell, for encouraging and supporting my research interests and for their mentorship on projects that led to various chapters within this book.

Thanks to Angela Ndalianis, Peter Coogan, Randy Duncan, David Lavery, and Rhonda Wilcox for inviting me to participate in conferences, allowing me to further my studies and make valuable connections.

A quick shout-out to Lorna Jowett is in order for convincing me *Dark Angel* was worthy of another look and that it spoke to the very themes I was interested in and concerned about.

To my writergrrrls, Lisa Farino and Rachel Bravmann, for their practical and emotional support—a special thanks to Rache for her thoughtful editorial advice and kind check-ins.

Thanks to the 84th Street crew for periodically stopping by to check on my progress and my spirits. I feel blessed to be part of such a warm community.

As I am certainly not the first woman to be curious about female representation in modern myth, I must sincerely stress my indebtedness to the works of herstorian Trina Robbins; scholars Kate Noble, Ruby Blondell, and Rhonda Wilcox; and cultural critic Roz Kaveney. Like the mythic characters that will be addressed in these chapters, I too am standing on the shoulders of Amazons before me.

And finally, to my husband Ryan—it's true what Virginia Woolf said about how in order to write, one needs money and a room of one's own. You have provided me with these two essential things, but also so much more. I love you more than I can ever say.

Introduction

*Everybody loves a hero. People line up for them, cheer them, scream their
names. And years later, they'll tell how they stood in the rain for hours just
to get a glimpse of the one who taught them how to hold on a second longer.
I believe there's a hero in all of us, that keeps us honest, gives us strength,
makes us noble, and finally allows us to die with pride.*

—*Spider-Man 2*

In Sam Raimi's 2002 film, *Spider-Man 2*, Aunt May tells her nephew, Peter
Parker, that she believes "there's a hero in all of us." If this is true, what
happens to our social consciousness if the presence of our mythic heroes
is—and has always been—overwhelmingly male? In a world where many
young girls would rather be Harry Potter than Hermione—or Peter Parker
than Mary Jane Watson—I often wonder where our "Wonder Women" are.

Well . . . there have been a few.

As a little girl in the 1970s, I adored the televised *Wonder Woman* series.
Each time the ever-graceful Lynda Carter transformed herself from Diana
Prince into the Amazon Princess by holding out her arms and spinning
from her alias into her true identity, my younger sister and I would hop
up out of our seats to twirl along with her. We hoped that by mimicking
her magic we too could possess the admirable powers of justice and truth,
compassion and love. Carter's pirouettes look a bit silly in retrospect, but as
a child, they meant possibility. My sister and I may never be endowed with
superpowers, though like all children, we certainly hoped we would be, and
as adults secretly still do. But seeing Wonder Woman's acts of bravery and
kindness, her reaching beyond the everyday, allowed us to see the potential
in ourselves.

Wonder Woman was joined by *Charlie's Angels* and *The Bionic Woman*,
each series an attempt to capitalize on the women's liberation movement of

the 1970s. In the subsequent backlash years of the 1980s, superwomen in modern myth enjoyed a sporadic presence at best, though the revitalized *Star Trek* franchise did feature women in positions of authority and leadership, such as Chief of Security Lieutenant Tasha Yar and Dr. Beverly Crusher. *She-Ra: Princess of Power*, a spin-off of the animated series *He-Man and the Masters of the Universe*, as well as Princess Leia of the *Star Wars* movies, showed young girls they could aspire to power—if they were royalty. The strongest women on American television were career women Murphy Brown and Claire Huxtable. While groundbreaking in their respective ways, they weren't exactly mythic—or even capable of more-than-human acts.

The Uncanny X-Men comics, as written by Chris Claremont, featured prominent females, including original member Jean Grey, as well as new characters Ororo Munroe, and her protégée Kitty Pryde. But superhero comics have not traditionally been written with a female audience in mind. The powers that be in the comics industry assume that girls don't read superhero comics, because they don't typically buy superhero comics, and therefore publications in that genre aren't typically made for girls. Needless to say, it's a tired cycle that many fans (and several creators) are still working to break.

Movie representations of superwomen historically haven't fared much better than their four-color sisters of the printed page. In the 1980s and early 1990s, action heroines Sarah Connor of the *Terminator* films, Ellen Ripley of the *Alien* franchise, and arguably, to an extent, Charly Baltimore of *The Long Kiss Goodnight* and Nikita of *La Femme Nikita*, were the proud few to infiltrate what continues to remain a male-dominated genre. Each of these characters left her mark in a revolutionary way, and yet each was also limited by socially accepted gender stereotypes that kept her from being radically progressive. To this day, superhero movies still focus on male characters, with women in the supportive roles of nurturer and love interest.

The few superhero films that do feature female leads have failed miserably at the box office; infamous examples *Elektra* and *Catwoman* were received with great negativity. But unlike *Spider-Man*, *X-Men*, or *Superman Returns*, these films were poorly, shamefully, and embarrassingly produced. Regardless of the lack of attention to the source material (which is often problematic to begin with), it's the lack of monetary success that captures a studio's attention, framing further disinterest in committing proper resources to female-centric projects. As in the comics industry, the powers that be assume audiences aren't interested in superwomen when, in fact, they just aren't interested in subpar movies about superheroes.

This lack of heroic female role models in popular culture can be distressing for a little girl, as well as for a grown woman. We're shown too many images of us as beauty queens, femme fatales, vixens, girlfriends, mothers, and damsels in need of rescuing. We *can* be these things, but we can also be more.

In the late 1990s, two serendipitous things happened on a personal level that led to the book you hold before you. I came to realize that even if they appear scarce, superwomen do exist—and not just as someone's expendable love interest or second-rate sidekick.

The first was that I met my husband, a man who had grown up fascinated by the stories surrounding both comics and their creators—something that as a woman I hadn't had much exposure to. Sure I'd watched *Wonder Woman*, and other television series based on comics, but my own experience with print comics was limited to the *Archies* tantalizingly placed at child's-eye level in the checkout line at the supermarket.[1]

So whenever we watched a superheroic film, be it *X-Men*, or *Spider-Man*, he would give me the full background mythos of the various characters. I learned what happens to a man when he has been bitten by a radioactive spider, and about the crucial difference between organic and manufactured web-slingers. I heard stories about the mutant threat and the dangers of angering a man who had previously been exposed to gamma rays. Listening to the stories he told, with their themes of loss, love, and redemption, I began to appreciate these tales on a new level and finally recognized that superhero stories are American culture's modern expression of myth.

Modern myth serves a function similar to that of ancient myth, namely, telling and hearing stories helps us make sense of our lives. Narratives reflect the world and comment on it as they document events and also imagine them. Stories meditate on human behavior and interrogate the meaning of big ideas: Good and Evil, Morality, Spirituality, Justice, Relationships, Community, Power, and Love. The same basic themes our ancestors contemplated, crafted to be relevant to *their* particular and specific time, place, and cultures, are continually revisited through the ages, part of humanity's endless search for meaning.

Myths can be fantasy and they can be real, and sometimes, they are reality wrapped in metaphor and thus used as a way of teaching values. Recognizable character types such as the Hero, the Mother, the Father, the Sidekick, the Trickster, and the Villain—which according to Carl Gustav Jung were a global phenomena embedded in the human unconscious—give us ideas about who we are, and who we do or do not want to be. When these archetypes—as Jung termed them—are used in stories they can teach us about our socially appropriate roles, how we fit into our communities, and about our human potential, both terrible and great.[2]

Archetypal themes and big ideas may retain their significance for any given culture, but the ways stories are told and characters presented must evolve as a particular society does. For example, myths were once part of an oral tradition, and then they were expressed through the written word. Later, we were able to experience the wonder of the world through cinema, radio, comic books, and television—and all of these are where we can find our modern mythology.

In light of this, it was troublesome to me that although women's roles have evolved, and in fact, female *and* male roles have changed, modern hero stories, like those of classic world myth, continue to focus on male experience and fantasy; and that women in these stories continue to fill the supporting roles of mothers, wives, temptresses, and goddesses. Additionally, because heroism is often confined to power fantasies, there is little room for female experiences to be considered heroic.

Now, not every audience will be able to identify with *Star War's* Luke Skywalker in his quest—even though he follows the archetypal hero's journey. But, we *all* need to be able to imagine that we are capable of destroying the Empire and saving the galaxy from oppression. Certainly, many humans have at times felt powerless, perhaps, to use an ancient example, like the mythic David, small and standing up against a world of Goliaths. We want to believe we are capable of phenomenal acts and we need stories to teach us that, indeed, no matter our gender, race, sexual preference, or physical challenges, we can be heroes.

As my curiosity was piqued, serendipity again stepped in. The second marker on my path to this book was that female superheroes began to appear on television screens in numbers I hadn't seen since I was a little girl. First came *Xena, Warrior Princess*, and soon after, *Buffy the Vampire Slayer*. Both had (and continue to possess) cult appeal, but the characters were also impressive enough to make their way into a larger social consciousness. They became icons, with a popularity and marketability that enabled the presence of even more female heroes in popular entertainment media.[3]

A combination of watching these innovative series and contemplating the stories my husband had shared led me to wonder about the history of superwomen in modern mythology. Buffy and Xena may be relatively well-known, but who are the overlooked, or at least quietly celebrated, characters? Where can we find stories about female agency and adventure? What about *our* feats of physical strength and our personal growth?

Wanting answers, I began to chronicle a history, which ultimately became Section I of this book, "Standing on the Shoulders of Amazons." This begins in the late 1930s and highlights characters from American popular culture, as well as a few British and East Asian influences, all the way from

Lois Lane and Wonder Woman up to the currently running (at time of writing) superwomen of television's *Heroes*.

This history, of course, cannot be all-inclusive. Throughout the book, when I have addressed a television show or film series, I have generally included the entire series as a complete text (and when I haven't I've noted otherwise). When I've mentioned a comic character, it has been in terms of a particular incarnation, story arc, or writer to make a point about a larger theme.[4] Those who are sticklers about canon will note that "retcons"—a narrative tactic that retroactively alters a previous story arc to change current continuity—may negate or alter a point that I have made. This is why I want to stress that while a character's history may be addressed, this book is about common narratives that recur in representations of heroic women. And there is always room for more histories, revised editions, and so on—especially as I hope this book inspires women to go out and study modern mythic women, as well as create them.

So, what *is* a superwoman?

She can be a spy, a secret agent, an assassin, a detective, a witch, a reporter, or a superhero. She becomes super by surpassing the limits of the human body and mind, either through rigorous training, an industrial accident, by virtue of being an alien, mutation, or advanced evolution.

Sometimes a woman is destined to be super. She can be prophesized and called to duty, or she can be created in a lab. She can be an Ink-stained Amazon gracing the pages of comics, or a warrior woman of the digital or silver screens.

For the purposes of consistency in this book, each of the characters I've chosen have, more often than not, met at least two of the four criteria, discussed in the following sections.

The Narrative Borrows from, or Resonates with, Classical Themes and/or Elements of World Mythology

Many serials, be they print, digital or film, have complex mythologies that appropriate and blend classic tropes, legendary quests, and symbolic archetypes.

Wonder Woman and *Xena, Warrior Princess* borrow from a combination of ancient Greek and Roman mythology to create hybrids of classic tales and modern politics, while series *Alias* and *Heroes* strive to establish their own unique mythos, with much less overt reliance upon the stories of our common past.

Regardless of the source material, these mythic stories transcend everyday experience. They tap into a larger tradition of storytelling that for millennia has allowed humans to fantasize about our potential. We see recognizable characters that are often the embodiment of an idea or an ideal, and because we so readily identify with them, their stories allow us to vicariously experience the extra-ordinary.

An Element of the Fantastic

Superwomen generally are involved in paranormal, mythic, or magical circumstances. It's important to note that in these types of stories "magic" is often translated into, or conflated with, science.

Agent Dana Scully of *The X-Files* frequently encountered fantastic circumstances. The extraterrestrial phenomena, religious mysticism, telepathy, extrasensory perception, and other acts of transcendence, which were the foundation of her investigations, forced her, and us, to suspend disbelief and engage with the extraordinary.

On *Buffy the Vampire Slayer*, Willow Rosenberg was adept at both science and magic. Though she was not the lead character, her contributions to the good fight were just as important as Buffy's.

Buffy herself had prophetic dreams, and Veronica Mars of *Veronica Mars* had slightly paranormal, if haunted, dreams that aided her investigations.

The birth of *Alias*'s Sydney Bristow was prophesized in the fifteenth century by the fictional Milo Rambaldi—a combination of Nostradamus and Leonardo da Vinci.

A Uniquely Identifiable Skill or Power

As noted above, superwomen are uncannily good at something that allows them to accomplish their tasks—often with flourish. Their capabilities are usually achieved through a combination of innate ability and intense training.

Each of the Potentials on *Buffy* could become the Slayer—a warrior girl of superstrength, precognitive dreams, and accelerated healing. But it is the skills they gain by rigorous practice that see them through their greatest battle.

CIA agent, Sydney Bristow, has a preternatural capacity for language, but was also schooled from an early age in espionage. Dr. Catherine Gale and Mrs. Emma Peel are extraordinarily intelligent and champions in martial arts. And though often the damsel-in-distress, Lois Lane's trademark moxie, and skill with the written word, has made her name practically synonymous with "investigative journalism."

A Mission or Purpose That Benefits the Greater Good

Finally, a superwoman must use her skills for good, otherwise she has the capacity to become a supervillain.[5] As Roz Kaveney points out in her book *Superheroes!*, "The mission is an important defining characteristic, as much so as [a superhero's] powers." It is this devotion to the mission that enables us to cast our widest net when identifying superwomen, because, as Kaveney notes, people who lack the traditional powers associated with superheroes are still generally considered superheroic if they share a commitment to the superhero mission of fighting for "truth, justice, and the protection of the innocent."[6]

This mission can be the altruistic teachings of Wonder Woman, or Sarah Connor protecting the savior of humanity (who also happens to be an innocent—her child). It can be Ororo Munroe and Jean Grey of the *X-Men*, offering their services at the very school that taught them, or The Powerpuff Girls saving the world before their bedtime.

* * *

Having identified the characters that meet these essential characteristics, and thus providing a comprehensive history of superwomen from the 1940s to the present day, we can better see the events that sparked their arrival, as well as the effects they did—or didn't—have on popular culture and consciousness. It's a fascinating question: How do stories reflect a changing society, and what effect do representations of gender have on social consciousness? Eccentric psychologist William Moulton Marston believed that young women needed to see a heroic image of themselves, and so created *Wonder Woman*. Sixty years later, writer, director, and feminist activist Joss Whedon said, "If I made a series of lectures on PBS on why there should be feminism, no one would be coming to the party, and it would be boring. The idea of changing culture is important to me and it can only be done in a popular medium."[7]

Whedon believes, as Marston did, in changing men's ideas about women, and women's ideas about what they are capable of, by using the power of storytelling. But both Wonder Woman and Buffy Summers were also enabled by the political trends of their time. Wonder Woman symbolized women's participation in the American homefront industry during the Second World War—a time when superheroes were the embodiment of American patriotism. But after the Rosie the Riveter era, post-war women, both mythic and real, were returned to the domestic sphere. And Buffy both grew out of, and spurred on, the Grrrl Power movement of the 1990s—a part of what some refer to as the Third Wave of Feminism.

Clearly, there have been progressive flows tempered with regressive ebbs in representations of superwomen in popular culture. But when chronicling characters in a linear history, a cyclic pattern appears of a progression, followed by the inevitable attempts to capitalize with copycats. Then there is typically a regression, or even an outright backlash, then an absence, again followed by the appearance of one or two influential characters and a repeat of the process.

Section II of this book, "Journey of the Female Hero," explores themes that are consistently present in representations of superwomen. The common narratives, motives, and character attributes addressed are the results of numerous and varied influences, including tropes from ancient storytelling, archetypal images, politics, cultural stereotypes about sex and gender, and occasionally, zeitgeist.

Themes to be covered in these chapters include feelings of love and acts of compassion. Be it maternal, romantic, or platonic, love has often been the motivating impetus for women. And it is perhaps because of this that female heroes are often shown working in tandem, either as a team, or as the sidekick to the professionally superior male (i.e., Dana Scully to Fox Mulder on *The X-Files*). This could easily be interpreted as a way of containing women's power by only depicting them in more traditional roles, that is, "mother," "love interest," or "assistant." It could also be suggested that a solo woman warrior is still too outrageous to be taken seriously and therefore requires assistance in her heroic ventures.

While readings like these may occasionally be the case, superwomen have also revolutionized depictions of collaboration in contemporary heroic narrative for women *and* for men.

Generally, teams of male heroes are brought together by chance (The A-Team) or because of convenience (The Justice League of America). They participate in missions together, simply because it's pragmatic to combine their skills. But women's desire for companionship (as with Xena and Gabrielle) and tendency to support and nourish the skills of those around them (as with Buffy) has raised the status of cohorts, teammates, and sidekicks. As scholar and educator Sharon Ross has noted, modern superwomen "are not heroes for other women so much as they are heroes *with* them."[8]

Whether these traits are innate or not, my purpose is to argue for deeper, more complex, and even multivalent readings. Our relationship with how gender is represented in popular culture will probably never be comfortable—and it most likely shouldn't be. But just because an image is-n't progressively satisfying, it doesn't mean there isn't pleasure or empower-ment to be found. Conversely, just because a character may have liberatory potential, it doesn't mean she, or he, shouldn't be met with critical engage-ment.

"Journey of the Female Hero" also examines the role of parents—who are just as dominant a presence in the hero's life as they are in ours. As fathers and mothers often have a separate and unique influence over us, each unit will be addressed in a separate chapter.

Single fathers and their superdaughters is an oft-recurring theme in the mythic origins of superwomen, many of whom are the product, or perhaps, result, of single fathers who work for the police or the military. Their moth-ers are almost always either dead, alcoholic, clueless, unmentioned, insane, or otherwise emotionally unavailable and out of the picture.

While mothers are absent from the female hero's life, they do play a valuable role in the journey of the heroic male. Because behind every great man, there's a great mother figure, right? John Connor has Sarah, Clark Kent has Martha, and Mulder, at least symbolically, has Scully—whose role as a maternal figure was explored throughout the series and took center stage with the character's pregnancy through much of season eight.

But can motherhood be heroic? Or is it always just a way of containing women's potential power by showing what sorts of heroism are socially ap-propriate for them? The lioness protecting her child is perhaps more palat-able to a general audience than vigilantism for its own sake. Indeed, women are often shown nurturing the savior of people, rather than protecting the community as a whole.[9]

While mythic moms are almost always kept in minor, secondary, or behind-the-scenes roles, several mother–daughter relationships are notably exceptional, as we'll see in Chapter 7, where we'll also look at images of women mentoring women. This is invaluable because when all we see are images of superwomen—even extremely talented and capable ones— receiving their training from only male teachers, gurus, sensei, and sages, it assumes that intellectual and physical power is masculine and that female knowledge has no value.

Section III, "The Mythmakers," looks at men and women in the USA and Great Britain who have created modern myths with a strong female presence.

While women writers, artists, and directors may have the potential to change how superwomen are produced or received, many shy away from outright statements that they are intentionally creating strong or feminist characters. Jane Espenson, who has worked with Joss Whedon, and Gail

Simone, a former hairdresser who now writes for DC Comics, have both stated that they *just write characters*, not specifically female characters. But they *are* women, and it's difficult to escape being gendered. Female-produced myths often have a slightly different flavor, taking on different issues, or exploring possibilities overlooked by male authors.[10]

Trina Robbins and Anne Timmons' teen comic book series *Go Girl!* has a functioning relationship between a mother and a daughter—a rarity in myth, while Gail Simone's run on *Birds of Prey* depicts women who actually talk like women. In movies, Angela Robinson's campy spy-fi film *D.E.B.S.* provides a feminist alternative to *Charlie's Angels*.

The "Conclusion" ponders the future of super*people*, and looks optimistically toward more complex myths where a range of identities is represented.

Reflecting back on those joyously dizzying pirouettes that made me believe I was becoming a superhero, I'm happy to say that my journey as a superwoman continues. I may not have a magic lasso, or even a tiara, but because of an Amazon Princess named Diana, I was able to recognize the hero in myself at an early age. I grew from a shy, geeky girl, into a confident, compassionate woman.

Wonder Woman's journey continues too. Once the sole warrior woman to fight gender stereotypes, she is now surrounded by an army of slayers, princesses, witches, mutants, and meta-humans. These women not only collaborate with one another, but with men as well. They are complicated, fleshed-out, damaged, driven, intelligent, and resourceful. Some are endowed with powers. Some are simply human. But they are all super.

SECTION I

Standing on the Shoulders of Amazons

The Birth of Modern Mythology and the Mother of Female Superheroes

"Aw, that's girl's stuff!" snorts our young comics reader. "Who wants to be a girl?" And that's the point; not even girls want to be girls so long as our feminine archetype lacks force, strength, power... The obvious remedy is to create a feminine character with all the strength of a Superman plus all the allure of a good and beautiful woman. This is what I recommended to the comics publishers.

—William M. Marston

Thus wrote Dr. William Moulton Marston in a 1943 essay for *The American Scholar*. Motivated by his disappointment in how he had seen women portrayed in the nascent, yet booming, medium of comic books, Marston created a superhero character the world would know as Wonder Woman—a lasting symbol of female power, independence, and sisterhood.[1]

There were already many remarkable women in both comic books and news strips by the time Wonder Woman debuted in late 1941, but the liberatory power of most of them was contained, even diminished, by the secondary status of their roles. There were female superheroes, yes, but more often there were girl sidekicks, girl heroes, girl sleuths, and girl reporters; "Girl," meaning not yet woman, not quite mature, not entirely whole. Girls *could* have careers, as long as they were culturally appropriate for their gender, but grown women were married and homemakers.

Beyond girls of books and radio shows, there were some flying aces and a spy or two, as well as a nominal number of costumed female action heroes in comics of the 1930s, 1940s, and 1950s.[2] But Wonder Woman would become the only female superhero of that era to rival the iconic status of Superman, a character widely recognized as the first modern superhero.

Superman was born in the 1930s, when Cleveland teenagers Jerry Siegel and Joe Shuster combined their love of science fiction stories, pulp magazines, adventure movies, radio serials, and Sunday newspaper funnies to forever change the world of mythic storytelling. A writer and an artist, respectively, the young men suffered numerous rejections until finally, in 1938, their amalgam of genre and form debuted in *Action Comics* #1.

Extraordinary beings possessing phenomenal strength have been around since stories were first told, but Siegel and Shuster's legacy to popular culture was a modern myth for modern times. By 1941, comics that featured superheroes—larger-than-life characters with a secret identity, a costume, and a greater purpose—were flying off newsstands and rolled up in the back pockets of a generation of children. As America prepared for its involvement in the Second World War, Superman, Batman, Captain America, and Captain Marvel were just a few of the names illustrating patriotism and bolstering hope: that families would be reunited from across the Atlantic Ocean; that the innocent would be saved and protected from our enemies; that justice would prevail; and that maybe beneath our seemingly frail exteriors, which were damaged by the Depression or stricken with polio, there existed warriors to entertain, lead, and inspire us toward greatness.[3]

But these growing ranks of superheroes were missing a super*woman* who could capture the national imagination as they did. She was soon to come from the unusual mind of Dr. William Moulton Marston.

Dr. Marston was a modern renaissance man, a Harvard-educated doctor and lawyer who was also a writer, an editorial consultant, and the inventor of the systolic blood pressure test—a precursor to what is known today as the polygraph lie detector test. He was also a notoriously shameless, yet successful, self-promoter. In the 1930s and 1940s, the comics industry was growing so fast that parents began to worry about this overwhelmingly new medium that was monopolizing their children's attention.[4] Savvy publishers quickly hired psychologists as editorial advisors, who also publicly gave their "expert" opinion on the value of comic books—namely, that they were good for children.

Marston was savvy as well, and saw an opportunity to promote himself. He had his girlfriend and assistant, Olive Byrne, "interview" him on the topic of children and comic books for the women's magazine *Family Circle*. The article caught the attention of All American Comics[5] executive

M.C. Gaines, who subsequently hired Marston as an editorial advisor and writer for the company. The position ultimately led to the creation of Wonder Woman.

Marston had observed that the majority of superheroes were men, and that women were relegated to secondary roles. He later reflected:

> It seemed to me, from a psychological angle, that the comics' worst offense was their blood-curdling masculinity. A male hero, at best, lacks the qualities of maternal love and tenderness which are as essential to a normal child as a breath of life. Suppose your child's ideal becomes a super*man* who uses his extraordinary power to help the weak. The most important ingredient in the human happiness recipe is still missing—*love*. It's smart to be strong. It's big to be generous. But it's sissified, according to exclusively masculine rules, to be tender, loving, affectionate, and alluring.[6]

What Marston rejected was not the presence of violence in comics (as other psychologists had and would) but the lack of multidimensional female characters. To him, masculinity was overshadowing femininity, and that was a disservice to both men and women alike. This was compounded by the fact that Marston had fairly radical ideas about sex and gender—ideas that would be subversively expressed in the comic he would come to write, but which were already overtly expressed in his other works, most notably his 1928 publication *The Emotions of Normal People*. In brief, Marston believed that women were the superior sex and that men should submit to what he called, "their loving dominance." These convictions were based on his pseudo-psycho-physiological theories regarding the human organism, including that a woman's body contained "twice as many love generating organs and endocrine mechanisms as the male."[7]

To further promote his ideology, Marston's formula for his superhero series consisted of a beautiful woman who fought for the greater good of humanity through her altruistic love. The doctor also went so far as to proclaim that Wonder Woman was "psychological propaganda" for the type of woman he believed would soon rule the world, and predicted our society would evolve into a matriarchy within a century—if only characters like his led the way. By using the Amazon Princess and her allies as role models, he hoped to show that any young girl could become a Wonder Woman if only she took the time and energy to properly train herself; if only she had an example to guide her.

Written by Marston under the pseudonym "Charles Moulton" (a combination of the names Maxwell Charles Gaines and William Moulton Marston) and drawn by Harry G. Peter, Wonder Woman first appeared in the December 1941 issue of *All Star Comics* #8. One month later she began a regular appearance in *Sensation Comics* #1, and an eponymous title, *Wonder Woman*, saw print six months later.

Wonder Woman's origin story tells us that she is Princess Diana of the matriarchal Paradise Island. The Amazons of this hidden island are peaceful, highly trained athletes who live an immortal existence free from the brutality of men. When their Queen, Hippolyte, desires a child she is instructed by Aphrodite to mold one from clay. So was born Diana, a child "as lovely as Aphrodite, as wise as Athena, with the speed of Mercury and the strength of Hercules."[8]

This first tale also tells us how Steve Trevor, a US army officer, comes to crash his plane on the women-only island. As he is nursed back to health, it is discovered through a sort of magic television that Trevor is fighting for America against the "forces of hate and oppression." Hippolyte consults the gods, who order that he immediately be returned to duty and that the strongest of the Amazons must return with him to help win the war. Athena proclaims America as "the last citadel of democracy, and of equal rights for women."

An athletic contest is held to find the strongest emissary. Diana has been forbidden to participate by her mother, but since she has fallen in love with Trevor—the only man she has ever seen—the princess disobeys her Queen by participating in disguise. She bests her competitors and wins the tournament. As Diana leaves for "man's world," she takes sacred totems with her: a magic Lasso of Truth formed from the girdle of Gaea (inspired by Marston's proto-polygraph) and bullet-proof bracelets—a reminder to never submit to the authority of any man. Her mission to protect America is alive in her star-spangled costume of red, white, and blue. She returns Steve Trevor to his base, and adopts a secret identity as "Diana Prince."

Marston freely borrowed from classic Greek and Roman culture, blending names, places, and customs with contemporary American values to create *his* mythic Amazons. The Amazons familiar to the ancient Greeks, however, were a legendary matriarchal society that took part in activities normally associated with Greek men such as hunting, farming and fighting. Stories of Amazons frequently placed them geographically near the southeastern shore of the Black Sea, around the city of Themiscyra. (Years later, in a *Wonder Woman* reboot, *Themyscira* would replace Paradise Island as the home of Marston's Amazons.) Historian Sue Blundell notes that for most writers of classical Greek texts the Amazons were "a phenomena of the distant past" and that no one had ever claimed to have seen or met one.[9]

The "outrageous" customs of the Amazons included members of the all-female society anonymously copulating with men twice a year.[10]

Of the resulting births, only female children remained with their mothers. Some stories tell that the males were given up for adoption, while others claim they were victims of infanticide. It was told that the Amazons removed their right breast, either with a knife or cauterization, in order to more proficiently wield weapons. Legends say that these women were horse riders and horse stealers, who fed their girl children on horse's milk to prevent breast development altogether.[11] Tall tales to be sure; vase paintings and other images almost always depict Amazons with two breasts. However, the Greek word *a-mazon* can be translated as "without a breast."[12]

Just as centuries later Marston wanted his stories about Wonder Woman to be psychological propaganda for the empowerment of women, it is argued that Amazonian myths served as "Athenian propaganda" for the proper behavior of women—yet another testament to the power of stories to influence societal ideas. As Ruby Blondell writes in her essay "How to Kill an Amazon," "in the Greek imaginary, Amazons function in many respects as an antithesis to 'civilized' society, and their myths enact a prohibition on disrupting the roles and relationships between the sexes enshrined in the institutions of marriage and the household."[13] For Athenians, these daughters of Ares represented female independence and bravery, which was as exciting as it was a threat to established social structures. Amazonian rejection of appropriate gender roles necessitated their defeat, and as a cautionary tale about the dangers of social transgression, Amazon defiance actually facilitated their mythic downfall.

In ancient Greece, myths were continually reimagined to serve a changing culture and politics—a tradition Marston continued by manipulating the raw power inherent in a story about a race of warrior women to make it relevant for his time and place. In his efforts to invert the classic myths about warrior women who were tamed by love and domination, he made a symbolic nod to them in the origins of his Amazon race. In *All Star Comics* #8, Marston retells the myth of Hercules' Ninth Labor (of which there are many classic versions)—to steal the magic girdle of the Amazon Queen, which was a gift to her from the goddess Aphrodite. Hippolyte tells her daughter Diana, "Hercules, by deceit and trickery, managed to secure my MAGIC GIRDLE—and soon we Amazons were taken into slavery. And Aphrodite, angry at me for having succumbed to the wiles of men, would do naught to help us!"[14] The Amazons continued to appeal to the goddess for help, and she eventually relents. But she decreed that the women must always wear the wrist bracelets fashioned by their captors as a reminder to be cautious of men. These became famous for being Wonder Woman's bullet-proof bracelets.[15]

Marston believed in the power of stories to influence children; if they were going to read comics, they should be given comics that mattered— words and pictures that could change ideas about gender roles, power structures, and war. Clearly, Marston's warrior women were much more playful than their mythic namesakes, and perhaps it is because he rewrote their myth for a modern consciousness that the word *Amazon* is no longer associated with the "bogeywomen" whose gender subversiveness was a threat to Athenian society. Instead, "Amazon" now generally connotes strength, independence, power, and sisterhood—ideas which Wonder Woman would symbolize during the Women's Liberation Movement of the 1960s and 1970s (indicating that American feminism during this time also influenced new associations with the word, as covered in Chapter 2).

Marston's fictional superwoman was also infused with aspects of the real females in his life—he lived with not one, but two wonder women, each phenomenal in their unique way. His legal wife, Elizabeth Holloway Marston, had three degrees herself, including one in psychology and one in law. She also assisted in the creation of the Amazon Princess. Olive Byrne was a former student and research assistant of William Marston who lived with the Marstons in a polyamorous relationship. The Marstons had two children of their own, and legally adopted Byrne's two children, also fathered by Marston. Each adult contributed to the workings of their household and all were an indispensable part of their harmonious family unit.

After Marston's death from skin cancer, Byrne raised the children and kept house while Holloway-Marston provided financial support. With her salary and Marston's royalties she was able to put all four children through college and Byrne through medical school. The women lived together until Byrne's death in the 1980s. Holloway-Marston died at the age of 100 in 1993.

Women in Extraordinary Roles

Wonder Woman had a definite impact on young girls of the 1940s and 1950s, but it's hard to find evidence of her inspirational impact on adult women venturing into the homefront workforce during the Second World War. Through observation we *can* say that she debuted at a time when real and fictional representations of strong, resourceful women were in relative abundance in both advertising and popular culture.

With America finally forced to enter the war with the bombing of Pearl Harbor on December 7, 1941, media images of self-sufficient and patriotic women became important, not only to American economics, but to the threatened morale of its people.

Women suddenly found themselves in liberating industrial positions. Encouraged by public service ads, movie reels, and other propaganda created by the Office of War Information, they patriotically stepped up to serve their country. Riveters built planes and the Women Airforce Service Pilots (WASPs) flew them. Women were nurses overseas and ballplayers at home. For the first time, they were not only *allowed* into exciting new positions in the public sphere, but were actually *encouraged* by those in power to be there, but only temporarily, and not without being subjected to misogyny, sexism, and racism (the last of which many white women sadly contributed to).

For the young girls that read *Wonder Woman*, and perhaps saw their mothers venturing into the same workforce as their fathers, opportunities for achievement were further emphasized via an inspirational recurring segment titled "Wonder Women of History." Written by tennis champion Alice Marble, these one-page inserts spotlighted women such as Amelia Earhart, Annie Oakley, and Florence Nightingale. This message of empowerment was consistently brought to young girls and grown women alike in the regular comic narrative as well.

We tend to romanticize women's involvement in homefront industry, but as with any story or image, the reality is always much more complex. The riveters embodied in Norman Rockwell's famous painting were expected to work in factories to make machines that would protect their husbands; they were also expected to be "good mothers" but had to work and rear without government-assisted childcare, or even, at the very least, daycare facilities at the factories where they labored.[16] The brave and talented WASPs, who transported planes from the factories to the ports and towed targets for artillery practice, were refused military status. One thousand American women ferried 12,650 planes and flew a total of 60 million miles during the war. Thirty-eight of them died in the line of duty. But because they weren't allowed official military status, their friends were forced to take up collections to send the bodies home. Female fliers were not even allowed to have an American flag placed over their coffins, despite having died in the service of their country.[17] Wonder Woman must have been ashamed.

The Newspaper Game Is for You!

The Intrepid Reporter is another archetype to come out of this era, and has remained as recognizable as the superhero, a character with whom the journalist has frequently shared a genre. And, some of the strongest representations of women in modern myth came in the form of "Girl" or "Women" reporters. As Gail Collins notes in *America's Women: 400 Years of Dolls,*

Drudges, Helpmates, and Heroines, the girl reporter was one of Hollywood's stock heroines "tough as nails but with a romantic streak."[18]

The epitome of this description is, of course, Lois Lane, possibly the second most recognizable female figure from comics after Wonder Woman— even though she actually debuted *three years prior* to the Amazon Princess. Just as superheroes came to be associated with the American values they fought for, the name "Lois Lane" to this day remains synonymous with gutsy investigative journalism.

Like Superman and his alter ego, Clark Kent, Lois has been around since the inaugural issue of *Action Comics* over 70 years ago, and though she predates Wonder Woman, it's doubtful anyone would call her the "mother of superwomen," as she is generally viewed as a supporting character. Regardless, her trademark moxie was present from the very beginning, as illustrated in Lois and Clark's initial scene together. Having finally agreed to give the awkward reporter "a break ... for a change," Lois and Clark head out for an evening of dinner and dancing. When a thug tries to cut in on a dance, Clark is forced to adhere to his secret identity as a submissive weakling. Lois, furious with her date for failing to defend her honor, slaps the mobster herself. She grabs her coat and hat, and Clark runs after her. As she climbs into a cab, her quick tongue and fiery temper lash out: "You asked me earlier in the evening why I avoid you. I'll tell you why now! Because you're a spineless, unbearable *coward*!"[19]

Later in the episode, Lois is abducted by the thug she had earlier refused. Superman arrives to rescue her, and thus the tone is set for a decades-long pattern of animosity, jealousy, and obsession. For the next half century, Lois will love Superman, Superman will be disguised as Clark Kent, Clark Kent will love Lois, Lois will dismiss Clark, Clark will scoop Lois' stories, and because of this, Lois' attempts to prove herself as a journalist will force her into increasingly dangerous stunts that require the Man of Steel to save her.

Comics historian Les Daniels has written that:

> On one level Lois Lane can be seen as a shallow gal who dismisses a decent guy (Clark, her coworker) while dreaming about a muscular member of another species. From today's perspective, it's easy to denounce Lois as the misogynistic fantasy of a disappointed male. Yet both men and women can relate to the pain of being judged by superficial standards, thus giving Clark Kent's trials and Superman's triumphs a broad appeal.[20]

The problem with Daniel's statement here is that it forces women to identify with Clark/Superman instead of with Lois—assuming the privilege of the male hero's perspective. Since the audience knows Clark's secret, we are apt to feel as frustrated as he does whenever Lois works against him or loses her temper because *we* know he's saving the world in his other identity, not simply dumping his work responsibilities on her.

But, even if Superman is our hero and Lois is a secondary character, it's better for the purposes of this book to consider her role in his mythos from what we can imagine is her perspective. It's certainly not the intended reading, but it will allow us to see how for many years Lois represented conflicted feelings toward women's roles in society and how she at least tried to face them as a superwoman.

In the early days of the Superman mythos, Lois was eager to be a news reporter, but wasn't often offered that type of career-making assignment— rather she was confined to "women's news." Once, when she asks her editor if she can report on a particularly exciting story, he tells her, "It's too important! This is no job for a girl!" When alone, Lois fumes, "No, job for a woman, eh? I've half a mind to...." She corrals Clark, who *had* received the said assignment, but instead of relaying the proper message to him she sends Clark on a fake mission so that she can cover the real deal.[21] In another episode, Lois actually slips the mild-mannered reporter a sedative![22] When Clark (who is, of course, immune to sedatives) realizes what she's done he muses, "Double-crossing a pal, eh? Just like a newspaperwoman!"[23]

While other men would be frustrated by Lois's expressions of vanity, acts of scheme and spunk, and insensitive public swooning over a romantic competitor, Clark is able to find her behavior amusing because it is *as* Superman that he will continually end up having to rescue this irrepressible newspaperwoman.[24] But because she doesn't know that Clark and Superman are one and the same, Clark's genuine expressions of concern come off feeling like a challenge to her journalistic capability. Who is the mild-mannered, ineffectual Clark Kent to tell the street-smart, quick-thinking, fast-talking Lois Lane what to do? The following exchange serves as a perfect example:

Clark: Stay clear of this yarn, it's dangerous!

Lois: You have a nerve ... telling *me* what to do!

Clark: I was only thinking of your welfare!

Lois: On the contrary, you were only thinking of *your* by-line! No, Clark, I'll do *what* I like, *when* I like, and *where* I like![25]

You Go Girl (Reporter)! Lois calls it as she sees it, as she has *every* opportunity to see it. Clark's continuous scooping of her stories and the realities of being a woman trying to maintain a career in the 1940s (even the realities of a fictional woman) would certainly lead Lois to feel she is being systematically pushed out of her job. Not to condone Lois's acts, drugging someone to scoop a story and see your boyfriend Superman, is extreme, but, at least in this era, the behavior of her sometimes nemesis/sometimes lover also leaves much to be desired.

Take this example from *Action Comics* #47, which follows a familiar formula: Clark and Lois are sent on an assignment and they discretely slip away from each other. Lois gets in over her head and Superman saves her. But the event is not her story to tell. Lois waves goodbye as her hero flies off: "So long, Superman, and thanks for a swell news story!" "Don't thank me yet," he yells back in response, "I have a hunch Clark Kent will get the story into print before you do!"[26] For the savior of the human race, he can be disturbingly cold and cruel.[27]

When Lois sends Clark on a wild goose chase, we think ill of her. But is she just supposed to sit back, be a good girl, and be happy that she gets to report at all? At what point does it become her prerogative to take charge and get the scoop? Isn't she asserting herself against what from her perspective is obvious journalistic one-upmanship? Clark has an unfair advantage that goes well beyond male privileging; he essentially gets to report on his own actions. To top it off, he taunts Lois for his own pleasure, though occasionally, out of the goodness of his heart, he'll throw her a newsworthy bone.

"Girl reporters" such as Lois continued to be a popular role for women in modern storytelling throughout the 1940s. Rosalind Russell starred as Hildy Johnson in *His Girl Friday* (1940), a film adaptation of the play *The Front Page*. Dale Messick's *Brenda Starr* (1940) sizzled in the dailies. Nancy Drew had even gotten into the journalism game in 1939, when Bonita Granville played the title character in the movie *Nancy Drew . . . Reporter*. Her line, "A reporter has the right to do things an ordinary person shouldn't," could just as easily have been a sentiment expressed by Ms. Lane, who was famous for sneaking into (and being rescued out of) places she wasn't supposed to be.[28]

And again, real and fictional women mirrored each other's achievements as America tried to make sense of the social upheaval caused by the war. According to the Library of Congress, which in 1995 featured an exhibit called "Women Come to the Front: Journalists, Photographers, and Broadcasters During World War II":

> For female journalists, World War II offered new professional opportunities. Talented and determined, dozens of women fought for—and won—the right to cover the biggest story of their lives. By war's end at least 127 American women had secured official military accreditation as war correspondents, if not actual frontline assignments. Other women journalists remained on the home front to document the ways in which the country changed dramatically under wartime conditions.[29]

Women's news, like Lois Lane's "sob sister" column, was a way to break into the profession, but the war allowed for much more active reporting, helped by none less than First Lady, Eleanor Roosevelt who facilitated women in journalism. During the Depression, when women were encouraged not to take jobs away from men, Mrs. Roosevelt "instituted a weekly women-only press conference to force news organizations to employ at least one female reporter. During World War II, many of the newswomen in the First Lady's circle served as war correspondents."[30]

Wonder Woman may have been the poster child for women's empowerment during the war years, but it's clear Lois Lane more accurately reflected social attitudes regarding women—particularly career women. They would both morph to fit with changing politics in subsequent years, but in the late 1930s and through the 1940s they set a precedent for subsequent new myths.

Post-Second World War and the 1950s

In the 1940s women had been represented in popular culture as strong, capable, and collaborative—a tactic necessary to keep American production flourishing while a war was fought overseas. But in the 1950s many women, both fictional and real, were returned to the traditionally defined domestic sphere. Even Wonder Woman wasn't exempt. She suffered a harsh blow when William Moulton Marston died in 1947, and his princess was left to generations of writers who didn't understand her revolutionary purpose. For example, "Wonder Women of History" was replaced with a feature that documented wedding customs across the globe. As Lillian S. Robinson writes in *Wonder Women: Feminisms and Superheroes,* "his utopian feminist dream died with him," and in these post-war years Wonder Woman declined "from an inconsistent, but unquestionably liberatory icon into something quite different."[31]

After Marston's death, Sheldon Meyer, editor, cartoonist, and family friend of the unusual clan took over writing Wonder Woman. Soon, he wished to return to his love of drawing, and Robert Kanigher, who had been writing another female character, Black Canary, was hired as his replacement. Kanigher served the dual role of writer and editor of *Wonder Woman* for the next 20 years.

According to Les Daniels, *Sensation Comics* was yet another title about to fold when an attempt to save it was by made by incorporating a romance theme.[32] In what can be assumed to be a correction to the gender reversal that made Wonder Woman so wonderful in the first place, the cover of *Sensation Comics* #94 (Nov.–Dec. 1949) depicts Steve Trevor carrying

Wonder Woman across a stream (presumably so she won't get her dainty self wet) as she gazes lovingly into his eyes. The cover blurb, meant to entice readers, reads "Only a call for help could prevent Wonder Woman from marrying Steve Trevor!" By 1950, *Sensation Comics* and *All Star Comics* had folded and only the eponymous *Wonder Woman* survived. But Kanigher had removed Etta Candy and the Holliday Girls—Wonder Woman's friends, protégées, and collaborators—from the narrative. Diana's origin story was also rewritten. Instead of being formed from clay, she was now the child of two members of the opposite sex. (One can only assume from the television of the time that they slept in separate beds.)[33]

In the late 1950s, the adventures of a teenaged Diana called, of course, Wonder Girl, were added to the Wonder Woman family. Continuing with the romance theme approach, Wonder Girl was given a boyfriend named Mer-Boy. This completely ignored the fact that Diana had never seen a man before Steve Trevor, although it could be argued that meant a *human* man. Drifting even further away from the independence and inspiration of the original Amazon Princess, another version of Diana soon followed in the chronicles of Wonder Tot—Diana as a toddler. For a while the adventures of Wonder Woman, Wonder Girl, and Wonder Tot were kept separate until all logic was thrown out in the 1961 story *The Impossible Day*.[34] In this tale, Hippolyta—now a much less Greek-looking blonde—uses a magic camera to take a photo of her daughter at these three stages in her life, which allows them to forthwith reside together in the present in several "impossible tales."[35]

Though characters must evolve to serve the purposes of their times, clearly this Wonder Woman was a devolvement, caught up in infantile— in some cases quite literally—adventures rather than her initial calling as a champion of female strength and love.

During this backlash to the empowering images of Wonder Woman and Rosie the Riveter, women in comics were often little more than simpering girlfriends who shopped, fainted, cried, and were obsessed with marriage. Lois Lane was *Superman's Girl Friend* instead of having a title in her own right like *Lois Lane, Star Reporter*. Batgirl consistently bungled missions, instead of truly being an asset to the dynamic duo, and usually needed to be saved, rather than actively doing the saving.

Super*girls*, rather than superwomen, were also a common post-war theme. Ironically, Supergirl (Superman's teenage cousin), whose very name embodied the infantilization of women with power, was one of the only lasting female sidekicks to come out of this era. With the rare exception, girl sidekicks were generally less capable than their male counterparts, of whom they were character spin-offs. Like the hero's love interest, though sometimes they were that too, supergirls often attempted to handle situations above and beyond their capabilities, which ultimately necessitated their rescue by the hero. Their bumbling incompetence reinforced the superiority of the male hero and the paternalism that plagued much of 1950s' media. The fact that the majority of supergirls had a familial relationship to the hero—cousin, niece, sister, and so on—reinforced a "father knows best" ideology. (Though to be fair, Mary Marvel was a teenage girl who held her own comic and was very popular with young girls.)

Additionally, after the war, public interest in superheroes declined as a sense of normalcy settled over the nation. As with the women of wartime industry, once the war was won, superheroes were no longer needed. Whereas caped crusaders and masked avengers had once dominated newsstand space, gaps left by discontinued titles were quickly filled by other genres. Horror comics, Westerns, funny animal stories, and romance comics rose to the fore, many of these directed toward a new market called "the teenager." By the end of 1948, most superhero comics had been canceled or converted to other genres. The survivors, mostly the big-name heroes, were being aimed more consciously at a juvenile audience.

But no matter the genre, one man viewed all comics as a danger to society and launched a crusade against them.

At the height of their popularity in the 1940s, hundreds of millions of comic magazines were sold every month. The relatively new medium that captivated the nation's children was beginning to alarm parents, and *Seduction of the Innocent*, a book written by Dr. Frederic Wertham and published in 1954, fueled their panic.

Frederic Wertham was a German-Jew, an intellectual, and an immigrant, whose writings on the harmful effects of racial segregation on children had helped end separate-but-equal education in the United States when they were used as evidence during Brown v. Board of Education. He was also renowned for establishing a clinic in Harlem for at-risk youth and their families to receive free psychological care. It was there that he made a connection between comic book violence and juvenile delinquency, though his was a controversial, and reductionist, assumption about cause and effect. As Trina Robbins snarkily notes, "Using the same logic, we could prove that tomatoes turn people into killers by showing that 99 percent of the residents of our prisons' death rows regularly eat tomatoes."[36] But she also points out:

> Whereas it was certainly true, as Wertham stated, that the vast majority of young criminals he studied were avid comic book readers, he neglected to mention that the vast majority of American children were avid comic book readers. And while some comics mentioned in Wertham's book were indeed objectionably violent,

gruesome, and sadistic, he tended to get carried away and lump all action comics under the title 'crime comics,' including even *Wonder Woman.*[37]

Wertham testified before the Senate Subcommittee on Juvenile Delinquency using evidence from his text, taking issue not only with the more gruesome horror comics, but with the violent acts of superheroes—that to him were reminiscent of Nazi oppression.[38] He was also appalled by Marston's delight in portraying bondage scenes, and criticized what he interpreted as homoerotic subtext in superhero comics, particularly in the mentorship of Batman to Robin.[39] He labeled Wonder Woman and her sometime-collaborators, the Holliday Girls, lesbians and claimed it would be detrimental to the mental health of children to be exposed to such menace. His testimony contributed to the cancellation of many superhero titles, as well as causing those that survived to take a more gentle tone as the Congressional hearings led comics publishers to create the Comics Code Authority—a self-regulatory organization that screened comics for adherence to specific standards. Regulations included a policy to present crimes so that they should never create sympathy for the criminal—making good and evil strictly black and white issues.[40] The code also stated that the treatment of love–romance stories should emphasize the value of the home and the sanctity of marriage.

Comics, once titillating, had become vanilla.

They were also competing with a new storytelling medium—television. Television sets had been available since the late 1920s, but were a rarity in American living rooms until the 1950s when post-war advances in technology and the lifting of rations on manufacturing materials led to mass production of television sets at affordable prices. This allowed for yet another way to capitalize on already familiar characters who were successful in other media such as comics, radio, and theatrical serials.

In fact, by the 1950s, stories featuring Superman and Lois were being told in all three of these mediums. In the theatrical serials, Kirk Alyn portrayed the Man of Steel and Noel Neill was Lois Lane. In 1951, a feature-length film, *Superman and the Mole Men*, was produced, which served as a combination pilot episode for the subsequent television series *The Adventures of Superman* (1952–8).[41] George Reeves portrayed the title character, and Phyllis Coates, who was known for her roles in science fiction B-movies, played Lois Lane.[42] When it was unclear whether the show would return for a second season, Coates took a job elsewhere, and Neill was called in to take her place when production did indeed resume. She went on to play Lois Lane for a total of five seasons.

But back in the comics one had to wonder whether Lois Lane was a star reporter or a desperate housewife. When the character finally got her own book in 1958, it was titled *Superman's Girl Friend Lois Lane*, as if she were a piece of property rather than someone who could be independently dynamic. Her accomplishments and stature as an independent woman continued to be diminished.

One of many tales that undermine Lois's talents and minimize her success as a reporter is 1960's "How Lois Lane Got Her Job" (*Superman's Girl Friend Lois Lane* #17 May 1960). The teaser narrative reads:

> As a girl reporter for the *Daily Planet* in Metropolis, Lois Lane has gained fame for her many headline stories through the years! But have you ever wondered just how she got her job? How her daring career of hunting down scoops began? Did her great friend, Superman, whose feats are always super-news, get her started? Well, you're in for a big surprise, as we give you the untold story of … How Lois Lane Got Her Job."[43]

The set-up is a party at the *Daily Planet* to celebrate the anniversary of the day Lois was hired at the prestigious news publication. Here she is praised as a famous and daring hunter of headlines. But again the joke is on Lois, as the ensuing tale exposes her inadequacy, "proving" that she is incapable of landing a scoop without assistance.

The teaser panel goes on to show Lois telling Superman, "You gave me many scoops, Superman … But only *after* I became a girl reporter! Those three Lois Lane Scoops" she says pointing to a bulletin board featuring her clips "won me my job, and I got them without your help!"

It turns out she didn't.

In order to get hired as a reporter, Lois Lane was tasked by Editor-in-Chief Perry White to bring him three scoops in three days, a feat which Lois accomplishes. As Lois begins to tell the tale of her first scoop, Superman's super-memory recalls that by chance he happened to instigate the very events that led her to successfully gather the material for her article. In each case Superman was coincidentally behind the scenes. And if it wasn't for some minor act on his part, Lois would never have completed her quest and been hired at the *Daily Planet*.

Even though it's stated time and again that Lois has talent, these stories are designed to illustrate her as magnificently inept. Lois had previously appeared in two issues of *Showcase* that focused on her character and that served as a test run for a possible Lois Lane spin-off series (*Superman's Pal, Jimmy Olsen* had already been running for several years). The sexism, and occasional outright misogyny, that plagued Lois for many years was not absent from these two 1957 issues. The first all-Lois issue, *Showcase Presents Superman's Girl Friend Lois Lane* (#9) depicts Lois on the cover as Mrs. Superman, scolding her husband for leaving her alone with their Super-Baby, whom she can't handle by herself. The cover of the second issue (#10) shows Superman reprimanding Lois for opening "The Forbidden Box from Krypton"—the allusion to Pandora's Box is made clear by Superman's commentary, "Lois—Your curiosity in opening that chest has released Three Super-Powers which may doom the world!"[44]

It's hard to decide which stereotype is more offensive, the housewife or the woman whose curiosity is a plague. But by the debut issue of Lois' eponymous title, a whole host of ugly, sexist assumptions about women were added. The first issue (March–April 1958) featured a cover story titled "The Witch of Metropolis." Even Daniels notes that the book "was a catalog of stereotypes—from hussy to helpmate to hag—but the series lasted 16 years."[45]

Throughout its run, the stories of *Superman's Girl Friend Lois Lane* would revolve around three insidious stereotypes concerning women: (1) they are obsessed with finding a husband; (2) they are a danger to themselves and others—and therefore must be looked after; and (3) they are rivals, prone to catfights, and as a result can never have authentic friendships.[46]

Fortunately, the possibilities of the 1940s were only temporarily quelled in the 1950s. The 1960s would get superwomen out of the kitchen and into something exciting.

2

Modern Myth, Meet Feminism

[After watching Cathy Gale *in* The Avengers*] Women were leaving their homes, their kitchens and their crèches in droves and going out and starting to throw men over their shoulders, which they've been doing ever since. It was sheer luck that the women's movement was starting to get going then.*

—Patrick Macnee[1]

The nineteen-seventies, as I look back, were a pretty good time for amazons.

—Michael Chabon[2]

Myth is complicated; stories, images, and representations reflect cultural trends as well as influence them. Additionally, those that reach a mass audience are generally made, manipulated, and marketed by those in positions of power and are representative of a small, stereotyped, or even imaginary population.

For example, Mrs. June Cleaver, the sweet and patient homemaker of television's *Leave It to Beaver*—a late-1950s series that revolved around a stereotypical suburban nuclear family—continues to serve as an American symbol of that era's real or imagined family values and cultural ideas about roles for women. Advertisements of the time further reinforced the "perfect" woman: tiny waist, ironed apron, and glistening pearls. Mothers had perfectly manicured hands, though they did all the cooking and cleaning, and wives usually deferred to their husband's judgment. One could easily assume that the life of a suburban housewife like the aforementioned Mrs. Cleaver was the only proper lifestyle choice for women and that, in fact, it was something to aspire to. But social assumptions about what women were (and were not) capable of had been irrevocably shattered by female accomplishments during the war, and not every woman longed to be in the kitchen—though entertainment of the time did little to reflect this. As Susan J. Douglas writes in *Where the Girls Are: Growing Up Female with the Mass Media*, when mothers sat down "to relax in front of the TV after a twelve- to fifteen-hour day, they were surrounded by allegories about masculine heroism and the sanctity of male gonads." Douglas adds, "Rarely, if ever, did they see any suggestion that the incessant, mundane, and often painful contortions of a woman's daily life might, in fact, be heroic too."[3]

In 1963, the fallacy of the content suburban housewife was exposed by the publication of Betty Friedan's *The Feminine Mystique*, which claimed that women had (falsely) been led to believe that the only ways in which they could find fulfillment was through marriage and motherhood. The book appealed to university-educated, white, middle-class women who were feeling dissatisfied with their lives—a plague Friedan called "the problem with no name." Women of color and working-class women had always worked both in and outside the home, so these feminist "revelations" often had little relevance to their lives; double shifts leave little time for the privilege of contemplating discontent, particularly when dealing with the very real issues of everyday survival.

But the 1960s were an era of many political movements, not just the Women's Liberation Movement (also called "The Second Wave of Feminism"[4]). The Civil Rights, Black Power, Youth (or Hippie), and Gay Rights Movements had all gained momentum during the 1960s and 1970s. Landmark events such as the assassinations of political and spiritual leaders Malcolm X and Dr. Martin Luther King, Jr., and of John F. Kennedy and Robert Kennedy, the formation of the National Organization for Women (NOW), the three-day music festival at Woodstock, the moon landing, and the Stonewall riots forever altered the American cultural landscape. In the midst of this cultural whirlwind, the shifting and often subversive political temper of the Baby Boomer generation came to be expressed through entertainment media of the 1960s.

Hailing Frequencies Open

Girls in space, be wary! (*Star Trek*[5])

William Moulton Marston had used comic books and stories about his character, Wonder Woman, to influence societal ideas, but while it were comic books that had once held captive audiences of children and adults alike, television was the new and exciting medium that post-war audiences were engaged with. It was through this new storytelling medium that Gene Roddenberry infused a progressive humanist philosophy into his science fiction series *Star Trek*.

In 1966, television audiences were introduced to the racially diverse and species-rich crew of the starship *Enterprise*, who were on a five-year mission to explore deep space. The inclusion of Majel Barrett as Number One, the ship's first officer, in the original pilot, "The Cage," did not sit well with network executives who weren't comfortable with depicting a woman so high in rank. Fearing Roddenberry's subversive approach would be offensive to audiences and advertisers, a second pilot was filmed, this time with both a new captain and a male first officer. Barrett, who would later marry Roddenberry, was now recast in a more feminine role as ship's nurse.

Nichelle Nichols was cast as one of the series's main characters, Lt. Nyota Uhura—a native of the United States of Africa and a top student at Starfleet Academy. In Nichols's autobiography, she writes that Uhura is derived from Uhuru, which is Swahili for "freedom" (as well as the title of a book she had been reading at her audition). She developed the biographical background for her character with Roddenberry—a friend, collaborator, and former lover. Contrary to how the character was actually presented, Nichols writes, "Uhura was far more than an intergalactic telephone operator. As head of Communications, she commanded a corps of largely unseen communications technicians, linguists, and other specialists who worked in the bowels of the *Enterprise*, in the 'comm-center.'" She adds, "Many times throughout the years I've referred to Uhura as my great-great-great-great-great-great-great-granddaughter of the twenty-third century."[6]

Nichols also strongly believed in Roddenberry's agenda:

Gene created in *Star Trek* a multidimensional, multiracial, multipurpose metaphor through which he could express his personal, progressive ideals....[7] More than anything else, Gene was a philosopher, a man who felt compelled to share his moral vision for the future of humanity with the world. In another time or place, he might have been a great teacher of history or philosophy. But in the mid-twentieth century he instinctively sought access to the most powerful communications medium in history: television.[8]

Roddenberry may have had a progressive vision of the future, let alone his present, but National Broadcasting Company (NBC) executives weren't keen on giving such a colorful crew what they considered to be excessive screen time. While promises were made that Sulu (George Takei), Uhura (Nichols), and Scotty (James Doohan) would feature prominently in future episodes, these turned out to be mere placations when the network stuck to a more familiar formula in which two or three men served as focus characters—in this case, Captain Kirk (William Shatner), Dr. McCoy (DeForest Kelley), and Mr. Spock (Leonard Nimoy).

Nichols, distressed over her increasingly diminished role and frustrated by the double whammy of sexism and racism she faced from network executives, decided to leave the series after the initial season. First drafts of scripts had displayed her character prominently, but by final cut, her lines were often limited to "Hailing frequencies open, Captain." Fortunately, for the marginalized everywhere, a spiritual leader serendipitously stepped in and that line would empower generations to come.

The day after she had given Roddenberry her resignation, Nichols attended a fundraising event for the National Association for the Advancement of Colored People (NAACP), where she was approached by a fan of *Star Trek*, and of Uhura. The fan was none other than civil rights activist and leader Dr. Martin Luther King, Jr. Though honored by his praise, Nichols informed him of her decision to leave the show. Dr. King replied:

> You *cannot* and you *must* not. Don't you realize how important your presence, your character is? Don't you realize this gift this man [Roddenberry] has given the world? Men and women of all races going forth in peaceful exploration, living as equals. You listen to me: Don't you see? This is not a Black role, and this is not a female role. You have the first nonstereotypical role on television, male or female. You have broken ground.[9]

He acknowledged that her decision was likely the result of having suffered prejudice, but that her role as Uhura had "changed the face of television forever." Because Nichols had portrayed a "character of dignity and grace and beauty and intelligence," she was a role model not just for Black children, but for *everyone*.[10]

Nichols stayed with the series and indeed became a role model for many, including actress Whoopi Goldberg, who had a recurring role on *Star Trek: The Next Generation*, and astronaut Dr. Mae Jemison, who was the first African American woman in space.[11]

Invisible Girls

Invisible Girl, first and perhaps most famous of Marvel's dazzling damsels. (Stan Lee[12])

The Invisible Girl was as wimpy as the weakest of comic book sidekicks. (Trina Robbins[13])

Though the 1960s comics industry touted women as equals, they were still consistently depicted in lesser positions, with weaker powers, or in roles more traditionally "suitable" to women. The maternal figure was embodied by Sue Storm of *The Fantastic Four*—a family team-up of superheroes. Jean Grey was another token female and the sex symbol desired by her male colleagues, the X-Men. Wonder Woman was stripped of her supernatural powers altogether, leaving behind her Amazonian heritage to become the owner of a clothing boutique and the protégée of a male mentor. But at least she was the proprietress of her business, and not just a shop girl. Thank Goddess for small favors.

In *The Super Women of Marvel*, a 1977 trade paperback collection of comics featuring the "fabulous females of Marvel," Stan Lee writes introductions to about a dozen stories—as well as a preface in which he states with unconvincing enthusiasm:

> We have been, we are, and we shall continue to make the strongest possible effort to bestow the cultural blessings of superherodom upon male and female alike. Let chauvinism be eschewed. Let equality prevail. Let historians of the future look back upon this era and proudly declare, " 'Twas Marvel that led the way! ..." For too many years the females have been relegated to mere supporting roles. We think it's time to change all that. It's time for the Super Women![14]

Invisible Girl, a.k.a. Sue Storm, perfectly illustrates the tensions inherent in cultural responses to the second wave of feminism. She was a contradiction—a superwoman whose power is the ability to be unseen. She premiered alongside the rest of the Fantastic Four in November of 1961 (*Fantastic Four* #1), when Stan Lee and artist Jack Kirby were tasked with the creation of Marvel's first superhero team—a response to the success of DC Comics's team-up book, *Justice League of America* (JLA).

According to Lee, Sue was a revelation, "After dreaming up the three male characters who'd provide the brawn for the ol' F.F., our next task was to make sure that the obligatory female was included on the team."[15] This "three guys and a girl" formula was typical of Marvel at the time, though Lee appears to believe that with Sue he was taking a radical departure from depictions of previous superwomen.

What few heroines there were all seemed to follow the same pattern. They weren't actually heroines at all; they were just the heroes' girlfriends. They worried when their man went off to fight the ferocious foe, and they usually spent the rest of the time tearfully imploring him to give up his dangerous calling . . . Well, right at the outset I determined to do all I could to change that pattern, to alter the formula. There must be a better way—or, at least a different way. And that's where little Susie comes in.[16]

Lee goes on to praise Marvel for not making her a clueless girlfriend, bossy, or an otherwise "pretty little pest." Instead of making Sue a *girlfriend*, they made her a *fiancée*. And not just that, but the fiancée of "the intellectual leader of the group."

"Did you get that?" Stan the man asks, in awe of their bold progressiveness, "Fiancée! She was actually engaged to Reed! They were gonna be married! And married they were, a few years later."[17]

Well, whoopee for Sue. Now that she's married, she can finally become the Invisible *Woman*, a.k.a. Mrs. Intellectual Leader Richards.

Over the years there have been varied interpretations of the symbolism of Sue's invisibility. One reading is that she illustrates the invisibility of women—a point explored with poignancy in James Sturm's 2003 graphic novel, *Fantastic Four: Unstable Molecules.*[18] For many readers, the passivity of being unseen diminished her contribution to the group by virtue of not being a proactive power. Sue later gained the ability to project limited force fields, although even that was often too much for her to physically handle. As Trina Robbins notes, Sue also "had a habit of fainting, becoming hysterical, or bursting into tears."[19] She conformed to other traditional norms as well; according to one letters column, her hobbies included "fashion, cooking, cosmetics and reading romance novels.[20]

To be fair to Lee, it's clear he had the best of intentions. He believed Sue participated as a full-fledged, equal member of the Fantastic Four. And at least she wasn't just a girlfriend.

Spy Girls

Meanwhile, in Britain, even before the Bond Phenomenon was ignited by film adaptations of Ian Fleming's novels about a rakish secret government agent, a spy-fi woman was dishing out judo chops on television and another was kicking ass in a daily news strip. Both dealt in espionage, but neither worked in an official capacity, preferring instead to handle matters on their own terms.

One was the extraordinary Modesty Blaise, who debuted in 1963 and starred in an eponymous panel strip written by Peter O'Donnell for *The Evening Standard.*

Modesty—a survivor, a force of nature, and a loyal friend—was formerly the leader of a global crime syndicate before retiring in her mid-20s. Along with her right-hand man, but never her romantic interest, Willie Garvin, she leads a life of leisure surrounded by the luxury her former crimes secured. But every now and then the unusual pair crave a good caper. Fortunately for their adventurous spirits trouble inevitably rears its head and they are once again destroying criminals and saving friends.

Modesty—highly trained, resourceful, and compassionate—remains one of the coolest, most complex, and intriguing superwomen of all time. She was a groundbreaking and progressive character that rivaled other spy-fi icons she was so often compared to—most notably and erroneously, James Bond. And though her continuing adventures were printed in *The Evening Standard* for over 40 years and she featured in 11 novels and two collections of short stories, all penned by O'Donnell, the name Modesty Blaise remains practically unknown to an American audience—and is increasingly unrecognized by a British one.[21]

But in 1960s Britain, popular culture must have been primed for female adventurers of complexity, independence, and sexual sophistication, because as Modesty Blaise was being envisioned, so was Cathy Gale—the first lead female character featured on *The Avengers* (1961–9).

The show, which was the longest-running secret agent series of the 1960s, had begun as a story about Doctor David Keel (Ian Hendry) whose fiancée was murdered by drug dealers. Keel teams up with shady secret agent John Steed (Patrick Macnee) to avenge his wife's death and put an end to her killers. When actor Hendry left the series after 26 episodes to pursue a film career, Macnee became the star of the show, and a search began for someone new to fill the role of Steed's partner. Series co-producers Sydney Newman and Leonard White thought perhaps this new character should be a woman—a radical move in the early 1960s, but as Newman recalls:

> Why shouldn't Hendry's role be played by a woman, I thought. God knows, women were, in life, doing incredible things.... A woman [on television] actively physical, attractive and demonstrating intelligence would certainly be fresh and different. Now, thinking about it, it was years ahead of the women's lib movement as recognized by the media today.[22]

The result was Dr. Catherine Gale, a character based on a number of remarkable women, including Margaret Bourke-White—a photographer for *Life* magazine, the anthropologist Margaret Mead, and a woman Newman had seen featured on the nightly news detailing her experience of the Mau Mau uprisings in colonial Kenya in which her husband and two young sons were slaughtered.

Gale was played by Honor Blackman, and in a direct nod to Newman's inspirations was an anthropologist and a photographer, and her family had been killed by the Kenyan Mau Mau. She was, by necessity, proficient with firearms and also an expert in judo. The death of her family and the political uprisings in Kenya caused her to return home to London, where she began work as a curator at the British Museum. It was through this job that she became professionally involved with John Steed.

Cathy Gale was not, at least initially, an official employee of Steed's agency. But she was his equal, if not his moral and intellectual superior. At the time, Blackman said, "I'm a first for television. The first feminist to come into a television serial; the first woman to fight back. Cathy is all anthropologist, an academic, all brain and what she doesn't have in the way of brawn, she makes up for in motorbikes, black boots, leather combat suits and judo."[23]

But two years later in 1964, Honor Blackman left *The Avengers* to take on the role of Pussy Galore, the infamous lesbian leader of an all-female Harlem crime gang in the film adaptation of Ian Fleming's *Goldfinger*. Series producers were interested in finding another fabulous femme to play partner to Macnee's Steed, and Honor Blackman's kinky boots were soon filled by the lovely Diana Rigg.

The source of the new character's name is an oft-told story. Marie Donaldson, the studio's press officer, was brainstorming about how the character needed to have "man appeal" and wrote a shorthand notation that read "M. Appeal." Thus was born Mrs. *Emma Peel*, a role model for liberated women, yet whose very name is an embodiment of her objectified sexuality.

And yet, Mrs. Peel *was* sexy, not just because Rigg was luminous, but because Emma was as witty and charming as Steed. She was a brilliant intellectual, could hold her own in a fight, and needed to be rescued only as often as her partner did. As *Salon* observed, even when Emma was put in a traditional damsel-in-distress situation, she responded without fear:

> She treated each threat as a mere annoyance, as something essentially beneath her.... The genius of Rigg's portrayal was that she did what generations of male heroes had done: made sexiness inseparable from competence, confidence and professionalism. Emma *does* show fear in the course of the episodes where, separated from Steed, she's stranded with some maniac in a remote place. But those flashes of fright never seriously challenged her nerve or resolve.[24]

Like Cathy, Emma was a widow; her test-pilot husband, Peter Peel, was missing in action and assumed deceased. Emma was at least a decade younger than her predecessor and provided contrast between herself and Steed; whereas he represented traditional notions of British identity, she was a symbol of the new mod style.

The Avengers, which had already influenced fashion with Gale's kinky, oiled, leather bodysuits, continued to be on the cutting edge of clothing design with Emma Peel's wardrobe. Her most famous outfit, the "Emmapeeler," was a feminine and feline piece designed by Alun Hughes for the series's transition to color transmission. These action suits were fashioned out of stretch jersey and Crimplene and decorated with buckles, braiding, and links. The kit was completed by the addition of matching booties made out of the same material. Hughes described Emma in these suits as being like "a cat in the night, prowling silently on her secret assignments, ready to strike at anyone who challenges her."[25]

With their fabulous style, witty banter, and sexual innuendo, Steed and Peel are the most famous Avengers team.[26] Together they faced a host of affable British eccentrics, including an upper-class chimney sweep very properly named, Bertram Fortescue Winthrop Smith; a feline enthusiast for the fictional PURRR (the Philanthropic Union for the Rescue, Relief and Recuperation of Cats); and various diabolical masterminds played by renowned guest actors such as Peter Cushing and Donald Sutherland.

The Avengers itself was filled with kinky fun, fashion, and storylines that often bordered on the absurd. As James Chapman notes in *Saints and Avengers*, the elegance and style of the episodes made nonsense of the laws of probability.[27] Steed and Peel were miniaturized; they had their consciousness placed in different bodies; Emma fought an adversary suspended from the ceiling in gravity boots; and perhaps, most astoundingly, they drank gallons of champagne and never seemed drunk—even though they themselves were ever-intoxicating. *Salon* observed, the message Steed sent Peel at the beginning of most episodes, "Mrs. Peel, we're needed," always in the most innovative and delightful way, "was an invitation to a party."[28]

Because the Cathy Gale episodes have never been broadcast in the USA, Emma Peel remains the definitive 1960s spy girl, and the partnership of Peel and Steed has come to be representative of modish London cool. The spy-fi series, and Emma Peel in particular, would inspire a radical change in a familiar American icon—one who was in danger of becoming obsolete.

The New Wonder Woman

In the late 1960s, Wonder Woman was a dying franchise, and efforts were made to revamp her for a modern audience. "The Diana Prince Era"—as it is now referred to—begins when the Amazons need to retreat in order to restore their mystic and sacred powers. As Steve Trevor is once again in danger, Diana feels she needs to stay in "Man's World" to aid her friend and love interest. To do so, she sacrifices her powers, her birthright, and her immortality, returning to America as human.

She's immediately recruited by a male mentor—a blind Asian martial arts expert named I Ching. Though now deprived of supernatural gifts, which include her costume and lasso of truth, she's still a well-trained athlete and quickly learns martial arts and other skills that enable her to continue fighting crime. Members of the team of writers and artists who worked on *Wonder Woman* during her spy-fi era (Issues 178–204) have acknowledged that Mrs. Peel's style was inspiration for the mod direction taken with the new Diana Prince, and this is most evident in her appearance, particularly her hairstyle and her Emmapeelers, but also in her partner I Ching's bowler and brolly, which mirrored John Steed.[29,30]

DC felt this "new" Diana captured the tone of the women's movement, but she actually contradicted the values of the original Wonder Woman. She had no qualms about killing and wasn't sure she enjoyed the company of women.[31] This drastic change of character alarmed a certain group of women, who would go on to make sure that Wonder Woman would always be seen as a champion of sisterhood.

In early 1971, groups of activists and writers met several times to discuss the possibilities of a publication that would connect women, address the changing social landscape, as well as opportunities and resources for women, and hopefully generate income. They toyed with the idea of a newsletter, but decided that a national magazine created and controlled by women would better serve their purposes. They wanted their publication to "be as serious, outrageous, satisfying, funky, intimate, global, compassionate, and full of change as women's lives really are."[32]

After many meetings and many plans, the founders began to look for financial backing. Many responses deemed a "special interest" magazine to be a poor investment, and the future editors of *Ms.* were told that only a handful of women were interested in "changing women's status" anyway.[33] Fortunately, two publishers stepped up to help out. Katherine Graham, one of the few women publishers in the country at the time, bought stock in the yet-unproduced publication. Then Clay Felker, who worked at *New York*, got the magazine to financially back a one-shot sample issue that would be packaged with their year-end double issue. The women of *Ms.* had full editorial freedom, and *New York* took the full financial risk. The preview issue sold out all 300,000 copies in less than two weeks.[34]

With the debut issue in July of 1972, Warner Communications became *Ms.* magazine's major investor. The initial collective of editors (there were no secretaries) ranged in age from 17 to 45. While some had received formal higher education, some hadn't. Still others had Ph.D.s. Some were mothers; some had never been married. Whether they were gay, straight, Black, White, Latino, urban, country, or male, "*Ms.*," they wrote, "had tapped an emerging and deep cultural change that was happening to us, and happening to our sisters."[35]

To the editors of *Ms.*, what had happened to one of their spiritual sisters and feminist inspirations was a travesty. That Diana, *the Amazon Princess*, had relinquished her supernatural powers was not a sign of liberation to them, but of disempowerment. According to activist Gloria Steinem, since "many of the founding editors [of *Ms.* magazine] had been rescued by Wonder Woman in their childhoods—they decided to rescue Wonder Woman in return,"[36] doing this in a number of ways. First, they featured an image of Wonder Woman in her original costume on their inaugural cover beneath a banner that read "Wonder Woman for President," and Joanne Edgar wrote a feature on the history of the Amazon Princess for the issue. In 1972, Warner published a hardcover "Ms. Book" called *Wonder Woman* that featured a collection of 13 Marston-penned stories from the 1940s, best exemplifying the feminist values of sisterhood, collaboration, empowerment, and compassion. Steinem contributed an introduction in which she wrote of what the character meant to her:

> All those doubts paled beside the relief, the sweet vengeance, the toe-wriggling pleasure of reading about a woman who was strong, beautiful and a fighter for social justice. A woman who strode forth, stopping wars and killing with one hand, distributing largesse and compassionate aid with the other. A Wonder Woman.[37]

Feminist and psychotherapist Phyllis Chesler contributed an interpretive essay on Amazon mythology.[38] As a result of the campaign, the following year in issue 204 of the *Wonder Woman* comic, Princess Diana returned to her mythic origins. Additionally, the placement of Wonder Woman on that initial cover and her adoption as a representative of feminist values forever sealed her status as a symbol of female empowerment.[39]

Marvel comics also latched onto the movement by marketing themselves as an equal opportunity employer of superheroines, as Stan Lee declared, "Even before women's lib became a household expression, I began to tire of the way some of our female characters were being depicted."[40] Whether or not this sentiment extended to Sue Storm, Lee notes that he was determined to feature as many females as possible in the Marvel roster of headliners.[41] A cynic could easily assume that since *Ms.* magazine was launched in 1972 and DC's *Wonder Woman* was relaunched in 1973, this desire was more about capitalizing on cultural trends and less about promoting equality. Trina Robbins has a more generous approach:

> Stan Lee tried to reach a girls' market again by bringing superheroines back into comics. Lee, who had been responsible for the great superheroine girls' club of the late forties, was the right man for the job. During the sixties, he had tackled

socially responsible subjects like ecology and racism. He had introduced several African American superheroes. And in 1972, he produced three comic books with female protagonists, all aimed at a female audience: a jungle adventure (*Shanna, the She-Devil*), an action-romance (*Night Nurse*), and a superheroine comic (*The Cat*)."[42]

Beware the Claws of the Cat! was one of the more interesting attempts to create a superhero comic with feminist leanings; she was female friendly and captured the spirit of the movement. The Cat, also known as Greer Nelson, is a young widow rediscovering her identity during the second wave of feminism.

Though bright and curious, Greer had always been tended to by the men in her life and never had a chance to explore her potential. She'd had some college, but dropped out when she married. Essentially going from her father's house to her husband's, Greer was clearly a victim of "the feminine mystique." When her husband, a police officer and the financial provider, dies in an off-duty incident, she is forced to hit the pavement to look for a job. But "Every interview was the same, and Women's Lib began to have new meaning for Greer." She's told by potential employers, "It's obvious that you're intelligent and capable, but I see *hundreds* of girls like you *every week*" and is then offered a pedestrian secretarial position.[43]

Greer is smart and determined, and while she once floated through the expected steps of a woman's life, the death of her husband, though grievous, provides her with liberatory opportunities. Serendipitously, Greer encounters one of her former college professors, Dr. Tumolo, a woman whom she'd greatly admired. In a rare depiction of female mentorship, Dr. Tumolo hires Greer to work at her lab. She includes the young widow in her experimental research and science projects, and spiritually supports Greer when she returns to college as an adult student. As Greer begins to gain confidence and self-awareness, she recognizes, "Dr. Tumolo really makes me *proud* to be a woman. I can't let her—or *myself*—down."[44]

Dr. Tumolo's ultimate experiment involves machine therapy that would "someday make it possible for *any woman* to totally fulfill her physical and mental *potential*—despite the *handicaps* that society places on her."[45] While the message resonates with consciousness-raising politics of Women's Liberation in the 1970s, the method by which Dr. Tumolo wishes to empower women is problematic at best. Using a machine to amplify women's abilities excuses them from the responsibility of empowering themselves. (But, no matter. It's just bad comic book science that serves as a MacGuffin.)

The machine is commandeered by Dr. Tumolo's benefactor (a man!), who proceeds to test it on a Stepfordesque blonde. But in a radical act (*and* everyday rebellion), the doctor conducts tests on her willing protégée as well. The scientific data confirms that "attitude" either aids or inhibits the effect of the results, and Greer's curiosity allows the machine to magnify her innate abilities. She is able to consume and process vast quantities of information, her athleticism is enhanced, and "Her intensified perceptions were like an embodiment of that mythical quality known as woman's intuition."[46]

But in the final panel, Greer reflects on her unease with changing gender roles—and her path for the future: "All our plans for the betterment of womankind—! I did what I set out to do, and I did it well—But have I misused my powers? Have I become a stronger woman—only to become a poorer human being?" The letters page of *The Cat* mimics this unease, as a reader inspired by Greer captures the need for complex superwomen:

> I have always felt the lack of, and rather wistfully longed for a superhero with whom I could identify more completely than I have been able to with, say, Sue Richards or Wanda or the Wasp: I was wishing for a smartypants, wise-cracking, strong, brave-courageous-and-bold, bouncebackable WOMAN; and, in the Cat, I think we see the beginnings of her. The idea of a strip where a woman is the hero, not the love-interest, and action is the main focus, completely boggles my human mind.[47]

Another reader is less comfortable with shifting cultural norms and writes: "Dear Stan, CLAWS OF THE CAT #1 proved to me that Marvel is turning into a bunch of radicals. Sure, it was a good story, but it was burdened down by Communistic phrases put out by Women's Lib."[48]

The author of this particular letter goes on to say that Women's Lib is a communist plot to overthrow the country by destroying family values. Marvel, in a true effort to reflect a brave new world, responds that they are making "an attempt to portray some of the real injustices and, indignities suffered by women in the context of a fast-paced action story." They don't claim to be socially conscious and remind the reader that the prime purpose of comics "is *entertainment*. If we can also educate, that's even better."

Another letter begins with praise: "Dear Stan, THE CLAWS OF THE CAT was well-written, well-drawn, well-inked, well-lettered, and well-colored," but takes an antagonistic approach when the writer concludes that the magazine will be "ruined by Women's Lib sayings." The writer, who does not give their real name, goes on: "Equal pay for equal work is fair and just, and it's the right way. But all that stuff about, 'male chauvinist pigs' and women being 'sex objects' is a lotta (CENSORED). Anyway, what's *wrong* with being a sex object?"[49]

Whatever Marvel's intentions and however well they did, or didn't, succeed in presenting social justice and civil rights issues, their response to this letter is truly laudable:

Apparently, you've never been whistled and leered at on a streetcorner. Or had a sensitive extremity pinched in an elevator car. Or been treated with disdain because you dared to show some grain of intelligence. Or been refused a job because you might become pregnant.

But those are the things that are wrong with being a "sex object." And the whole point is ... people shouldn't be treated as *any* kind of object! We don't consume human beings the way we do noodle soup. Or at least ... we're not *supposed* to. Think of it.[50]

The title lasted only four issues. Perhaps the failure was a symptom of reader response, or lack of sales. Or perhaps it was simply that the artists and writers were too busy with other projects. The first two issues had been drawn by Marie Severin, but when she took over as head of the coloring department, she had no more time for *The Cat*. Linda Fite, who had written all four issues, married another employee of Marvel, and in a very un-Cat move, "left the ranks of Marveldom for the brave new world of Motherhood!"[51]

The Cat could have been a complex representative of superwomen, and an inspirational role model. Stan Lee praises the way the series captured an "awareness of the new spirit" and "the new mood of independence of women." But her potential was quashed, barely before it began. Girls and women alike would find their role model in another comic book superwoman, albeit in a new form.

Fighting for Your Rights, in Your Satin Tights

All the world is waiting for you ... and the powers you possess. (*Wonder Woman* Theme Song)

Just as the *Wonder Woman* comic empowered a generation of girls in the 1940s, *Wonder Woman* the television show (1975–9) did the same for children in the 1970s.[52] The title character was embodied with perfection by the endearing Lynda Carter and had enormous influence on a generation of girls, who, through her, saw the potential in themselves.

An animated Wonder Woman had been featured on Hanna-Barbera's *Super Friends* (1973) series, and two early attempts to translate Wonder Woman to prime-time television had failed. The first was a 1967 spoofy pilot called "Who's Afraid of Diana Prince?" written by Stan Hart and Larry

Siegel. William Dozier, executive producer of the *Batman* television series, had commissioned the script and served as the producer. Less than five minutes of the script was filmed, and it was never broadcast.

The second attempt occurred in 1974 when Cathy Lee Crosby, playing a blonde Wonder Woman, starred in a made-for-television movie, simply titled *Wonder Woman*, that wasn't well received. Fortunately for those in need of a superwoman, the next year ABC broadcast a new pilot, *The New Original Wonder Woman*, starring Lynda Carter. The former Miss World USA was statuesque, lovely, and had the dark tresses of a Greek. Her poise and temper secured her status as the definitive incarnation of the Amazon Princess.[53]

Wonder Woman writer and artist, Phil Jimenez, has said of Lynda Carter that "She is the living, physical, embodiment of this character" and that what he took from her "was a sense of grace and style and dignity."[54] Artist Alex Ross observed that even in a costume that resembled a swimming suit, Carter was able to take Wonder Woman and make her what the character essentially is, "an object of energy in motion, not . . . of corrupted sexuality or . . . something that is just for the boys."[55] Indeed, Carter's combination of kindness and power inspired countless girls to imitate her; donning the stars, stripes, and tiara come Halloween, and also during evenings at home, when they played less formal versions of pretend in their jammies and Underoos.[56] And Wonder Woman was just *cool*. She had a groovy theme song that accompanied her adventures and emphasized her awesomeness. She could lift and carry the weight of a grown man, throw a perfect lasso, and compel people to tell the truth. She was powerful without sacrificing compassion, and "wonder" didn't even begin to describe the feeling of watching, or imitating, her.

Though the show began in October 1976, storylines in the first season drew from the comics of the Second World War era and retained Marston's feminist message. Wonder Woman adopted the secret identity of Yeoman Diana Prince at the military base where Steve Trevor (Lyle Waggoner) was stationed. She frequently rescued Steve, even though he was a war hero. And she always appealed to a villainess's intelligence and womanhood in an attempt to rehabilitate her—a feminist play on the male hero's desire to "save" the femme fatale with romance.

Even when the villainess cannot be redeemed, Wonder Woman refuses to give up hope. For example, when she fails to convince the Baroness Von Gunther that freedom and democracy are causes more worthy of her intelligence than the Nazi agenda, she still believes the Baroness can learn from her experience and become a better person. Steve is impressed with Diana's understanding, compassion, and belief that people can change. "Yes," she says, "Where I was raised, we were taught that good must triumph over evil; and that women, and men, can learn."[57]

ABC dropped the series after the first season, and CBS picked it up for two more, moving the narrative to a more contemporary 1970s. The immortal Wonder Woman had not physically aged, and she once again left Paradise Island for America where she now aided Steve Trevor's son (in what was essentially the same character, and again played by Waggoner).

In a 2004 interview with Wonder Woman expert Andy Mangels, Carter said of the character she embodied so enchantingly that she intentionally infused Diana with altruism, compassion, and a deep sense of humanity. She wanted Wonder Woman to represent "kindness and goodness and hope and dreams and all the wonderful, human yearnings that we all have. To do the right thing and to have a happy life. She wanted everyone to have that."[58]

When asked by Mangels what she thinks her legacy of playing Wonder Woman is, Carter responds gracefully:

> I'd like to think that *Wonder Woman* had something to do with part of the change in terms of affecting a generation of young people and how they viewed women, and how women viewed themselves. You know, I certainly hear it often enough.[59]

Wonder Woman certainly was a superwoman who helped others believe in themselves. Indeed, in the true spirit of Wonder Woman, Carter says, "You know that if you can affect one person's life in your entire lifetime in a positive way that your life is worth living?"[60]

Charlie's Angels

Television series in the mid-to-late 1970s attempted to capitalize on the feminist movement, and several shows featured women in genre roles that were strong in spirit, if stereotypically feminine in appearance. This meant devising a way to appeal to the changing social consciousness of women viewers while not alienating men. The solution was The Kick-Ass Babe— a talented and capable woman whose beauty deflected the focus from her otherwise transgressive acts. Women could identify with—or aspire to be— these lovely ladies, while men would not be threatened by depictions of female independence, as they would instead be focused on the eye candy. *Charlie's Angels* (1976–81) is the perfect example of a series that successfully managed to walk this line. While less charged than Marston's creation and political agenda, the Angels nevertheless serve as a critical bridge from the progressive 1960s to the backlash of the 1980s.

Aaron Spelling had already produced a show featuring a superwoman in the 1965–6 run of *Honey West*—a series loosely based on the detective novels by the husband-and-wife team, Gloria and Forest Fickling, under the pseudonym G.G. Fickling, and starring Anne Francis. In 1976, the same year that saw the emergence of *Wonder Woman* and *The Bionic Woman*, he produced a show with not one, but three extraordinary women.

And whether or not you were a teenage girl in America in the 1970s, you can probably recite the story:

Once upon a time there were three little girls who went to the police academy—two in Los Angeles, the other in San Francisco and they were each assigned very hazardous duties. But I took them away from all that, and now they work for me. My name is Charlie.

Sabrina Duncan (Kate Jackson), Jill Munroe (Farrah Fawcett), and Kelly Garrett (Jaclyn Smith) were the original three women chosen by Charles Townsend (voiced by John Forsythe) to work in his private detective agency as his operatives, or "Angels." When an Angel left, the character was replaced so that they were always a trio, and so through the years, Kris Munroe (Cheryl Ladd), Tiffany Wells (Shelly Hack), and Julie Rogers (Tanya Roberts) all took an angelic turn.

Though labeled by the media as "jiggle TV"—a derisive term used to describe the physical attributes of the sexy young stars—such a critique is reductive and ignores the possibility of substance or merit within the program. For example, in subsequent years, women, reconciling their own pleasure of experiencing a show with three generally autonomous women, with the objectification of those very women, have cautiously, yet also passionately, praised *Charlie's Angels* for its positive depictions of intelligent women working together. Douglas writes, "It was watching this—women working together to solve a problem and capture, and sometimes kill, really awful, sadistic men, while having great hairdos and clothes—that engaged [us]."[61]

Sherrie A. Inness observes that while

The show's popularity was always based more on the sexual appeal of the actresses who played the Angels than on the intricacy of its plots[62] . . . The Angels did much of their own footwork to solve their cases, they were nearly always more intelligent than their male colleagues and opponents, and, despite the fact that the show was produced by a man and many of the writers were men, the Angels were not completely controlled by men. Though they had a subordinate relationship to their boss, Charlie, the Angels were generally free to pursue their own plans because Charlie was only a disembodied voice . . . We need to remember that in the 1970s the Angels represented a step forward for women.[63]

Elyce Rae Helford, editor of the anthology *Fantasy Girls: Gender in the New Universe of Science Fiction and Fantasy Television*, takes a more cautious approach when she writes that even though:

> *Charlie's Angels* offered strong female role models to young, white, middle-class '70s girls, for example, it also limited how we could think about the relationship between power and attractiveness to men and about the importance of fitting cultural expectations of age, race, class, and sexual orientation if we wanted to push the boundaries of feminine behavioral norms.[64]

While the Angels provided assistance to women from all walks of life, their core group never included any women of color. To find such diversity, we have to look in an unexpected genre, but first, one more beautiful blonde.

Na-na-na-na-na-na-na . . .

There has been some debate over whether or not Jaime Sommers (Lindsay Wagner) cost as much as Steve Austin (Lee Majors)—-a bionically enhanced man with the decidedly famous price tag of 6 million dollars. In the opening credits to *The Bionic Woman*, her cost is listed as "Classified," and in the pilot "Welcome Home Jaime," she suggests to Oscar Goldman—head of the Office of Scientific Intelligence (OSI)—that she must have cost as much as Steve. Goldman replies, "Well, not quite"; he smiles and adds gently, "The parts are smaller, after all."[65]

Jaime first appeared on *The Six Million Dollar Man* (1974–8). After the death of her parents when she was 16, Steve Austin's parents, Helen and Jim, became her legal guardians. Jaime and Steve were high school sweethearts, but they parted ways when Steve left to join the space program. On a return visit home to Ojai, California, they rekindled their romance and Steve proposed. At this point, Steve had already been in the accident that would lead him to be bionic and to work for the OSI. When Jaime is critically injured in a skydiving accident, Steve convinces Oscar Goldman to save her. Both of her legs, her right ear, and her right arm were replaced. At first, the couple work together on missions for the OSI, but soon Jaime's body begins to reject the bionics. After a death and revival, Jaime eventually adjusts to her new body, though unfortunately she suffers from amnesia. Any memory of her previous life causes crippling headaches that ultimately require more surgical procedures. Finally, her memory is restored, all but her life with Steve.[66]

Jaime, like the Angels, illustrates many of the contradictions inherent in mythic depictions of superwomen during the second wave of feminism.

She's blonde, athletic (at 27 years of age, she was a tennis professional with enough skill to beat Billie Jean King), and beautiful—all qualities that reinforce normative standards for women. On the flip side, she's almost 30, single and happy that way. She's also a professional, teaching sixth, seventh, and eighth graders with discipline problems at a local military base in Ojai.

Jaime's intelligence and humor make her one of the more complex of 1970s television superwomen. When it's determined that she has only partial memory recovery, her response to her doctors is gracious, brave, and pragmatic: "I'll simply have to take the life, and limbs, that you two gave me and live one day at a time."[67] Her loyalty is an asset as well. When Oscar wonders if it's fair to continue to use Jaime in service of the OSI, considering she'd already been through so much, Jaime insists:

> *Oscar:* Okay, I'll tell you what. When you get settled up in Ojai, we'll decide then.
>
> *Jaime:* Oscar, if I don't get an assignment from you very soon, I'm just going to show up and I'm gonna kick your door down.
>
> *Oscar:* Ah, you're just the one who can do it.
>
> *Jaime:* And don't you forget it.[68]

Oscar and Jaime's relationship is grounded in mutual respect and admiration, and though they are employer and employee (as well as friends), Jaime never allows Goldman to treat her paternalistically. When it appears that Jaime might be in danger, Oscar tries to convince her to move to a location where she may be safer. But Jaime is resolute, "Sooner or later I'm going to have to make a stand for myself."

And she can certainly take care of herself.

B-Movie Vixens: Superwomen Belted, Buckled, and Booted

Oh, you're cute . . . like a velvet glove cast in iron. (*Faster, Pussycat! Kill! Kill!*)

Don't try that machismo charm on her—She's a liberated Woman! (*Coffy*)

There are a handful of female action characters that appeared in the 1960s and 1970s that aren't superwomen per se, but who have served as nontraditional antecedents. The villainesses, covert operatives, assassins, and street-fighting foxy mamas of B-movies provided bad-girl alternatives to the admittedly jiggly, though intelligent, blondes of *Bionic Woman* and *Charlie's Angels*.

For example, within seconds of watching Tura Satana's portrayal of Varla in the 1965 Russ Meyer classic "ode to the violence in women," *Faster, Pussycat! Kill! Kill!*, it's difficult not to be mesmerized; her thrall is uncanny.[69] Satana is uniquely beautiful, an unexpected mix of Japanese, Cheyenne, and Scots-Irish. Her curves are kickin', her cleavage unparalleled, and her stare arresting; Satana could steal the show simply with her formidable presence. But it's so much more that makes her role as the vicious Varla memorable.

The movie begins with a wacky pseudo-beatnik/pseudo–Rod Serling introduction over an *Outer Limits*–esque screen:

> Ladies and Gentlemen, welcome to Violence. The word and the act. While violence cloaks itself in a plethora of disguises, its favorite mantle still remains—sex. Violence devours all it touches, its voracious appetite rarely fulfilled. Yet violence doesn't only destroy. It creates and moulds as well. Let's examine closely then this dangerously evil creation, this new breed encased and contained within the supple skin of woman. The softness is there, the unmistakable smell of female. The surface shiny and silken. The body yielding yet wanton. But a word of caution: handle with care and don't drop your guard. This rapacious new breed prowls both alone and in packs. Operating at any level, at any time, anywhere and with anybody. Who are they? One might be your secretary, your doctor's receptionist, or a *dancer in a go-go club!*[70]

And the go-go dancing commences. Odd-angled camera shots show close-ups of Varla, Rosie, and Billie (Satana, Haji, and Lori Williams, respectively) shimmying with fervor. Satana's contortions are especially remarkable, but of course, this former burlesque dancer *is* the woman who claims to have taught Elvis how to gyrate and grind.

After work, entertainment for the grrrls consists of driving Porsches at top speeds in the Mojave desert, playing chicken, bisexuality (or as one character calls it, an "AM/FM" sexuality), skinny dipping, smokes, and booze.

Varla is icy cool and wildly psychotic. She's the unspoken leader of this gang of go-go dancers, one of whom describes her as being "like a velvet glove cast in iron." Varla's sexuality and hard personality are an intimidating intoxication that allows her to easily manipulate others.

While taking a break from joy riding in the desert, the women come across a cocky young man named Tommy and his annoying, bikini-clad girlfriend, Linda (Susan Bernard). Tommy's a member of a driving club and wants to do some timing out on the flats. Perky Linda is prepared with a stopwatch, but Varla goads Tommy into a race by letting him know that she's a better driver than he could ever be: "I don't beat clocks, just people."

A gauntlet is thrown, and Varla wins the race. Tommy, feeling emasculated, attempts to beat her another way—with his fists—-but he chose to mess with a woman who could more than take care of herself. Varla breaks his back and kidnaps his girlfriend. (And that's just the first 20 minutes of *Faster, Pussycat! Kill! Kill!*)

From a contemporary perspective, it's as if Quentin Tarantino, John Waters, and Ed Wood had made a film together. It's exploitative to the max, yet also oddly and mildly empowering—without ever really intending to be. The clothes are fabulous, as is the wickedly bad dialogue. The delivery is delicious too. All of Varla's lines are shouted—a ludicrous technique that Waters would incorporate into some of his own work. *Faster, Pussycat! Kill! Kill!* is offensive and thrilling; a bad grrrl *Thelma and Louise* meets *Kill Bill* meets *Priscilla Queen of the Desert* meets *Glen or Glenda*; with lots of camera angles swiped from Orson Wells' *Citizen Kane*. As writer David Schmader has said of *Showgirls*, another awesomely awful film, and it's a fitting commentary here too, "The subtext is staggering until you notice there is no subtext."[71]

Writer/director Russ Meyer—famous for his depictions of full-figured women—has said, "I personally prefer the aggressive female . . . the super-woman."[72] As with William Moulton Marston, creator of Wonder Woman, his desire is not to experience a heroic woman but a dominant one. Because there's essentialism in the work of both these men, their belief that women are the superior sex makes for a difficult feminist interpretation. Conversely, just because Marston and Meyer had fetishistic leanings (bondage and breasts, respectively), it doesn't mean that feminist potential can't be found in their works—women are able to find inspiration in Wonder Woman's altruism and empowerment in Varla's karate chops.

Here, though, in the world of the Pussycats, the deepest message about gender (and female bodies) is that women have just as much potential for selfish and evil behavior as men. What is unique, or at least was in 1965, was to see a woman who was capable of defending herself.

Tura Satana featured in another pseudo-feminist B-film that needs mentioning, Ted V. Mikels's *The Doll Squad* (1973)—an enjoyable mess of a low-budget production about an undercover group of female commandoes that like *Faster, Pussycat! Kill! Kill!* is unexpectedly deserving of a positive feminist interpretation.

Responding to a threat made by the requisite villain, a senator and his assistant type the vital details of what will become an imperative, yet dangerous, mission into a computer that then determines the right group of individuals to handle the job. The computer suggests as most capable the Doll Squad, under the leadership of Sabrina Kincaid. Sabrina, played by Francine York, is a savvy redhead—smart and professional—but in her mid-riff tops and blazers, she looks more like a madame than a government employee. She assembles her team of "Dolls" from several disparate places, both likely and unusual: a dojo, a library, a laboratory, a swim club, and a burlesque club.[73] In a rarity for a youth-obsessed culture, not a single woman in the Doll Squad appears to be under 30. In fact, in 1973, York was 35 and Satana was 38.

The Dolls must stop the villain—who turns out to be Sabrina's ex-lover—from releasing a strain of the bubonic plague through rats systematically released around the globe—a diabolical plan ensuring world domination by an elite few who have been properly inoculated. As one Internet Movie Database commenter so elegantly puts it, the film is "marvelous crap."[74]

The "crap" should be clear from the description of the plot, but what's surprisingly marvelous is the respect afforded to Sabrina and the autonomy she receives from the men who hire her services as a strategist, an agent, and an assassin. Her opinion and expertise are considered essential from the start. Indeed, the senator's assistant informs his boss, "Unless she asks for help—it's her ballgame down to the last inning." A decidedly male analogy—but Sabrina is granted the authority to handle the situation without interference, and without concern for her gender.

Taking no prisoners, ruthless with a knife, and proficient with various weaponry and fighting arts, the Dolls—Sabrina, Lavelle, Liz, Sharon, and Kim—overtake the compound and save the world.[75]

Not bad for a "crappy" B-movie.

A Whole Lotta Woman

Nowhere are the tensions between empowerment and exploitation more exaggerated than in the Blaxploitation films of the 1970s, particularly those that starred the extraordinary Pam Grier. While on the one hand the genre's depiction of pimps, whores, drug pushers, drug addicts, and easy women reinforced negative stereotypes about African Americans, Greer's roles also presented a tough, independent woman who worked (albeit above the law) to protect her community. The actress's ability to make an impression, with generally weak material, sealed her status as one of the premiere action heroines of film, and certainly, outside of martial arts cinema, one of the only ones of color.

Greer's ability to make an impression is what landed her a movie role in the first place. Initially, she was a receptionist for American International Pictures (AIP), a film production company famous for its low-budget features. But Grier ultimately starred in a series of films for them, beginning with *Coffy* in 1973. The whole of the film involves the eponymous character seeking to destroy the network of drug pushers that led her younger sister to be a recovering junkie in a juvenile rehabilitation center. Stereotypes about the Black community are laid thick; not only is Coffy's baby sister a recovering addict—her older sister is a "hustler" and her brother is an addict as well. Additionally, there are an absurd number of gratuitous breast shots, which are titillating or distressing, depending on your opinion.

The concerns of those who criticized Blaxploitation for its emphasis on racial stereotypes, sex, and violence were certainly not without merit. But on the other hand, Grier's characters also presented a type of Black woman that hadn't really been seen on screen before. Before her, roles for African American women were generally limited to the often racist character types of Mammy, Jezebel, and Aunt Jemima roles.[76] Whether the characters portrayed by Grier (or any of her contemporaries, such as Tamara Dobson of *Cleopatra Jones* fame) simply replaced one stereotype for another is debatable. What *is* clear, as Yvonne D. Sims points out is that

> Before the 1960s, African American actresses dominated [the aforementioned] categories and were rarely seen in complex, multi-faceted roles. Blaxploitation films changed that by showing tough, no-nonsense women who were capable of holding their own among men and using justifiable violence to achieve their ultimate objective.[77]

One example of this takes place in the aforementioned *Coffy*, in which our superwoman's mission is clear from the very first scene. The film opens with Coffy fooling around with a man in bed. Her breasts are exposed over the top of her dress, and as he fondles her, she stops him and asks to have a hit of smack first. He calls out to a man in the other room, who is busy preparing the drug, to hurry up. Coffy has her bedmate get up to turn off the light; he does so thinking he's about to get real lucky, only to turn back around and see Coffy standing in shadow with a shotgun pointed right at his head. "This is the end of your life you rotten motherfuckin' dope pusher!" she proclaims before blowing his brains out. She then moves on to his partner with the gun and a syringe filled with an overdose of heroin. "My name is Coffy," she tells him, further explaining, "LuBelle Coffin's my little sister. Shooting smack at 11 and you got her on it you dirty shake! Her whole life is gone, she can never get it back, and you're living *real* good. That ain't right. It ain't right!"

Coffy, a nurse turned vigilante, has by the end of the movie murdered or maimed the system of dope pushers and mobsters that contributed to her sister's condition, telling one, in fact, as she shoots him that the bullet is a gift from her baby sister.[78]

Pam Grier is proud of the roles she created, and scoffs at any controversy concerning them. In 1979, she told *Essence* magazine, "I created a new kind of screen woman, physically strong and active, she was able to look after herself and others. If you think about it, you'll see she was the prototype for the more recent and very popular white Bionic and Wonder Women."[79] With conviction she added:

> I make no apologies for the women I created. Actually, I *re*created. When I grew up I knew a certain kind of Black woman who was the sole support of her family and who would, if you disrespected her, beat you into the cement. She was the glue that held her family together, got them through. I admired her greatly. I still do. And she still exists. I brought that lady to the screen—played her to the bone.[80]

Jamaica Kincaid wrote in a 1975 cover story for *Ms.* that although Grier "can so effortlessly dominate a scene everything and everyone else in it become incidental … [*Coffy, Foxy Brown, Sheba, Baby,* and *Friday Foster*] are mostly simplistic, sensational, violent, and technically faulty."[81] But Kincaid also praises them for being "the only films to come out of Hollywood in a long time to show us a woman who is independent, resourceful, self-confident, strong, and courageous. Above all, they are the only films to show us a woman who triumphs!"[82]

***

The B-movie vixens made famous by actresses Tura Satana and Pam Grier would pave the way for more mainstream female action heroes, but these latter women would time and again conform to more normative stands of beauty.

As Sherrie Inness notes, popular media has the "power to present images of women that have the potential to change social reality."[83] As we'll see in Chapter 4, there are many women and men who grew up with the superwomen of the 1960s and 1970s and positively internalized the images they saw. In turn, they have worked to inspire, create, and be heroic themselves.

3

Women of Steel: The Buff and the Backlash

No man may have me, unless he's beaten me in a fair fight.

—*Red Sonja*[1]

Many feminists consider the 1980s to be a backlash period in politics and popular culture, a topic Susan Faludi explored at length in her book *Backlash: The Undeclared War Against American Women*. She describes this backlash as "an attempt to retract the handful of small and hard-won victories that the feminist movement [of the previous decade] did manage to win for women" and observes that the political and mass media response of the 1980s insinuates "that the very steps that have elevated women's position have actually led to their downfall."[2] Yet she also notes that while fear of feminism "is a sort of perpetual viral condition in our culture," it is not always in an active stage. As Faludi puts it, "symptoms subside and resurface periodically."[3] Take for example the propaganda machine that was put into motion during the Second World War to inspire women's participation in industry and the subsequent backlash media of the post-war era described in Chapter 1.

The "symptoms" Faludi refers to had already begun to resurface toward the end of the 1970s. The trend of superwomen in popular culture, inspired by the progressive political movements of the late 1960s and early 1970s, began to lose momentum in tandem with road blocks faced by participants in the Women's Liberation Movement—namely, an increasingly conservative US government. In a major letdown, the Equal Rights Amendment to the US Constitution, which would have guaranteed equal rights under the law regardless of sex, fell three states short of ratification. Mass media played its role too, inflating ideological disputes between prominent feminist leaders as well as trivializing feminist concerns. For example, *TIME* magazine referred to a disagreement between Betty Friedan and Gloria Steinem as "a bit of sisterly hair-pulling"[4]—a comment that simultaneously evokes the "catfight" and the age-old trope of the older woman in competition with the young beautiful maiden. Media also introduced a different myth of the superwoman, the insidious image of the "woman who does it all," career, sex goddessdom, motherhood, and homemaker extraordinaire, and then tried to convince us that striving to be this unattainable and fallacious idol was what real women wanted and that any complaints other women had about it were the fault of feminism.

The slowing momentum of the feminist movement was mirrored in popular culture. While superwomen in the 1970s had at the very least represented a restrained progressiveness, most of their followers in the 1980s (with the exception of a notable few) further exaggerated perceived contradictions between femininity and feminism. Films in the 1980s focused heavily on hyper-masculinity, and superwomen who did manage to grace the popular landscape were for the most part peripheral.

One of the most recognized of these was, in fact, a little sister. She was Princess Leia Organa of *Star Wars* (1977) and one of the last mythic women to appear on screen in the 1970s. She was initially presented as a character with feminist potential, but the possibilities were wasted with each subsequent picture of the original trilogy.

Writer and director George Lucas was famously influenced by Joseph Campbell's book *The Hero with a Thousand Faces*—a study that detailed the archetypal stages involved in the journey, or quest, of the mythic hero. But this quest is generally considered a metaphor for the discovery of male identity, and women's involvement in the hero's journey has limited them to the roles of the goddess who aids, the mother, the temptress, or the lover/prize.

The initial movie focuses on how a disenchanted Luke Skywalker (Mark Hamill) is introduced to his destiny as a heroic figure called a Jedi. His journey begins with the discovery of a secret holographic message from a beautiful princess requesting assistance. When he finally meets Leia (Carrie Fisher) and attempts to rescue her, it's immediately clear that she's a leader who is used to calling the shots. Rather than swooning over her rag-tag team of "saviors," she tells them, "I don't know who you are or where you've come from, but from now on you'll do as I say, okay?" Her delivery makes it clear this is a statement, not a question.

She's also resilient; by the time Luke finds her, she's withstood torture without betraying the location of her rebel base. Here Leia is a senator, a spy, and one of the leaders of a political rebellion. She's snappy and savvy, and about business first. Though she has just witnessed the destruction of her home planet, Alderaan, her first concern is not herself, but to review the contents of a valuable secret document that will aid the rebels in their mission. Her response to a concerned colleague is brave: "We have no time for sorrows, Commander. You must use the information in this R-2 unit to help plan the attack—it's our only hope."

In the second film, *The Empire Strikes Back* (1980), when it's believed that our hero Luke may be sacrificing the good of the many for the good of a few with his decision to leave training before it's completed, his mentor Obi Wan Kenobi says, "That boy is our last hope." Yoda, Luke's other mentor with whom he has been recently studying, replies, "No. There is another." It's a reference to Leia, who in *Return of the Jedi* (1983) is revealed to be Luke's twin sister (the children had been separated at birth and raised in secret—an attempt to ensure their safety from their murderous father). The possibility of Leia as a mythic warrior hero is brought up only once again in the Star Wars movies, in *Return of the Jedi*:

> *Luke:* If I don't make it back, you're the only hope for the Alliance.
>
> *Leia:* Luke, don't talk that way. You have a power I don't understand and could never have.
>
> *Luke:* You're wrong, Leia. You have that power too. In time you'll learn to use it as I have. The Force runs strong in my family. My father has it. I have it. And ... my sister has it. Yes. It's you, Leia.
>
> *Leia:* I know. Somehow, I've always known.[5]

To be fair, the theme of Leia as Jedi (in this mythos, the ultimate in respected, and spiritual, heroism) is picked up in the subsequent authorized novels. But as the films progress from the 1970s to the 1980s, Leia morphs from a smart-mouthed, passionate, cinnamon-bunned political rebel to a love interest, slave, and sister—the latter recalling the sidekick trope in comics where the hero has a kid sister or cousin. (While the authorized novels are considered canonical, the mainstream familiarity with the films makes such a special-interest tie-in trivial in relation to a discussion regarding mass cultural attitudes about gender.)

While the paramount image of Luke is of him holding his Samurai-esque lightsaber, and young boys across the globe have reenacted lightsaber battles for over 30 years now, the most striking image of Leia is of her in a metal bikini. The "Slave Leia" outfit—as it has come to be known—ensures her status not as an icon of female empowerment and political influence (as she was in the first, and arguably second, film installments) but as an object of heterosexual male fantasy. The pervasive, and perverse, popularity of the outfit is seen throughout popular culture—from parades of "Slave Leias" at Comic Con International to Ross Gellar of the television series *Friends* admitting it's one of his sexual fantasies. Admittedly, Leia's bikini is memorable precisely because it ignited a generation of young boys' first "funny feelings" and thus serves as nostalgia for sexual awakening. But it's also troublesome that an outfit a powerful woman was forced to wear in a tactic meant to demean and objectify her, and in which she may have been sexually assaulted (her captor, Jabba, does feel her up with his suggestive tail), has become one of the dominant images of Leia.

Pumping Steel: The Valkyrie Thief and the Swordswoman

Superwomen in the 1980s often took the form of the Action Babe—a hard-bodied, modern Amazon following in the vein of Arnold Schwarzenegger and Sylvester Stallone.[6] Her body may have been as emphasized as Leia's was, but unlike Princess Organa, her physical skills were as emphasized as her physical appearance. One of the first action babes appeared in *Conan the Barbarian* (1982) as the love interest, partner, and inspiration of the title character. Valeria, played by dancer Sandahl Bergman, was a thief and lone warrior woman until she came across Conan (Arnold Schwarzenegger) and his traveling companion Subotai (Gerry Lopez). Together, they burgle one of the temples belonging to the villainous Thulsa Doom. And after, Valeria and Conan fall in love.

John Milius, who co-wrote the film with Oliver Stone and also directed the picture, says he loves the character Valeria, "because it's not the usual girl in one of these movies, you know that she could kill any one of them. She's the real thing."[7] Milius had seen Bergman in *All That Jazz* and notes, "When I saw Sandahl, *I fell in love*. I mean Sandahl was a *Valkyrie*. She's a *Valkyrie*."[8]

Tall and lithe, Valeria is physically spectacular, and Bergman's training as a dancer lends her movement, power, and grace.[9] In a film where the plot revolves around the "Riddle of Steel"—a question of what is more powerful, weapons or the spirit of the flesh—it's clear that even though Valeria ultimately dies, the strength of her body, and in fact strength of spirit, rivals that of Conan.[10]

Valeria even has life after death. She is reborn as a Valkyrie—one of those great warrior women of Norse mythology. In Conan's most difficult battle, her spirit appears to fight alongside him at a crucial moment, keeping an earlier promise: "If I were dead and you were still fighting for life, I'd come back from the darkness. Back from the pit of hell to fight at your side." A vision in her shining silver armor, Valeria galvanizes a fallen Conan with her mantra, "Do you want to live forever?"[11]

While Valeria is a notable action babe, ultimately she is not at the center of the story. It's Conan's quest and his revenge.

Conan the Destroyer (1984) followed *Conan the Barbarian*, and in 1985, the film *Red Sonja* became the final installment in an increasingly disappointing trilogy, the characters of which had been loosely based on the 1930s pulp writings of Robert E. Howard. Red Sonya had appeared in only one of his stories, "The Shadow of the Vulture," as a pistol-wielding Russian in the sixteenth century. In the 1970s, the character was adapted by Roy Thomas and Barry Windsor-Smith of Marvel comics for their *Conan* title. The spelling of her name was changed from Sonya to *Sonja*, and her origins were moved from Russia to Conan's fictional prehistoric "Hyborian Age." Her deftness with a pistol was changed to mastery of the sword.

Though she began as a supporting character, Sonja proved popular enough to support an eponymous title. Stan Lee referred to her as "the ultimate female warrior" and suggested that because Sonja is depicted as holding her own against any combatant—regardless of gender—"perhaps through the medium of the contemporary comicbook [sic], society may inch itself a bit closer to the time when we judge an individual on his or her own merit, rather than the accident of sex."[12] As will be clear, the 1980s film focuses more on Sonja's gender than on her skills.

Red Sonja, the movie, borrows elements from the comic, although it's not a verbatim retelling of anything from that medium but rather an attempt to capitalize on the sword and sorcery trend of the early 1980s.[13] This fierce warrior with flaming red hair lived in a savage world, and her quest begins with an act of violence against her. After Sonja has refused her sexual advances, the evil Queen Gedren orders that Sonja's family be murdered and her home burned to the ground, and has her guards rape the defiant young woman. That night, Sonja (Brigitte Nielsen) is visited by a goddess apparition who takes pity on the girl and becomes her benefactor.

Sonja is given a sword arm with unequaled strength so that she may seek justice and exact vengeance against Gedren (Sandahl Bergman[14]). She trains with a Chinese swordmaster and becomes a master herself. Though the grandmaster praises his finest student, and even provides her with a sword, he fears for Sonja's well-being. In a bit of backlash rhetoric, he tells her, "Sonja—you must learn to like men a little better. We are not all evil." And adds, "In life all is not swordplay. Hatred of men, in a lovely young woman, it could be your downfall."

It is then that Lord Kalidor (Arnold Schwarzenegger, in a not-quite-Conan role) arrives on a mission to tell Sonja that her sister Varna, a priestess, is dying. The priestesses Varna resides with were about to destroy an object of great power called the Talisman, an undertaking that Kalidor was sent to observe, though only women may safely touch this green and glowing sacred orb. Before the task could be completed, Gedren and her minions arrived, sacked the temple, and stole the Talisman. Gedren is hell bent on world domination, at any cost, even if, as Sonja learns from Varna, that cost is the very destruction of the world Gedren seeks to possess. It seems the Talisman is unstable and must be destroyed within 13 days or the world will end.

Perhaps it is a stretch to read much into a script as frivolous as that of *Red Sonja*. Alas, one could argue that the destruction of a strictly female power, that is, the Talisman, signals a shift from pagan worship to the monotheistic, male focused, Judeo-Christian religions. (Additionally, the number 13 is associated with sacred femininity.)

Relinquishment of independence and power is echoed in Sonja's personal journey; Yvonne Tasker notes that "An analysis of the ideological terms at work in a film like *Red Sonja* is not difficult—the film follows Sonja's journey to a 'normal' sexual identity."[15]

Sonja appears to be a vision of female independence, but her autonomy will be revealed as mere illusion throughout the course of the narrative. Here, a "normal" sexual identity will include nurturing a child, learning that not all men are evil through a romance with the gentle and respectful Kalidor, and the destruction of female threat.

Initially, when Kalidor attempts to accompany Sonja on her mission to destroy Gedren, she refuses his assistance, telling him, "I don't need any man's help," and ventures forth on her own. Kalidor, amused by the feisty warrior's stubbornness, follows and aids Sonja on her journey—whether she wants him to or not. Later he tells her, "You didn't seem to want a man's help—but you needed it." The few men in Sonja's life assume they know what's best for her and that she is incapable of taking care of herself—the movie will ultimately prove them right, giving preference to male wisdom over female action.

Additionally, as will be addressed in Chapter 8, there are common, even overused, narrative impetuses for acceptable female violence, including the experience of sexual abuse and the protection of children. While still seemingly on a solitary journey, Sonja comes upon a kingdom destroyed by Gedren. The only inhabitants that remain are Prince Tarn—a 10-year-old boy—and his servant, Falkon. Thus begins Sonja's return to a normative gendered identity; after an initial irritation with the bratty prince, she begins to train, and eventually nurture, the child. Many feminist critics, though certainly not all, have pointed out that the actual or spiritual role of "Mother" is used as a way of justifying a women's capacity for violence. It is also argued that linking a powerful woman with a traditionally gendered role or attribute limits her potential transgressiveness, as well as decreases the possibility of being perceived as threatening (read: "sexually unavailable") to a male audience.

Because of the assault on her, Sonja has adopted the position of a virgin swordswoman in order to protect her own chastity. In ancient Greek mythology, the virgin goddesses, Athena, Aphrodite, and Artemis, did not refrain from having sexual identities, or engaging in sexual pleasure—rather they chose whom to share their bodies with and when. Therefore, "Virgin" did not mean abstinent, but reflected a conscious control over one's body. Of the virgin goddess archetype, psychoanalyst Jean Shinoda Bolen wrote that it represents "the independent, self-sufficient quality in women." Women who identify with this archetype are driven by what is important to them, are focused and autonomous, actively seek their goals, and are both competent and self-sufficient.[16] Clearly, though this description applies to Sonja at the start of the narrative, toward the end her autonomy is questionable. She ultimately does give herself to Kalidor willingly, but it's difficult to say whether or not she will retain her solid identity after the credits roll.

Sonja sets her ground rules. Although they appear muddled, they stress her mastery of the sword, and by extension, the protection of her body—a body that has been abused and that she must reclaim ownership of.[17] A scene between her and Kalidor at their camp illustrates Sonja's position:

Sonja: No man may have me, unless he's beaten me in a fair fight.

Kalidor: So, the only man that can have you, is one who's trying to kill you. That's logic.

(Sonja goes and lies down. Kalidor picks up his sword and holds it to her throat.)

Kalidor: If you yield only to a conqueror, then prepare to be conquered.

Sonja: Don't be a fool, I don't want to kill you.

Kalidor: Try it.

It is guaranteed that no man can beat Sonja, and thus she is assured safety from further assault. But she is also taken with Kalidor, impressed by his tenacity, his physical beauty, and his relative tenderness. The unsubtle anti-feminist message is that strong, independent women may *say* they don't need or want men, but what they *really* want is to be conquered. When

Sonja and Kalidor do draw swords, playfully, even the child prince notes, "Why does she fight so hard? She doesn't want to win."

Sonja's tenderness toward this child, and her eventual submission to Kalidor, will restore her to her rightful place as Woman. Red Sonja has the potential to be a transgressive character; she's skilled with a sword, has a beneficent goddess, and is independent. But as the narrative in this film is constructed to lead her back to a normative femininity, Sonja is not subversive, simply confused.[18]

Killing Monsters

Get away from her, you Bitch! (*Aliens*)

Superwomen in the early 1980s, such as Valeria and Red Sonja, lacked the cultural impact of their mid-to-late-1970s sisters, but two characters emerged in the later half of the decade that became landmarks. One was Lieutenant Ellen Ripley in *Aliens* (1986), played by Sigourney Weaver in a reprisal of her role from 1979's *Alien*. The other was Sarah Connor, the damsel-in-distress who evolved into a warrior in the *Terminator* franchise. These two phenomenal characters are linked by the creative intention of writer and director James Cameron.

Ridley Scott's *Alien* was a horror film that focused on an ensemble cast, in which the characters were written as gender neutral so that they could be played by either a woman or a man. *Aliens* the sequel was a combat movie that really brought Ripley to the fore. In a genre dominated by male characters, it was *her* strength and possibility as a female character that interested Cameron. As Weaver herself noted in an interview for *TIME* magazine, "Usually women in films have had to carry the burden of sympathy, only coming to life when a man enters. Doesn't everyone know that women are incredibly strong?"[19] Cameron recognized that indeed they are.

Aliens takes place 57 years after the events of the first movie. After defeating the alien and bedding down for hypersleep, Ripley's ship drifted off course until it was eventually discovered by a deep salvage team. Remarkably, Ripley is alive and healthy, but the world she has returned to is unfamiliar. Her daughter, who was ten years old when Ripley left, has died of old age, and "The Company" for which she worked puts her on trial for destroying their costly property (the starship *Nostromo*), though it was decades ago and for a damn good reason. They don't believe Ripley encountered a hostile alien life form; there is no evidence of the original encounter, her crew is dead, and since her previous visit to the planet LV-426, a colony of terraformers has been long established.

Subsequently, Ripley's flight license is suspended and she is forced to take up a manual labor position at a loading dock to support herself financially. That is, until company man Burke (Paul Reiser) informs her that his organization has recently lost contact with the inhabitants of the LV-426 colony, and they suspect Ripley's aliens are to blame. They want her to accompany a group of marines out to the planet as a consultant, and although she at first declines, she's plagued by nightmares she needs to purge, and ultimately agrees.

Upon arrival at LV-426, it's discovered that there is only one survivor out of a population of 158—a feral little girl named Rebecca Jorden has managed to survive by hiding in the air ducts. Ripley, who is the only other person alive to have experienced the aliens, attempts to connect with the terrified child:

> *Ripley:* I don't know how you managed to stay alive, Rebecca. But you are one brave kid.
> *(The child finally looks up out of her catatonic state.)*
> *Rebecca:* Newt. My name is Newt.[20]

Much has been made about the bond between Ripley and Newt (played with great bravery by a winsome Carrie Henn). Some critics have observed that the child serves to re-emotionalize the distant Ripley. Others have noted that Newt serves as a surrogate for the daughter Ripley lost. And many have suggested that introducing a maternal relationship emphasizes her femininity, again providing a socially acceptable "excuse" for female violence. While all of these observations have merit, most fail to recognize that Newt herself is a subversive figure. If it's rare to see a woman at the center of an action movie, surely it's rarer to see a girl child. Sherrie A. Inness notes that Newt and the tough Latina marine, Private First Class Jenette Vasquez (Jenette Goldstein), offer alternative versions of female toughness in a film that is itself "a meditation on toughness and the nature of being heroic."[21]

Roz Kaveney, in her case study of the Alien franchise, makes an astute interpretation when she notes that

> critics have overstated the extent to which Ripley is the Mother and the extent to which her protection of Newt is solely and wholly a matter of paying her debt to the daughter whom she inadvertently abandoned—Newt is also another self who has experiences more like Ripley's than anyone else's and has to be protected for that reason.[22]

More often than not, Ripley treats Newt not as a child, but with the honesty and respect one would give an equal. When the formerly confident marines begin to waver, Ripley goes so far as to hold Newt up as an example of bravery by reminding them that a little girl managed to survive for weeks without weapons or training. Ripley's also aware that Newt knows the score, and therefore never lies to her. A mother would be tempted to comfort the child by saying that everything would be alright, but Ripley doesn't insult Newt's experience or resolve.

Ripley is one of the first recognizable female action heroes of American mainstream cinema—an impressive feat in an era where John McClane of the *Die Hard* films and Sylvester Stallone's character Rambo were the norm. *Aliens* proved that with the right creative team, a female lead could carry an action film to positive audience reception. As producer Gale Ann Hurd noted, "I really appreciate the way audiences respond [to *Aliens*]. They buy it. We don't get people, even rednecks, leaving the theatre saying 'That was stupid. No woman would do that.' You don't have to be a liberal ERA supporter to root for Ripley."[23]

Cameron told *TIME* that Aliens is about "finding personal resources: will, courage, whatever."[24] Weaver, who structured herself "to play Ripley like Henry V and like the women warriors of classic Chinese literature,"[25] has said, "real strength and unpredictability comes from not having an obvious weapon."[26] Perhaps this is why she and Newt prevail.

James Cameron's next warrior woman, Sarah Connor (Linda Hamilton), is an unexpected hero, and in *Terminator* (1984) she evolves from an unassuming diner waitress to a damsel-in-distress, to an archetypal Final Girl,[27] and ultimately, in the last scene, the epitome of determination. It is not until *Terminator 2: Judgment Day* (1991) that she becomes a true action hero.

Terminator is a successful mixture of genres; it's a love story, a work of science fiction, and a horror film. In brief, two individuals have been sent back in time from the year 2029 to 1984 in order to find a Los Angeles resident named Sarah Connor. One is an assassin—a cybernetic organism called a "Terminator" (Arnold Schwarzenegger) that was sent back to murder Sarah before she can give birth to the child who will become the leader of a resistance movement against an army of sentient machines. The other is a human named Kyle Reese (Michael Biehn)—a soldier for the resistance sent on a mission by Sarah's future son to protect her (and unbeknownst to Reese, actually father the child).

Reese informs Sarah of the danger she's in and the terrible events to come. In the future, machines made by a company called Cyberdyne Systems will become self-aware and decide that humans are a threat to their existence. The machines will subsequently launch a nuclear war and attempt to either destroy or enslave humanity. A war between humans and cyborgs ensues. At first, Sarah doesn't believe Reese, despite the fact that every woman named Sarah Connor in the area is being systematically killed. But when it becomes clear that he is the only person who can possibly protect her from the Terminator, she goes into hiding with him. In a bit of mind-bending irony, Reese teaches Sarah some of the basics of soldiering that she in turn will one day teach the resistance. But she still can't quite believe that the actions of a waitress in her 20s will be so crucial to the fate of humanity.

> *Sarah:* Are you sure you have the right person?
>
> *Reese:* I'm sure.
>
> *Sarah:* Come on. Do I look like the mother of the future? I mean, am I tough? Organized? I can't even balance my checkbook.

Sarah and Reese fall in love, and in a rare case, the *male love interest* dies to further the *heroine's* story. Alone with the Terminator, Sarah discovers resolve she never knew she had. She stops the machine herself and with a new fierceness says, "You're terminated, fucker." (It's a rather Pam Grier sentiment.) As Inness points out in *Tough Girls*, "the woman who says these words is very different from the one who claimed that she could not balance her checkbook."[28] In the film's final scene, we see Sarah planning for the future, for hers, for her son John's, and for that of all humanity.

In *Terminator 2*, we see a very different Sarah, one whose every move is informed by a consuming resolve. Her singular focus is to protect John, and if possible, prevent Judgment Day (the day the machines launch a nuclear attack) from ever happening so that he may not have to face such a tragic destiny, and perhaps, so that she may one day relax her oppressive vigilance.

While *Terminator* is most remembered for its original and intriguing story, *Terminator 2* is most remembered for its special effects—and for Hamilton's *astounding* physique. It's important to note that *Terminator 2* has become so familiar—so ingrained in American popular culture—that it's difficult to remember just how radical Sarah Connor was in this 1991 release, as well as how unexpected Hamilton's embodiment was, having transformed from the soft, romantic lead of television's *Beauty and the Beast* to a hard-bodied warrior woman.

As with Ripley, feminist critics have debated the symbolic meaning of Hamilton's physical metamorphosis. Just as important as academic theory, though, is audience reception and internalization. An anecdote from anti-violence activist, Martha McCaughey, proves valuable. In *Reel Knockouts: Violent Women in the Movies*, she writes that she generally had a negative response to violent scenes in films—and therefore avoided films with violence. She shares her reaction to the experience of viewing Sarah Connor in *Terminator 2* and the potentiality of tough female icons:

> My usual anger at the violence changed dramatically when I watched *Terminator 2* in 1991. Sarah Connor's competence with weapons and hand-to-hand combat exhilarated me. I remember driving my car home differently from the theater that day, flexing my arms as I clutched the steering wheel. That's when I realized that men must feel this way after seeing movies—all the time. My anger changed to envy; I could understand the power of seeing one's sex made heroic on-screen and wanted to feel that way more often. I realized that my own lectures on sexual assault failed to give women any feelings of strength and that this new strategy promised much for teachers and activists.[29]

***

Some critics have praised these hard-bodied women with guns and attitude as offering a symbolically transgressive iconography—others questioned whether or not the characters could truly provide alternative visions of womanhood if only their bodies, and not their spirits, changed. Was "musculinity," as Yvonne Tasker called "the masculinization of the female body," truly radical?[30] Debates continue about whether or not Action Babes of the 1980s were "men-in-drag" or women made masculine by their guns and muscles, but kept feminine by their adopted or actual children. Perhaps they were revolutionary characters in and of themselves, simply because they presented images of women that had rarely been seen before in American cinema, outside of B-movies.

"Change has to be envisioned before it can begin," wrote Gloria Steinem,[31] and though the images of Ellen Ripley and Sarah Connor provide many contradictions to be addressed, they also, as McCaughey notes, provide inspiration for envisioning changes in how gender is perceived and how women choose to walk heroically in the world.

4

Super Grrrl Power in the 1990s and the Turn of the Twenty-First Century

Sugar. Spice. And everything nice. These were the ingredients chosen to create the perfect little girls.

—Introduction to *The Powerpuff Girls*

All right, yes, date and shop and hang out and go to school and save the world from unspeakable demons. You know, I wanna do girlie stuff.

—*Buffy the Vampire Slayer*[1]

The American 1990s: The Hill–Thomas hearing. An unprecedented number of women elected to the US Senate. Revolution, grrrl style. A president who championed his wife as a political leader as capable as he was—if not more so. *Sassy* magazine, girlie culture, and the introduction of a superwoman who will forever be held up as the standard of excellence. And, as always, feminism both made gains and was frustrated by road blocks.

Meanwhile, young women both in Olympia, Washington, and in Washington, D.C. began holding meetings to discuss an approach to dealing with sexism, particularly within the punk music scene. These self-proclaimed "Riot Grrrls" promoted a DIY lifestyle, formed bands, and waxed revolutionary in self-published zines—small expressive magazines comprised photocopy and staples. Riot Grrrls pushed the envelope of "acceptable" topics to discuss in their publications and their music. Their lyrics addressed rape, sexual harassment, incest, homosexuality, abortion, and a "sex-positive" approach to feminism. Unlike traditional publications, zines were not reliant on advertising revenue, enabling grrrls to address controversial issues without threat of censorship or bankruptcy. These activists, artists, and writers offered each other support and encouragement, as they simultaneously critiqued the system, networked, and heroically combated injustice.

Outlets such as publication, performance, and meetings—much like the consciousness-raising groups of the 1970s era—empowered girls, and grrrls, to have a voice. In a 1994 issue of *Ms.* magazine, Kathleen Hanna, one of the pioneers of the movement, reflected that the riot grrrl phenomenon "shows how hungry so many women are to connect with each other."[2] According to the Experience Music Project's online Riot Grrrl retrospective, the brief yet influential movement was "instrumental in helping young women navigate the cultural and political terrain of the 1990s."[3]

Women looking for meaningful friendships, or at the very least a respectful feeling of sisterhood, had rarely seen such images of themselves in the media. Zines, and later the Internet, would serves as innovative methods of communication and thus provide women with unprecedented access to making their critiques of culture, and of those who have power over the creation of entertainment, public opinion.

BUST and Girlie Culture: Revolution? Or Feminism Lite?

This was not going to be Ms. *magazine for juniors, but rather* Sassy *for grown-ups.* (*The Bust Guide to the New Girl Order*[4])

With the exception of *Sassy*[5]—a hip, frank, and much loved American magazine that empowered teenage girls—the mainstream media deeply misinterpreted the Riot Grrrl movement, trivializing it as a "trend" when it was actually the emergence of young women, who grew up with the hard-won gains of second wave feminism, finding ways to make feminism relevant for themselves and for the twenty-first century. Understanding they had grown up with civil rights that their mothers hadn't had, they also recognized gender and racial discrimination, sexual harassment, and domestic abuse were still very real issues. Though they continued to see images of themselves in the media that didn't reflect who they really were physically or spiritually, they also recognized that the media had influenced them in positive ways.

Editors Debbie Stoller and Michelle Karp, and art director Laurie Henzel, took this influence and expounded on it in the pages of their own zine, *BUST*—a publication that celebrated sex, female experience, and popular culture, as well as promoted a philosophy called "Girl Culture." In their book *Manifesta*, Amy Richards and Jennifer Baumgardner define Girlies as

> adult women, usually in their mid-twenties to late thirties, whose feminist principles are based on a reclaiming of girl culture (or feminine accoutrements that were tossed out with sexism during the Second Wave), be it Barbie, housekeeping, or girl talk.[6]

The founders of *BUST*, eager to continue the conversation started by *Sassy*, were able to further push topical boundaries through the medium of zines, and eventually their own glossy rag, where they continue to champion, valorize, and document the pop culture inspirations that help define them as women, and as feminists.

Critics of Girlie Feminism have questioned whether or not this philosophy can be productive. In an essay for a *BUST* anthology, Stoller writes, "it's much more fun to be an activist when it involves sitting on your couch, munching popcorn, and watching the boob tube instead of marching for hours on the hot concrete sidewalks of Washington D.C."[7] Second wave feminists have interpreted such sentiments as suggesting that young women take the hard-won freedoms of their foremothers for granted. Even self-proclaimed "Third Wave" feminists Baumgardner and Richards, who appreciate the attention Girlies have brought to feminist issues, have said they wish that "Girlie feminists would organize as well as they onanize ... being a woman in the world requires not just saying 'I believe in equal pay for equal work' but knowing how to fight for it."[8]

Stoller argues that

> it's not just a cop-out that so many feminists of our generation have turned their attention to the media as ground zero in the fight for women's rights. It's clear to any of us who grew up in the '60s and '70s that the mass media have a massive influence on how we think about ourselves and the world around us.[9]

She observes that for many contemporary women, icons such as Pam Grier and Tura Satana (who have both been interviewed in the pages of *BUST*) as well as Audrey Hepburn, Bette Davis, Chrissie Hynde, and Tina Turner "have been as central in developing our idea of twentieth-century womanhood as Mom and Gloria Steinem."[10]

Stoller goes on to stress that

> Our appreciation for the power of the media also explains why today's rebels are making 'zines, building Web sites, and recording rock songs rather than holding rallies: we know that we can effect change through pop culture; that it's worth our while to channel our effort through TV channels.[11]

But a fair question remains: is simply saying you're a feminist activist enough?

As Rachel Fudge rightly argued in *Bitch*, a magazine dedicated to the critique of popular culture from a variety of feminist perspectives:

"Girl power" as articulated in the mass media (and mass marketing) is often misrepresented as de facto feminism, when in fact it's a diluted imitation of female empowerment. Indeed, for some people, it's a way to bypass the complexities of feminism—it's a lot easier to wear a "girls kick ass" t-shirt than to learn how to defend yourself physically. The problem with girl power is that all too often it relies on style over substance, baby tees over action. While girl power and the accompanying mania for girl culture has certainly helped spread pro-feminist, pro-female messages throughout the land, it also threatens to turn empowerment into yet another product.[12]

On the other hand, an affirming mantra such as "Girls Kick Ass" has the power to reinforce a positive self-image, helping us walk taller, speak louder, and apologize less. What can't we accomplish if we believe in ourselves? If we believe that we are superwomen, we have the strength to try and change the world.

So who kicks ass?

Skating the Edge

Edgy, dangerous, and seductive are words that aptly describe Aeon Flux— one of the first superwomen to appear in the USA in the 1990s. As neither hero nor villain, Aeon was a hypnotic force appearing in a series of animated shorts for MTV's progressive program, *Liquid Television* (1991). Intended to help the station find a new identity by moving away from its musical roots,[13] *Liquid Television* was comprised of arty, and often abstract, shorts that appealed to the late-night youth market.

Aeon Flux was developed when Peter Chung, a Korean-born and American-raised artist, was approached by Colossal Pictures—a San Francisco–based company producing *Liquid Television* for MTV. They asked Chung to contribute something that would be very "spy vs. spy like," but in his unique style.[14] Chung, who had been working on the children's program *Rugrats*, was frustrated with the limits of working with characters who were babies and looked forward to a project that could be radically different.

The autonomy of the project allowed Chung to take an experimental approach. In the spirit of his influences; German expressionism; the work of French artist Moebius; and directors Alfred Hitchcock, Stanley Kubrick, and Michelangelo Antonioni,[15] Chung employed unique editing techniques intended to break with cinematic conventions.[16] Everything about Aeon—her clothes, body, dancer's movement, and environment— was tailored to seduce the viewer and keep them watching, even if the narrative was completely confounding. A lack of dialogue in the original shorts contributed to this sense of disorientation and intrigue.

Aeon Flux was conceived as a 12-minute pilot that aired over six segments throughout the first season of *Liquid Television*.[17] Action without explanation, the shorts were perverse, smart, and disturbing. Aeon lives in a dystopian future world made up of two neighboring societies, Monica and Bregna (which were once united as Berognica and are now separated by a wall[18]). The Monicans are an anarchist society, while the Bregnans live in a formal and scientifically advanced state run by Aeon's lover/nemesis Trevor Goodchild. In *The Herodotus File*, a companion text to the series that features "classified intelligence" on the infamous operative, Aeon's specialities are listed as assassination, seduction, domination, and modeling for foot fetishists. Though she's clearly artistically presented as disproportioned, she is listed as having the impossible weight of 108 pounds for an athletic 5'8" tall woman.[19] The file also notes that in background interviews on Aeon, "the term 'independent' was used more than once by informants in describing the subject, and our experience has been that 'independence' translates to 'unpredictability.'" (Recall Sigourney Weaver's comment in the preceding chapter on how unpredictability is a powerful weapon.)

Aeon is an expert in espionage and accountable to no one, her allegiances never revealed. Chung says he "tried to eliminate anything that would allow you to predict her actions" and that

> Aeon has no family, or ties to anyone. Any dramatic points a screenwriter can score by holding family members hostage (or killing!) reveal nothing about her as a unique individual. Too easy. It's shorthand. We assume anyone is going to feel an emotional attachment to their sibling. That tells me nothing about her. Her worth (to us) is her responsibility and hers alone. The point is, we all define our own worth. It's the main point of the series, actually.[20]

He was clearly not intending to create a character that supported a political agenda or that represented an ideology. He says,

> The single most important thing about the character was that she's self-motivated. That she does not belong to any kind of organization, she's not fighting crime, she's not trying to uphold the law, she's not upholding an ideology, or fighting for her country. Everything she does is personal.

He also wasn't interested in something that would be either escapist or didactic, but in "shifting perceptions," which in itself has the possibility to be revolutionary.[21] With *Aeon Flux*, Chung was tapping into what he saw as the nonsensical absurdity of Hollywood action movies and infused it with Art (yes, capital "A" art). He chose to reject a narrative message in favor of a viewing experience.[22]

Aeon's lack of a discernable agenda doesn't negate an interpretation of her as heroic—the audience simply isn't privy to the details of her mission. We know only that she's *very* good at what she does. Additionally, the focus on her barely clothed and catlike body, or on her active sexuality, doesn't necessarily detract from her impact as a warrior woman. As scholar Dawn Heinecken observes, "Aeon is a dominatrix designed to titillate MTV's youthful, male audience ... [yet] in spite of her obvious sexual appeal, Aeon is never pure spectacle."[23] Heinecken also suggests that "*Aeon Flux*'s presence on MTV guaranteed Aeon a unique position in the emerging pantheon of female heroes," noting that "MTV has had a pronounced effect on contemporary visual culture, influencing both the style and content of much recent media."[24]

Chung wanted the character to die at the end of the pilot because he thought it would be subversive—as well as illustrate the futility of her mission. He commented that "Not only does she die, but she actually fails to accomplish anything really."[25] With the half-hour show, he decided that dying was "going to be her thing. She was going to die in every episode."[26]

On one level, this sentiment could easily be read as misogynist pleasure in finding new ways to kill the superwoman. But Chung's philosophy seemed to be one of narrative practicality, rather than an anti-woman sentiment: "If you start with the premise that she's always going to die, you can have her do things that a normal character in a recurring series wouldn't do."[27] An alternate reading of Aeon's death at the end of each episode would suggest that it illustrates her very nature. Death, return, and timelessness are embodied in her name "Aeon" (or eon), which means eternity. Flux is defined as something that is in continuous change or that flows in and out. Heinecken notes that "Aeon's name suggests her association with natural processes, evoking endless ebb and flow as well as the cycle of life and death. Likewise, the character of Aeon frequently dies, only to reappear in the next episode."[28] One of the key themes in the archetypal journey of the hero is a death and rebirth, and it seems that one of the key elements in the journey of the *female* hero is a repetition of these themes.

Her Courage Will Change the World

You're a warrior princess and I'm an Amazon princess. That is going to make such a great story. (*Xena, Warrior Princess*[29])

Xena was an icon, a warrior, a tragic hero, and one of the most emotionally complex female heroes of the 1990s and early twenty-first century—certainly one of the most impressive of any era. The character first appeared on TV in a three-episode arc on *Hercules, The Legendary Journeys*—itself a new age reimagining of Herakles with Kevin Sorbo in the title role. Rob Talpert, a producer and collaborator on *Hercules*, had wanted to do a female action TV show or female action superhero. He admits that he could think only in terms of *Wonder Woman* and *Charlie's Angels*, which he felt was limiting. He preferred to do something fresh and exciting, something that would diverge from the mold. Upon seeing the film *A Chinese Ghost Story* (1987), he thought, "what if we had a *bad* woman?"[30] Xena, created to fulfill that desire, was destined to die in her third appearance on *Hercules*,[31] but interest in the flawed character led to a series spin-off, *Xena, Warrior Princess* (1995–2001): a combination of high-concept camp and tribute to Asian action cinema, with twists on world mythology and ancient history.[32]

On *Hercules*, Xena (Lucy Lawless) was initially the "bad woman" Talpert had envisioned. As a result of her contact with Hercules, who helped to "unchain" her heart, and out of the narrative necessity of developing an ongoing series, Xena begins a quest for redemption. Although she declines Hercules's offer of companionship on her journey, she eventually accepts the friendship of a plucky village girl named Gabrielle (Renee O'Connor).

In the pilot episode for *Xena, Warrior Princess*, "Sins of the Past," Xena travels home to Amphipolis in an attempt to make amends with her estranged mother Cyrene.[33]

On her journey home, Xena encounters the farm girl who will become her soul mate. When she arrives in the village of Potidaea, Gabrielle and the other young women of the community have just been abducted by slavers. Xena uses her warrior skills to rescue them. Gabrielle, amazed by Xena's prowess, wants to accompany the warrior woman on her travels. Xena refuses. But Gabrielle is desperate for a life other than the one she is supposed to lead, and rather than marry her betrothed, bear children, and work on the farm, she wants to pursue a life where she can be a bard and a just warrior.

Gabrielle: You've got to take me with you, and teach me everything you know. You can't leave me here.

Xena: Why?

Gabrielle: Did you see the guy they want me to marry?

Xena: He looks like a gentle soul—that's rare in a man.

Gabrielle: It's not the gentle part I have a problem with. It's the dull, stupid part. Xena, I'm not cut out for this village life. I was born to do so much more.

Xena: I travel alone.[34]

Xena advises Gabrielle not to follow her, but the feisty girl does so anyway. When Xena's attempts to reconcile with her mother and the villagers fail, Gabrielle intervenes, bravely telling these strangers, "Now, you don't know me. I'm new in town. But, I can assure you, Xena is a changed woman. I saw her do some heroic things in the name of good."[35] Later, when a distraught Xena visits her brother Lyceus's grave, she tells him, "I wish you were here. It's hard to be alone." The tenacious Gabrielle has followed Xena again, and in her compassion responds, "You are not alone."

By the end of the episode, Xena has successfully saved her people from an invading army and received forgiveness from her mother. She soon continues her quest to right the wrongs she has done. Xena still can't shake Gabrielle and ultimately gives into the young woman's request.

Xena: You know where I'm headed there'll be trouble.

Gabrielle: I know.

Xena: Then why would you want to go into that with me?

Gabrielle: That's what friends do. They stand by each other when there's trouble.

Xena: Alright ... friend.[36]

Xena is interesting first because she initially rejects romance—the traditional motivation for a female character—for an exploration, healing, and development of the self. Second, *Xena, Warrior Princess* is radical in that it presents a story of female friendship with mutual respect between friends. Women are too often presented in competition with each other—and though Xena and Gabrielle do experience a controversial rift in Third season, their relationship is rooted in their care for each other. Otherworldly interference may have caused them to become enemies for a time, but their respect and awe of one another, as well as their belief in forgiveness, soon reunited them as best friends, partners, and depending on the reading of the viewer, lovers.

The series rejected historical accuracy in favor of sending the warrior pair from Greece to China, India, and Rome. They are allied with the Amazons—Gabrielle is even made a queen of their people—battle Caesar, help empower Helen of Troy, encounter gods and goddesses from the Greek and Norse pantheons, and learn from the Prophet Eli, a clear stand-in for Jesus Christ.

Rob Talpert promised viewers that although Xena would have male lovers to appease the network executives (who had also asked that the "girl sidekick" be replaced with a male), the superwoman would never settle down with any of them. And when the series' producers discovered that audiences were viewing Xena and Gabrielle as having a romantic same-sex relationship—even as lesbian icons—they played to that interpretation on a not-too-subtle subtextual level (which still managed to go over many viewer's heads). Openly gay *Xena* producer, Liz Friedman, has said of what fans call "The Subtext" that she's "always been a big believer in the power of popular culture. The best way to convey more challenging ideas is to make something that functions on a mainstream level but that has a subtext people can pick up on—or not."[37]

The show explored themes generally attributed to stories about the male hero: redemption, friendship, and bravery. And Xena's gender was never considered either an asset by her allies or a liability by her enemies. In her world, it was natural for both men and women to be warriors.

And for many of us in the audience, the combination of her attitude and her physique was a revelation. In the *Village Voice*, Stacey D'Erasmo wrote that Xena was "like something out of [a] Russ Meyer [film]"[38]— once again situating the roots of modern action heroines in the fierce and statuesque women of B-movies.

Some may argue that Xena's bulging breastplate and short leather skirt detract from her feminist potential by focusing on her body as a sexual object. Ditto for Gabrielle's half tops. Xena and Gabrielle will be feminist role models for some viewers, while others will feel that their skimpy outfits force them to conform to standards of femininity. Some will champion them as lesbian icons, while others will believe that the refusal to admit outright that the two women are in a homosexual relationship is a disappointing cop-out. Regardless, they are both characters that have made an impact on personal politics and the cultural landscape by providing courage to those who saw them as role models and internalized their values. Furthermore, we as audience don't need to take an either/or approach to superwomen. We can look critically at the social implications of the over-emphasis on sexuality as well as thrill at watching displays of confidence and power. Because an individual audience can engage with a representation as entertainment or as message, the relationship will never be static.

One Girl in All the World

If the apocalypse comes, beep me. (*Buffy the Vampire Slayer*[39])

Possibly the most celebrated superwoman of the 1990s in both the USA and the UK is Buffy Summers—a smart-talking, ass-kicking, vampire-slaying, demon-hunting, gum-chewing, teenage cheerleader in Southern California.

She was created by Joss Whedon—a third-generation script writer: his father wrote scripts for *The Electric Company, Alice*, and *The Golden Girls*— among others—and his grandfather worked on *The Donna Reed Show*. Whedon's mother, Lee Stearns, was a feminist and a high school teacher. Whedon notes that she was an enormous influence on him and on the woman-friendly values that shape his work. As described to the *New York Times*, "She was very smart, uncompromising, cool as hell."[40]

Whedon attended Wesleyan University, where he studied film and immersed himself in feminism and gender studies. After graduation he worked on the television series *Roseanne* and has since created three broadcast television shows; scripted or doctored several movie scripts, including *Toy Story, Speed*, and *X-Men*; wrote and directed the film *Serenity* based on his canceled-too-soon sci-fi Western television series, *Firefly*; and wrote a comic book series based on a future Slayer eponymously titled *Fray*, as well as many issues of the *Astonishing X-Men* line.[41]

The original screenplay for *Buffy the Vampire Slayer* (1992) came out of the desire to create a B-movie with a strong female protagonist, but also a "world in which adolescent boys would see a girl who takes charge as the sexiest goddamn thing they ever saw."[42] (And Whedon means "sexy" in an I-respect-and-admire-your-kick-ass-power kind of way, *not* a fetishized-object-created-for-the-male-gaze kind of way.) As an adolescent, Whedon was dissatisfied with the lack of empowered women in popular culture—particularly in comic books—though he admittedly had a crush on Kitty Pryde, of *The X-Men*, whom he has noted as "a figure of both affection and identification."[43] He adds that "the idea for *Buffy the Vampire Slayer* came from that same lack I had felt as a child. Where are the girls? Girls who can fight, who can stand up for themselves, who have opinions and fears and cute outfits? Buffy was designed to fill that void in movies, and then, ultimately, TV."[44]

The project was the result of a combination of influences: *Night of the Comet* (1984), a post-apocalyptic horror/comedy featuring two smart sisters with Valley Girl vocabularies—one of which is a cheerleader; *Near Dark* (1987), a Kathryn Bigelow written and directed vampire movie that played with genre; comic books and superhero tropes, particularly that of *The X-Men*; his mother; and his frustration with horror films where the blonde girl turns down an alley and gets killed. He wanted that girl to turn around and kick some ass.

Fran Rubel Kuzui fell in love with the script the moment she saw the cheeky title and optioned it with the intention to direct. But in opposition to Whedon's intent, she saw the movie as being more comedic than scary and was interested in approaching the script from a pop or pulp sensibility rather than as a genre piece.[45] After a series of rewrites, some encouraged by Kuzui, and many notoriously forced or adlibbed by Donald Sutherland, Whedon became despondent as he saw his female hero slip further and further from his original vision. When the film premiered, he sat in the theater crying, thinking he would never work again.[46]

Fortunately, five years later, Whedon was offered the chance to bring that original vision to the small screen. *Buffy the Vampire Slayer* (1997–2003) was a mid-season replacement on the WB network (owned by Warner Brothers) and moved to United Paramount Network (UPN) for its final two seasons. No one expected it to last past the first 13 episodes, if more than a few. Sarah Michelle Gellar, who played the titular character, has recalled that friends gently told her, "Don't worry, you'll get a pilot next season," and adds that "People pitied me—*pitied* me. We couldn't pay directors to come here. Nobody wanted to be on our show. And look what happened."[47]

One problem for many viewers was that getting past the title required effort. But as Tim Goodman noted in *The San Francisco Chronicle*, "any fan of the series—and one of the best-kept secrets of television was that the fan base spanned preteens to card-carrying AARPers—knew that 'Buffy' was never as silly as its title." He adds that "The title may have deterred people from watching. But that title also meant that people had to look beyond it, not to judge the show on its face, to open their minds to possibility."[48]

The title itself was of great importance to Whedon, as he wanted to create a character that nobody would expect to be a hero. "Buffy" was the name he came up with that he took the least seriously. In an interview for ign.com, he said that

> [T]here is no way you could hear the name Buffy and think 'This is an important person.' To juxtapose that with Vampire Slayer, just felt like that kind of thing—a B movie. But a B movie that had something more going on. That was my dream. The network begged me to change the title. I was like, 'You don't understand. It has to be this. This is what it is.' To this day, everyone says, 'Oh, the title kept it from being taken seriously.' I'm like, 'Well, f*** them. It's a B movie, and if you don't love B movies, then I won't let you play in my clubhouse.'[49]

The B-movie title was carried over to the WB (the network protested), but the show, unlike the movie, was anything but camp. *Buffy the Vampire Slayer* addressed a veritable encyclopedia of themes: bravery, redemption, insecurity, the death of loved ones, love affairs, failed romance, sexuality, self-destruction, addiction, friendship, family, sacrifice, spiritual evolution, and personal development through a combination of myth, philosophy, feminist ideals, metaphor, folklore and fairy tale, and literary and pop culture references. Seven seasons of well-planned and intricate story arcs rooted in Whedon's number one mission statement for the show, "the joy of female power: having it, using it, sharing it," inspired passionate loyalty in fans and a fair amount of scholarly attention.[50]

The series was based on the idea that high school is hell—and anyone who survives it is a hero. The school that Buffy attends literally sits on top of a Hellmouth, and the demons that she and her friends fight serve as metaphors for the challenges we all face—only the use of metaphor enhances the exaggeration of adolescent experience. For example, after Buffy has sex with her gentle and loyal lover, Angel, he turns into a monster.[51] In another episode, a classmate turns invisible because no one notices her.

The basics of the Slayer myth tell us that "In every generation there is a Chosen One. She alone will stand against the vampires, the demons and the forces of darkness. She is The Slayer."[52] Similarly to Wonder Woman's Amazon Sisters, Slayers are women who have existed for countless generations—perhaps even since the dawn of humanity. But unlike the women of Paradise Island, Slayers are mystically connected, and only one is supposed to exist at any given time. Therefore, when one girl dies, another is "called" to her sacred service. Once the new Slayer is "activated" and found, she is trained by the Watcher's Council, a group of specialists in mysticism and demonology based in England.

The series's pilot "Welcome to the Hellmouth" loosely picks up where the movie left off. Buffy's Watcher has died, and she's been kicked out of her Los Angeles High School for burning down the gym (because it was full of vampires, natch). Her parents have gotten divorced, and Buffy has moved with her mother to the fictitious Sunnydale, California, for a fresh start. Before she can even begin to settle in, however, she encounters her new Watcher, a librarian named Rupert Giles (Anthony Stewart Head). He's pleased to see her, having been trained for his role as a mentor, but she rejects her calling in hopes of living a normal life, insisting she's "just a girl."

> *Buffy:* Oh, why can't you people just leave me alone?
>
> *Giles:* Because you are the Slayer. Into each generation a Slayer is born, one girl in all the world, a Chosen One, one born with the strength and skill to hunt the vampires ...
>
> *Buffy:* ... with the strength and skill to hunt the vampires, to stop the spread of their evil blah, blah, blah ... I've heard it, okay?[53]

When a classmate turns up dead, and another is abducted, Buffy steps up to her slaying responsibilities—but on her own terms. New friends,

Xander Harris (Nicholas Brendan), a geek with heart, and Willow Rosenberg (Alyson Hannigan), a computer nerd who later becomes a Wiccan, stumble upon Buffy's secret and become her trusted allies. The group begin to refer to themselves in jest as "The Scoobies"— a nod to the mystery-solving team of Hanna-Barbera's *Scooby-Doo*. Over the course of the series, the Scoobies will expand to include ex-snobette Cordelia Chase (Charisma Carpenter), the werewolf and guitarist Oz (Seth Green), an ex-vengeance demon named Anya, the Wiccan Tara Maclay (Amber Benson), and in the fifth season, the mysterious introduction of a pre-teen addition to the Summers family in the form of little sister Dawn (Michelle Trachtenberg). They are frequently aided by Angel (David Boreanaz)—a vampire cursed with a soul, and later Spike (James Marsters), a vampire made impotent by a chip implanted in his brain by a secret government organization.[54] Faith (Eliza Dushku), a rogue vampire slayer accidentally called after the temporary death of Buffy, is their sometimes ally and sometimes nemesis. In the final season, the Scoobies are joined by the geeky, yet loveable, Andrew Wells (Tom Lenk); the son of a previous Slayer, Robin Wood (D. B. Woodside); and an army of young women from across the globe who have the potential to be called as Slayer—should Buffy or Faith die, aptly called "Potentials."

Like William Moulton Marston before him, Whedon recognized the revolutionary power of using a popular medium to change societal ideas about gender roles.[55] As he told writer Emily Nussbaum for a 2002 article in the *New York Times*,

> If I made a series of lectures on PBS on why there should be feminism, no one would be coming to the party, and it would be boring. The idea of changing culture is important to me and it can only be done in a popular medium.[56]

Whedon intended Buffy to be a feminist icon, but he also wanted to create something that would appeal to young boys who would likely not notice the feminist message, but might internalize it. Like it or not, part of selling young heterosexual men on a strong female character is making the kick-ass woman a babe. Fortunately, Whedon walked this line with admirable responsibility. He told *BUST* magazine that he

> would like sexuality to be part of the show. And I would like the attractive people to be present. I'm not going to lie—that's part of it. But at the same time, I try not to be exploitative. They're not running around in bikinis. There's a comfort zone, and they wear things they're comfortable with.[57]

Buffy is even written to be self-aware of her babeness, as well as her self-expression through fashion. When she goes undercover with her boyfriend's covert military operation, Buffy's told by their leader that she should consider a less revealing ensemble:

> *Walsh:* You might want to be suited up for this.
>
> *Buffy:* Oh, you mean the camo and stuff. I thought about it, but on me it's gonna look all Private Benjamin. Don't worry, I've patrolled in this halter many times.[58]

Rachel Fudge observes in an article for *Bitch* that "As cute and perky and scantily clad as she is, [Buffy's] not overtly sexualized *within* the show, which is a pretty dramatic shift from the jiggle-core of most other kung fu–fighting women on TV."[59] Irene Carres has commented similarly, "Buffy does not simply stand around looking pretty in her stylish clothes. She is physically and mentally active in saving the world, her body symbolizing a kind of resilience, strength and confidence recent to television's representation of the female body."[60]

With *Buffy the Vampire Slayer*, Whedon took the model of female heroism first illustrated (of course, literally *and* figuratively) in the original Wonder Woman comics—and later seen in the televised series—and he *rocked the mythic genre*. Inspired by values championed during the second wave of feminism, he created a new heroic archetype with the character of Buffy and the mythology of the Buffyverse. Whedon believes that

> People cared for her because she fulfilled a need for a female hero, which is distinctly different from a heroine. While a heroine is the protagonist, generally speaking, somebody swoops in and saves her. A hero is a more complex figure and has to deal with all the traditional rites of passage. Everything Luke Skywalker had to go through, Buffy had to go through, and then some.[61]

Whedon proved that a female hero could have the values of a Wonder Woman, as well as a complex emotional life. Therefore, while Wonder Woman will always remain a symbol of female empowerment, Amazons now have sisters in Slayers.

Kiss My Genetically Engineered Ass!

Girls kick ass; says so on the t-shirt. (*Dark Angel*[62])

The critical and cult success of *Buffy the Vampire Slayer* allowed for an explosion of superwomen on American television, some intriguing and some mediocre. A short list includes: Sydney Bristow of *Alias*, the Halliwell sisters of *Charmed*, the *Birds of Prey*, Turanga Leila of *Futurama*, Chloe Sullivan of *Smallville*, the women of Whedon's own shows *Angel* and *Firefly*, Veronica

Mars of her eponymous show, the children's programs *The Powerpuff Girls* (originally called "The Whoop-Ass Girls") and *Kim Possible*, and Claire Bennett and Monica Dawson of *Heroes*—many of which will appear in the following chapters.

One of the more conceptually interesting of the Post-Buffy superwomen is Max Guevara (Jessica Alba) of *Dark Angel* (2000–2). The character and series were co-created by Charles Eglee (*Moonlighting*) and James Cameron (*Terminator, Aliens*) and set in a near-future Seattle, Washington—a place they saw as representing the city of the future.

Max is an X-5—a child of the fifth generation of transgenic progeny created by a secret organization called Manticore. Cameron explains, "Max" is short for "maximum." "She's the maximum girl," he says, adding, "She's kind of a revved up version of us. She's not a machine. She's not a cyborg. She's the nth degree of human potential."[63] Max herself later explains how she's made up of the genetics of many remarkable people—with a little cat DNA thrown in for enhanced reflexes, "With my DNA I'm pretty much a blood relative to everybody who's been anybody *ever*. Churchill. Einstein. Pocahontas."[64]

Max's past is revealed through flashbacks. In the year 2009, she and 11 of her "siblings" escaped from their Manticore prison in Gillette, Wyoming, and the abusive training of Donald Lydecker (John Savage). The children all have visible barcodes on the backs of their necks, which are genetically embedded in their DNA and mark them as property. But rather than address each other by their assigned numbers, the independent spirits of the children, and their affections for each other, have led them to give each other real names.

During the escape, Max becomes separated from the other X-5s. Shortly after the breakout, in an unrelated incident, terrorists set off an electromagnetic pulse that wipes out most computer technology and records—effectively turning the USA from superpower to third-world country overnight. Cameron and Eglee have said that they wanted to create a world that would resemble America's depression of the 1930s; society would be corrupt, gangsters would take advantage, and the average person would be an underdog in need of a hero. Max would be the "avenging angel" of the story.

When we first meet our superwoman in post-Pulse Seattle, she has spent the past ten years searching for her family. During the day, Max works for a bike messenger service with her friends, Original Cindy (Valarie Rae Miller), an African American and a lesbian—certainly a first for network television; Sketchy (Richard Gunn), a ne'er do well that Max and Cindy consistently have to bail out of trouble; and Herbal Thought

(Alimi Ballard), a Rastafarian who frequently reminds his friends that even in times of trouble, Jah's plan is "all good, all the time." In keeping with the theme of names that reflect identities, their boss, Reagan Ronald (J. C. MacKenzie), is nicknamed "Normal."

Max funds the search for her siblings through cat burglary; her touch of feline DNA literally makes her a pop culture descendent of Catwoman, a.k.a. "The Princess of Plunder." (Indeed, Alba has said of the series, "It's like 'Matrix'/Catwoman/'Mission Impossible' all rolled into one!"[65]) It is during one of her heists, in which she attempts to steal a statue of the Egyptian goddess Bast, that she meets Logan Cale (Michael Weatherly). She quickly realizes he's the famous, yet anonymous, underground cyber-journalist "Eyes Only"—a cable hacker that in the words of Eglee "has pissed so many people off by trying to expose them that he has to file his pieces from the anonymity of cyberspace."[66] Logan, who has access to all kinds of secret information, deduces that Max is one of the escaped X-5s and offers to help find her family if she'll help him protect an important witness. Max refuses at first, but when Logan is permanently disabled as a result of shielding the witness himself, she begins to use her strengths for others. Thus begins her quest for self, justice, and community—as well as family.

Eglee wanted hip-hop music to play a major role in the show, believing that it was the dominant musical influence in the country. He also strived to have a multi-ethnic cast that would reflect the future face of humanity. The creators liked Alba because, as Eglee notes, the physical traits of her ethnicity are non-specific and interesting and would support their mission of representing a racial melting pot.[67] He told *SciFi Weekly* that

> we wanted a performer who [would give] a sense that maybe her DNA had been selected across the spectrum of human and even feline DNA. And Jessica brings this kind of unusual, exotic quality. You can't quite put your finger on her. You don't quite know where's she's from. You don't quite know what she is.

He adds, "She looks like she belongs to all of humanity, and not just part of it."[68] Alba, who is of Danish and Mexican descent, has echoed these sentiments, "Max is mixed up [ethnically] just like most people in the U.S. There's no purely one race, especially here."[69]

Science Fiction and Fantasy genres have always provided space for exploring issues of gender, sexuality, the body, class, and race, though this has certainly been more prevalent in literature than television, which is dependent on advertising revenues and thus subject to the tolerances of a consumer market. Until the twenty-first-century debuts of *Battlestar Galactica*, *LOST*, and *Heroes*—which feature ensemble casts of various and often mixed ethnicities—television series have been predominantly White, thus privileging hegemonic experience and standards of beauty.

The rare exception does exist. The original *Star Trek* ensemble included a Black actress and an Asian man. The character Mr. Spock, played by the White Leonard Nimoy, was the product of miscegenation (he was half-human, half-Vulcan) and even in an enlightened twenty-third century was frequently teased by the ship's doctor for his difference. His mixed-race heritage did not sit well with network executives, who wanted to play down controversial themes, but Roddenberry's humanist agenda prompted him to continue to use thinly veiled metaphor in his narratives to reflect racial tensions in the USA.[70]

On *Buffy the Vampire Slayer*, "Otherness" was also cloaked in metaphor.[71] Buffy's status as a Slayer, and thus a superhero, set her apart from the norm. Vampires and demons were also representative of difference, as were the awkward teenage natures of social outsiders Xander and Willow.

Dark Angel takes the concept of difference, or Otherness, to a new and more explicit level, particularly in its second season after Max releases all the genetic progeny of Manticore into the relatively normative world.[72]

The series addressed other issues concerning social justice such as class, sex trafficking, child abuse, scientific ethics, misuse of power, and access to medical care, as well as the human issues that were the very lifeline of *Buffy the Vampire Slayer*: the differently abled, family, friendship, redemption, a just cause, and noble action.

Scholar Lorna Jowett also points out that "Unlike other 'girl' action heroes who are generally white, middle class and at school or in college, Max has to work for a living—the double life of the superhero is shifted into different class territory."[73] She also notes that "*Dark Angel* may lack the humour and/or camp of, for example, *Buffy*, *Xena*, or *Farscape*, but it provides a much more obvious political and social context for its representation of gender."[74]

Dark Angel certainly has its flaws. Some of the hip-hop dialogue comes across as forced, while the combination of hip-hop, cyberpunk, biopunk, post-apocalyptic, conspiracy, and social justice themes can at times feel cluttered and directionless. And the episodes don't do well as stand-alones—watching the show in serial order gives a better feel for the provocative messages within the narrative. Like *Buffy the Vampire Slayer* and *Xena*, it can simultaneously be watched through many lenses and interpreted on many levels. It's a show about a female hero seeking redemption and family, about the state of American politics, and/or about pure sci-fi, cyberpunk entertainment.

The integrity of the core themes, as well as Alba's earnestness, makes it worth watching. As Teresa Blythe noted in *Sojourners Magazine*, "We certainly shouldn't ignore [*Dark Angel*] because it's not perfect. Powerful and popular visual stories raise key [cultural] questions and can help us become engaged with television in a new and productive way."[75] It can also give us new insight into our own lives and present new perspectives, perhaps even a new understanding, of the world we live in.

Max represents an independent, progressively motivated, just woman who speaks her mind and ultimately does what is right. As Alba says of the character she helped create, "She's confident. She's a smart-ass. She's honest. She doesn't feel the need to put on a façade for anyone."

Surely admirable traits for any superwoman.

Superwomen in the Movies

Superwomen in the 1990s and early twenty-first century flourished on television. Some influenced societal ideas about cultural gender roles, definitions of heroism, power, and sexuality, while others were shallow capitalizations on Girl Power trends.

Films of this time that featured superwomen fall into this latter category. Weak scripts, hurried effects, and one-dimensional characters plagued features such as *Lara Croft: Tomb Raider* (2001) and *Catwoman* (2004). The tongue-in-cheek (and ultra Girlie) *Charlie's Angels* (2000), produced by Drew Barrymore, consciously foregrounded style over substance. The critics of *Heroine Content*, a website devoted to feminist and anti-racist thoughts on women kicking ass, are disappointed in the Angels' displays of "free-market feminism . . . a kind of feminism that focuses on individual women doing whatever they want and not on any systematic change." But their review of the film also calls out the laudable depiction of female friendship. Reviewer Grace points out that "Dylan, Natalie, and Alex are honest-to-God friends. They aren't in competition, they don't fight for affection from their paternal boss or go for the same guys. They compliment each other and take care of each other. They seem to have fun together."[76]

So is a movie like *Charlie's Angels* embarrassing exploitation, or is there feminist potential to be found? The answer depends on the perspective of the viewer, and any one viewer can interpret or internalize depictions of a superwoman in myriad ways. And over the past decade, women who grew up with these formative pop culture images have since created spaces to discuss them. The Xeroxed zines, *BUST* and *Bitch*, evolved into newsstand publications. The Internet continues to provide communities and resources for women looking to make sense of images of themselves and for questioning the lack of more diverse representation. To invoke Debbie Stoller once again,

> Our favored weapon in this war against warped images of women is the smart chick's version of the kung fu kick: we study it, then slice it and dice it, dissecting its context and content to reveal its underlying and often contradictory meanings. Like our '70s sisters who proclaimed that the personal is political, we know that so, too, is the popular.[77]

When looking at superwomen, action heroines and kick-ass babes, there are no definitive answers to the question, "Is this feminist?" But we *can* note that many of the superwomen in this chapter *were* created with the intention of redefining notions about gender and heroism. As with all creative media, the ultimate interpretation resides within the minds of viewers, shaped as they are by personal experiences and intellectual perspectives.

SECTION II
Journey of the Female Hero

5

Love Will Bring You to Your Gift

On Redemption, Collaboration, and Compassion

Empathy is really the most revolutionary emotion.

—Gloria Steinem (*Town Hall, Seattle,* 2007)

"Love"—a complicated concept if there ever was one. Buffy is told by her spirit guide that love will bring her to her gift. William Marston's Wonder Woman is made of love, simply because she has the body of a woman. He even wrote that "Man's use of force without love brings evil and unhappiness. But Wonder Woman has force bound by love and with her strength, represents what every woman should be and really *is*."[1] In Luc Besson's film *The Fifth Element,* the eponymous character finds that the only reason to save our tragic world is for love. And for a time, Xena's companion Gabrielle follows a pacifist philosophy called "The Way of Love."[2]

Often with women, *love* is stressed again and again—making it necessary to wonder about this particular emotion, or ethic, consistently being linked to the source of a female hero's strength. Does love constitute a reimagining of heroism? It's certainly a different motivation from that of a quest for a prize, be it grail, fleece, dragon, or damsel. It is also a break from the "Lone Wolf" model of heroism, which is rooted in traditional uber-masculinity and isolationism.[3]

Does the suggestion of love as strength, or as gift, embrace innately female characteristics? Does it infuse what is "naturally" powerful about women into a liberating archetype? Or does it reinforce stereotypes about how women should behave as self-sacrificing nurturers? The assumption that love is inherent in women, but not in men, is a sticky, even sexist concept, and the idea that a female superhero's greatest gift is her nurturing temperament or her ability to love selflessly certainly has the potential to reinforce stereotypical feminine ideals. But there's evidence that love in the superwoman *does* in fact present a reimagining of heroism. Wonder Woman, Xena and Gabrielle, Buffy and the Scoobies, and Max Guevara (among others) are compelled by their values, which are in turn reinforced by love— a power greater than any of their physical skills. Their love is the impetus, but becomes integral to their strength, and thus the success of their missions. These superwomen illustrate a new form of heroism for popular culture that is based on loving compassion, and compassion itself is a heroic act.

The connection between "Love" and superwomen can at first seem troublesome, as it evokes notions of heroines in the traditional sense—of fair maidens and damsels in need of rescue by the hero of the story. But superwomen are *not* heroines in the traditional sense. Love, as it's used in stories about the female heroes described throughout this chapter, underscores three intertwined themes: redemption, collaboration, and compassion.

Redemption comes through a personal quest to make amends for past wrongs, often with guidance from a partner or a community. This definition of redemption emphasizes the belief that there is an innate good in all of us and allows for second chances. And many superwomen believe that anyone can change and grow into a better person.

In the original *Wonder Woman* series, this is seen as reformation, and in *Buffy* and *Xena*, it is seen as redemption. (The difference between *reformation* and *redemption* may seem subtle, but the nuance is crucial when evaluating the evolution of emotional complexity in depictions of superheroes in modern myth.) In the early Wonder Woman mythos, "Redemption" came through imprisonment and "love re-education." Villainesses were taken to Paradise Island's sister oasis, Transformation Island (originally named *Reform* Island), a place where "bad" women were taught to be "good" women. Here, good is of course equated with loving—in keeping with Marston's theories of the good and beautiful woman who should rule the world with her altruistic love.[4] In the Buffyverse, the individual human or demon in question is provided with the agency to decide what kind of life to live and what kind of person they want to be. (And just about anyone who has met Buffy is indeed influenced by her compassionate example to better themselves.) Along with female power, redemption is one of the overriding themes of the Whedonverse. Writer/director Joss Whedon has said,

> Redemption has become one of the most important themes in my work ...I think as you make your way through life it's hard to maintain a moral structure, and that difficulty and the process of coming out the other side of a dark, even psychological time [adolescence] is to me the most important part of adulthood ...I think to an extent every human being needs to be redeemed somewhat or at least needs to look at themselves and say, 'I've made mistakes, I'm off course, I need to change.' Which is probably the hardest thing for a human being to do and maybe that's why it interests me so.[5]

Choosing to live by a love ethic, writes bell hooks, "ensures that relationships in our lives, including encounters with strangers, nurture our spiritual growth."[6] Though Xena strives for redemption by helping those in need, a love ethic does not come easily to her. Fortunately, Gabrielle's stalwart morality helps bring Xena time and again to a place where she is capable of acting out of compassion. Indeed, hooks notes that "Those who choose to walk on love's path are well served if they have a guide. That guide can enable us to overcome fear if we trust that they will not lead us astray or abandon us along the way."[7] Clearly Gabrielle is Xena's guide on the path to redemption. Their mutual admiration is evident in their passionate praise of each other, as well as their sincere declarations of love and friendship, but it was Gabrielle's understanding of right and wrong that informed nearly every step they took. In the series finale, Xena tells her life partner, "if there is a reason for our travels together—it's because I had to learn from you, enough to know the final, the good, the right thing to do."[8]

Gabrielle had studied The Way of Love from a prophet named Eli (Timothy Omundson). In the Season 4 episode, appropriately titled "The Way," he taught her that the only way to end the "cycle of violence that has ravaged the Earth for centuries" is through nonviolence—a practice that is antithetical to Xena's warrior nature. In the same episode, the warrior princess learns from her own spiritual teacher, Krishna, that to fully tap into *her* strength she too must embrace "The Way."

Xena: The way? I've heard about the way in Greece, Ch'in, Anatoli, and now India. I don't get it. The way is not for people like me.

Krishna: You're wrong. You're very close to the way now. However, missing it by the width of a hair is the same as missing it by the height of a mountain.

Xena: I'm close? I don't think so. I don't have the patience of Gabrielle, the love of Eli, or the serenity of my mentor, Lao Ma. I'm just an angry, ass-kicking ...

Krishna: Warrior.

Xena: Yes, a warrior.[9]

Xena learns that "The Way of the Warrior" is a path that is just as valid and necessary as Gabrielle's, and though their paths are different, they walk them together.[10] When Xena apologizes for a time when she feels she's taken Gabrielle away from *her* truth, Gabrielle reconciles their ways of being. "Don't be sorry," she says, adding, "Xena, do you think I could have understood the power of selfless love if it weren't for our friendship?"[11]

Later, Gabrielle abandons the Way of Love for an even higher power. In "The Ides of March" (4.21), she dispenses with her pacifism when Xena is critically injured. With a violent rage rarely seen in her, Gabrielle destroys a troop of Roman soldiers attempting to finish off the paralyzed warrior princess. Though she is wounded, a horrified Xena feels responsible, thinking she has again caused Gabrielle to walk a spiritually false path: "I made you leave the way of love. It was my fault." Gabrielle reminds her that she had a choice, "do nothing or save my friend." With conviction she adds, "I chose the way of friendship."[12]

As Dana Hlusko rightly noted in an article for *Whoosh!*, compassion is the foundation for the Way of Friendship. She writes that with this concept Gabrielle designed a valid philosophy of life, one that was an even higher developed model than the Way of Love. Hlusko also points out that "These are not mutually exclusive 'ways.' They are tightly integrated in a service oriented, compassionate way of life." Most profoundly she adds, "One cannot live the Way of Friendship if one cannot love."[13]

When we are introduced to Max Guevara of *Dark Angel*, she like Xena is more interested in self-preservation than in helping others. But like *Spider-Man's* Peter Parker, who initially ignored his uncle's advice that "with great power comes great responsibility," a mistake that resulted in a death Peter could have prevented, so too will Max encounter a life-altering situation that her involvement could have averted. Her military training will cause her to be cautious, defiant even, but she'll also realize that she not only has the power to make a difference, but, like all of us, the responsibility to do so.[14]

As Lorna Jowett observed, in the beginning of the series,

> Max is recognizably the pragmatic, amoral thief who cares only for her own gain... She initially assists Logan because a 'friend of [hers] died on account of' the villain of the week (Pilot), in other words, for personal, not political reasons.[15]

But personal reasons are often the motivation for heroic acts. And for Max, especially as a transgenic—or symbolic—Other, the personal will become political.[16]

After Max's initial break-in at Logan's, he tracks her down, hoping to enlist her superhuman assistance (see Chapter 4). She can't believe that he's interested only in exposing corruption and not, like most everyone else in the post-Pulse States, after the almighty dollar. She asks, "What's your shot in all this? I mean being a famous, underground, pirate cyber-journalist can't be much of a payday." Logan explains that his parents "were loaded," he believes in making a difference, and uses his resources to do so. He encourages Max to use hers, but her response is that she's more interested in riding her motorcycle than giving herself a headache over stuff she can't do anything about. Logan reprimands her, lecturing, "You accept the way things are ... you're an active participant in making them worse." A defensive Max responds with trademark sass, "Is the social studies class over for today?"[17]

Logan wants Max to protect a key witness in a trial against a man named Sonrisa who has been replacing crucial medicine for war veterans with sugar pills and then selling the real deal for a marked-up price in Canada. The self-protective Max refuses, but when her friend Theo dies as a result of the false treatment, and she catches a news report detailing the kidnapping of the witness' daughter, as Logan is shot and his bodyguard killed, our hero steps up to the proverbial plate. Whether Max is driven by guilt or a desire for social justice is up in the air at this point. She saves Logan from a second assassination attempt and rescues the abducted child. She even executes a plan that takes down Sonrisa and his organization.

Logan thinks that Max's involvement means he's cracked her "bioengineered military-issue armor plating [to find her] beating heart"—and perhaps her sense of social responsibility. But she's wary, telling him she's "not signing up to join the Logan Cale brigade for the defense of widows, small children, and lost animals."[18] He entices her with an offer of exchange—information on the whereabouts of her X-5 siblings (which his clandestine investigations have led him to be aware of) for help with legwork. He produces a file on her brother, Zack, and in the closing narrated voice-over, Max says,

> I knew it. I always knew Zack was out there somewhere, but you know, just my luck this guy Logan had to be the one to find him. Now he figures I'm going to go and do the right thing because I owe him. Like I even care.[19]

Max does care and does do "the right thing." But not because Logan tells her to. (Although more often than not the "right" thing will be determined, designated, and validated by Logan—who has no problem manipulating Max for his own agenda, no matter how socially conscious or righteous it may be.)[20] Much of Max's motivation comes from finding and protecting her family—initially the X-5s she escaped with and later the majority of transgenics bred by Manticore. But she's also consistently faced with situations that allow her to heal the wounds of her own past by helping others move ahead in their lives. For instance, in "Flushed" (1.2), after a series of events lead to her arrest, she encounters Maria, a young woman being sexually abused by the prison's warden. Max, who had lived with a foster family after her escape from Manticore, has long felt guilt over not protecting her foster sister from similar abuse—even when she could have done so with her training. But Manticore's training also taught her that "You engage an adversary only if it is consistent with the overall strategic objective. Failing that, you will initiate a tactical withdrawal."[21] The child Max's objective was self-preservation, doing whatever she could to resist recapture. But she regrets leaving without the abused girl and doesn't make the same mistake twice—rescuing Maria and having Logan connect the young girl with a loving adoptive family. When Max thanks Logan, he reminds her, "You were the one who cared enough about this girl to go in and get her out. You did a good thing, Max." She replies, "Better late than never."[22]

Max will continue to learn that the "objective"—as dictated by her military training—is the last thing that matters. People—*good* people, friends, family, and the disenfranchised are what're truly important.

Notably, both Max and Buffy Summers reject patriarchal systems of behavior in favor of lived knowledge: experience, gut feelings, friendship, and context-based decision-making. When Max finally reunites with Zack, he chastises her for her emotional attachments. As Jowett observes, "Fairly early the show emphasizes that while staying in Seattle puts Max in danger of recapture by Manticore, over and over she chooses to remain with her various communities." Zack believes Max has allowed her tactical judgment to be clouded by feelings and emotions that will ultimately cost her her freedom. But, like Buffy, her emotions give her power.

And so do her friends.

***

Collaboration with friends, family, or community is common to the female hero—not because she is incapable of succeeding on her own, but because she is more successful when she recognizes, encourages, and utilizes the talents of others. This support system is essential to the evolution of her spirit—which will ultimately make her a better warrior. Additionally, in stories about the female hero, the sidekick—who is traditionally of lesser power than the hero, generally in need of rescue, and often serves the narrative purpose of comic relief—is elevated to the role of hero themselves through collaborative contribution.[23]

Xena was one of the first superwomen to be depicted as having complex and meaningful female friendships and as a participant in female communities. While Gabrielle is the single most important relationship in Xena's life, the warrior princess has also been involved in several mentor/protégée relationships with other women (even more notable because the learning and teaching were reciprocal). These include Helen of Troy, whom in the series's trademark rewriting of myth, Xena and Gabrielle liberate and empower; Lao Ma, a Chinese philosopher and ghost writer for Lao Tzu; and M'Lia, a Gaelic slave who taught Xena "The Pinch."[24] The Amazons also serve as an extended family of sorts, particularly as Gabrielle was gifted with leadership of their nation. In the episode, "Is There a Doctor in the House?," when the pair encounter Ephiny (Danielle Cormack), the Amazon who trained Gabrielle, in labor and alone in the middle of a battlefield, they protect and assist her and reassure her that her friends and family are there to support her.

> *Ephiny:* Family?
>
> *Gabrielle:* Hey—I'm your sister Amazon, remember? Xena and I will take care of you.[25]

Sherrie A. Inness notes in *Tough Girls: Women Warriors and Wonder Women in Popular Culture*: "Friendships are rare for tough women because such relationships can undermine the cool, aloof attitude of the tough hero …[but] *Xena* shows that toughness in women does not have to be antithetical to friendship." The modern superwoman deviates from the Lone Wolf model of heroism by being able to be both independent and part of a community. "The result," Inness writes, "is a new vision of toughness that emphasizes both her physical toughness and her connection to other women."[26] Here, the warrior princess demonstrates her priorities when she declares, "I'm gonna find a safe place for Ephiny to have her baby. And *then* I'm gonna stop this war."[27]

Xena populates her family with a variety of people, from Gabrielle and Joxer (Ted Raimi), to Ephiny and the other Amazons. It could even be argued that the gods, Ares (Kevin Smith) and Aphrodite (Alexandra Tydings), are part of her extended family.

Chosen families also play a large part in *Buffy the Vampire Slayer*, *Angel*, and *Firefly*. Joss Whedon has noted that he is much more interested in the created family than in families of origin, and in telling stories in which the chosen family is depicted as being more lasting and loving.[28] hooks also reflects on the value, and the healing power, of such a family:

> If we do not experience love in our extended families of origin (which is the first site for community offered to us), the other place where children in particular have the opportunity to build community and know love is in friendship. Since we choose our friends, many of us, from childhood on into our adulthood, have looked to

friends for the care, respect, knowledge and all-around nurturance of our growth that we did not find in the family.[29]

She goes on to add that "Many of us learn as children that friendship should never be seen as just as important as family ties. However, friendship is the place in which a great majority of us have our first glimpse of redemptive love and caring community."[30]

Nowhere in this series is this sentiment more poignantly put than in the Season 5 episode, "Family," in which Willow's girlfriend Tara Maclay—a relative newbie to the tight-knit Scooby Gang—approaches her 20th birthday. Willow's excited for the impending celebration, but the rest of the Scoobies, who admittedly like Tara very much, have yet to get to know her.

Unexpectedly, Tara's father, brother, and cousin arrive in Sunnydale with the intention of taking her back home with them. They've let her attend some college, but maintain that now her duty is to care for the men of her family, rather than dabble in alternative lifestyles. Her proficiency in magic especially alarms them, as they claim the Maclay women turn "demon" on their 20th birthday. Tara's terrified that if the Scoobies find out about this they will reject her; to keep her secret, she casts a spell that makes them unable to see her demon side. Unfortunately, the spell backfires when it renders the Scoobies unable to see *any* demons, and at the magic shop that Giles owns, they are attacked by what they believe is an invisible enemy.

Buffy, of course, defeats the demons, and as Tara reverses the spell, she apologizes and begins to cry. The Maclays have arrived on the scene:

Mr. Maclay: I don't understand.

Buffy: (*arms folded, looking at Tara*) I'm not sure I do either.

Tara: I'm sorry. I'm s-s-so sorry. (*sniffling*) I was, I was trying to hide. I didn't want you to see what I am.

Willow: Tara, what?

Buffy: What do you mean, what you are?

Mr. Maclay: Demon. The women in our family have demon in them. Her mother had it. That's where the magic comes from. We came to take her home before ... well, before things like ... (*points at a dead demon*) this started happening.

It's obvious that Tara doesn't want to leave and she and Willow are distraught. Buffy and Giles are disappointed in her seeming betrayal of their trust, but cautiously weigh the circumstances. Every one of the Scoobies has made a life-threatening mistake and been forgiven, protected, and loved.

Mr. Maclay:	You're going to do what's right, Tara. Now, I'm taking you out of here before somebody *does* get killed. The girl belongs with her family. I hope that's clear to the rest of you.
Buffy:	It is. You want her, Mr. Maclay? You can go ahead and take her. You just gotta go through me.
Mr. Maclay:	What?
Buffy:	You heard me. You wanna take Tara out of here against her will? You gotta come through me.
Dawn:	And me!

(Tara smiles.)

Mr. Maclay:	Is this a joke? I'm not gonna be threatened by two little girls.
Dawn:	You don't wanna mess with us.
Buffy:	She's a hair-puller.
Giles:	And … you're not just dealing with, uh, two little girls.

(Tara smiles even more.)

Xander:	You're dealing with all of us.[31]

Tara's father is furious and insists that "you people have no right to interfere with Tara's affairs. *We* are her blood kin! Who the hell are you?"

Giles, Dawn, Buffy, Willow, Tara, Xander, and Anya stand in solidarity, even Spike is included in the background. Buffy states with resolute love, "We're family."[32]

Tara has no demon in her—the accusation was a misogynist ploy by the Maclay men to keep their women oppressed. But it wouldn't have mattered to the Scooby family. As Jes Battis observes in his book, *Blood Relations: Chosen Families in Buffy the Vampire Slayer and Angel,* in Whedon's created families,

> You can be a werewolf, a vampire, an ex-vengeance-demon, a witch, a covert government agent—you can even be queer, which is still a stumbling block for most primetime offerings. Heredity, biology, genetics, appearance, class, gender, sexuality … none of these signifiers are crucially definitive within the Buffyverse. Your access to the Scooby Gang is based on your commitment to its mission, and your inherent sense of loyalty. Once you're in, you're loved—it's that simple.[33]

According to Battis, this episode illustrates that for the Scoobies, "blood kin" will never be as powerful as "family." Rather, in the Buffyverse, family is measured by emotional attachment, not heredity.[34] He adds that Buffy reorders the definition of family so that it encompasses members based on compassion rather than genetics and is therefore a perfect example of caring community.[35]

Of heroic collaboration and community, Sharon Ross writes, "while traditional heroes of the past have been made tough via their individualism and their ability to confront obstacles by themselves, modern female heroes such as Buffy, Willow, Xena and Gabrielle grow as heroes because of their friends."[36] She adds that they "are not heroes *for* other women so much as they are heroes *with* them (emphasis in original)."[37] Of course, on *Buffy*, it's necessary to add that women are also heroes *with* men. Instead of being the "one girl in all the world," Buffy rejects the traditional solitary mission of the Slayer. She chooses to collaborate with her friends, women and men working on equal footing—spiritually and even occasionally physically—forming a symbiotic entity or "group" hero, as in the episode "Primeval" (4.21).[38]

In this final battle of Season 4, Buffy and the Scoobies join together to defeat the "Big Bad" of the season, an uber-enemy named Adam. The group discusses how to extract Adam's power source, a uranium core embedded in his half-human, half-monster body. Willow suggests a magical solution:

Willow: What about magic? Some kind of, I don't know … uranium extracting spell?

(Everyone looks at her in disbelief.)
Willow: I know. I'm reaching.

(Giles stands up.)
Giles: Perhaps a paralyzing spell.

(He walks over to the bookshelf and pulls a book off.)
Giles: Only I can't perform the incantation for this.

Willow: Right. Don't you have to speak it in Sumerian or something?

Giles: I do speak Sumerian. It's not that. Only an experienced witch can incant it, and you'd have to be within striking distance of this object.

Xander: See what you get for takin' French instead of Sumerian?

Buffy: What was I thinking?

Xander: So no problem, all we need is combo Buffy—her with Slayer strength, Giles' multi-lingual know how, and Willow's witchy power.

(Giles looks at him.)
Xander: Yeah, don't tell me. I'm just full of helpful suggestions.

Giles: As a matter of fact, you are.[39]

The friends agree to do a "joining" spell so that each of the Scoobies' individual strengths will be embodied in Buffy. In doing this, the Scoobies create the ultimate superhero—and not just on special occasions such as this particular episode, but throughout the series run, though in a more figurative sense. The joining spell is yet another metaphor indicative of the "high school *is* hell" based series that illustrates what we can do heroically with our lives when we have the strength, trust, support, and love of our friends. Buffy may be the heroic vessel, but her friends are her heroic source. As Jana Reiss notes in her book *What Would Buffy Do? The Vampire Slayer as Spiritual Guide:*

> In Buffy's world the most powerful individuals are those with a strong support-system—friends and family members who share responsibility and heartache and who encourage one another to fight the good fight. The show doesn't preach about friendship ... instead, *Buffy* shows us the power of friendship in action and prompts us to ask ourselves why friendship makes us so much stronger.[40]

The obvious question that follows is, "Why aren't the X-Men and the Justice League of America also examples of this kind of 'group' hero?" The answer is that the JLA are solitary heroes who happen to periodically work together, and though the X-Men are something of a created family, they don't always demonstrate the depth of connection the Scoobies share. These individualistic superheroes don't play off each other's talents and don't seem to be inspired by one another, no matter how much respect they have for their colleagues. In contrast, the Scoobies have a familial love for one another that is fueled by their profound connectivity. Comparing the JLA to the Scooby Gang is like comparing co-workers to soul mates.

Through the Scoobies' enlightened example of collaboration, our traditional understanding of heroic tropes is once again rocked by Whedon. Though old-standard Jungian archetypes are recognizable in the Buffyverse, in Whedon's mythological world, the hero/ine, the sidekick, the lover, the sage, the trickster, and the great mother, all become champions whose unique capacities are of equal heroic importance. They are much more than a team—they are a heroic entity.

Max Guevara also has female friends, though unfortunately they are too often peripheral to the story. Her roommate Kendra disappears midway through the first season of *Dark Angel* when she moves in with her boyfriend, and interactions with Original Cindy are brief. As with Buffy Summers, Max's family is a combination of choice and origin and includes her "Sister Girl" Original Cindy, the X-5s she trained (and escaped) with, *their* children, and Logan Cale. Max's love for her family helps her evolve from a pouty, jaded, uber-sultry, and understandably self-protective girl to a courageous leader—a superwoman. This evolution is hinted at from the very beginning of the series, in Max's initial encounter with Logan when his eye catches the statuette she was in the process of stealing:

Logan: You have good taste. French, 1920s, a tribute to Chitarus.

Max: Whoever that is.

Logan: Oh. So, what? You liked it 'cause it was shiny?

Max: No. Because it's the Egyptian goddess Bast—the goddess who comprehends all goddesses, eye of Ra, protector, avenger, destroyer; giver of life who lives forever.[41]

Bast is depicted as a woman with the head of a lion or in the full form of a domestic cat. It's not a stretch to say that Max is an avatar of this goddess—especially as in Season 2 we see her fully come into her role as a compassionate leader, who protects her family and her communities.

In the beginning of Season 2, when Logan and Max have exposed the location of Manticore, the organization sets fire to the facility without evacuating its transgenic population. But Max arrives and releases her brothers and sisters from what would have been a fiery tomb. Many have never been outside the Manticore grounds, most have been trained as soldiers, several have been tortured to madness, and some look so different from humans as a result of their animal DNA that they could only be called "freaks." Survival for many will be difficult, as Max continually points out, people fear what's different.

Contrary to her "like I care" attitude expressed in the pilot, Max takes responsibility for releasing the transgenics into an unfamiliar and unfriendly world. Over the course of the season, she aids transgenics in need and stops those who abuse their power or jeopardize others with exposure. By season's end, when the transgenics have been exposed to the public, and the public responds with bigotry, Max will fight for the rights of her "Freak Nation" to exist.

Max would not have done this, in fact *could not have done this*, without compassion and love, both her own capacity for it and the nurturing support of her family and friends. Echoing Max's namesake, Guevara, who said that "the true revolutionary is guided by a great feeling of love" and that a "love of living humanity will be transformed into actual deeds," hooks has written that "All the great social movements for freedom and justice in our society have promoted a love ethic. Concern for the collective good of our nation, city, or neighbor rooted in the values of love makes us all seek to nurture and protect that good."[42]

Max has become the protector/avenger.

Love is redemptive; it heals and inspires—but so does the ability to forgive and be forgiven, which is made possible by compassion. As bell hooks wrote in *All About Love: New Visions*: "Making amends both to ourselves and to others is the gift compassion and forgiveness offers us."[43] Xena's story is a quest to make amends for the sins of her past, and though the theme is never explicitly called out on *Dark Angel*, Max continually encounters people in need who echo her past mistakes. Her assistance allows her to somewhat absolve her guilt over choices she wishes she'd made differently, if not, at least, to forgive herself for her own regrets.

Compassion is an act of selfless love often born out of empathy and an essential component of the love ethic that drives heroes to action without expectation of reward. Superman acts out of his love for his adopted home world, and as that great mantra from the Spider-Man mythos points out, there is an understanding that "with great power comes great responsibility," which underscores that our gifts are to be used for the greater good. They protect because it is just, as do superwomen, but again, the latter take heroic themes to a higher level. Their compassionate actions not only save others, but also *inspire* them to find and perfect the heroic in themselves.

On *Xena, Warrior Princess*, Xena and Gabrielle's long and tragic history with a woman named Callisto serves to show how a pivotal act of compassion can forever effect all lives involved.

When Callisto (Hudson Leick) was a child, her family was killed when Xena's army ravaged her village. Orphaned and alone, she swore revenge on the warrior princess. As an adult she does this in a number of ways: she raids villages in Xena's name to sully her reformed reputation, kills Gabrielle's husband, orchestrates the death of Xena's son, causes a rift between Xena and Gabrielle, steals Xena's body, and influences events from beyond the grave that ultimately lead to Xena's and Gabrielle's crucifixion in "The Ides of March" (4.21).

In the Season 5 premiere, "Fallen Angel," the pair are on their way to Heaven when Callisto organizes an attack on them with an army of demons from hell. Xena makes it to Paradise, but Gabrielle is not so lucky. The archangel Michael allows Xena to undergo a purification process and become a higher angel in order to rescue her companion. But he warns her that her capacity for compassion is now heightened and that the suffering she'll see in Hell will break her heart. He adds that if they can't rescue Gabrielle, Xena might be tempted to save her from her pain, and there's only one way to do that: "You would have to take on her guilt, and free her from her suffering—by giving her your light." This sacrifice would release Gabrielle from Hell, but doom Xena to stay there for eternity.

The angels manage to save Gabrielle before she becomes a full demon, but when Xena sees Callisto—suffering, demonic, and full of rage—her heart does break. Callisto seethes and shouts, "I will *never* stop hating you, Xena, do you hear me?! Never! You killed my *family*! My soul! My reason to live and love! And I will spend eternity seeking revenge!" Xena, angelic with tears in her eyes, simply whispers, "No."[44]

When Gabrielle arrives in heaven and her partner is nowhere to be found, Michael informs her that "Xena gave herself up—to save one of the damned." When Gabrielle learns just who Xena sacrificed herself for, she's horrified, turning to Michael and screaming, "This is insane. You call this justice?" Michael answers that "Xena called it justice" and encourages Gabrielle to respect Xena's decision to suffer in Callisto's place.

Callisto has no memory of who she was before she died, and in Heaven she's the kind and gentle spirit she would have been had Xena not killed her family. Gabrielle forgives Callisto for her past misdeeds, and in doing so, becomes an archangel herself. Callisto waits in Paradise as Gabrielle and the archangels attempt to now rescue the warrior princess.

As the angelic Gabrielle battles the now demonic Xena, the Earthly Eli is distraught over his inability to protect his friends. Questioning his way, he receives a vision of Callisto, telling him that "Love *is* the way" and "go to them." With Callisto's heavenly aid, Eli brings Xena and Gabrielle back to life, healing them with both his and Callisto's love. Xena's act of self-less compassion will heal once more; Callisto will later choose to be reborn through Xena, which will bring them both back that which they caused each other to lose—family.

If Xena and Gabrielle are archangels, and Max Guevara is symbolic of Bast, then Wonder Woman and Buffy illustrate a Bodhisattva ideology, as embodied by the Bodhisattva of compassion, Avalokiteshvara, best known by the name Kwan Yin.[45]

Bodhisattvas do not teach; rather they lead by example. Kwan Yin, in all her names, helps others to realize their potential through example and chooses to delay enlightenment in order to walk in the world helping others become the heroes of their own lives.[46] This is an approach adopted by the superwomen addressed in this chapter.

As noted in Chapter 1, William Moulton Marston created in Wonder Woman a warrior who fought for the greater good of humanity through an altruistic love. He'd felt that the "bloodcurdling masculinity" exhibited by men was detrimental to society, and his belief that women are fundamentally different from men led him to suggest that women should rule the world, precisely because they *are* women. With the character of Wonder Woman, he took the characteristics of love and compassion, which he believed to be natural to women, and made them heroic by giving women a superhero of their own.

Wonder Woman's Bodhisattva nature is realized when she gives up her immortality to help America win the Second World War. Her initial motives for leaving Paradise Island may include an adolescent crush on Steve Trevor, but once in America she inspires women to lead successful lives regardless of whether or not they had men in them. In one issue of the comic book, the Holliday Girls thank Wonder Woman for helping them. They helped themselves, she replies; she only showed them how.[47]

Contemporary superwomen also have a Bodhisattva nature, but Buffy and her companions illustrate more complex notions about heroic example. Although they don't always want to be the hero—a staple of the heroic archetype, according to Joseph Campbell's oft-referenced model—they are compelled to continue down their heroic pathways. For example, even with Buffy's occasional lack of faith in her sacred calling or in the merits of humanity, it is more often her Bodhisattva nature, than her duty as a Slayer, that compels her to continue to exhibit compassion regardless of exhaustion or discouragement.

Buffy's acts of love and compassion are relatively unique not only in the world of superheroes, but also in the world of Slayers. She breaks the mold in her own mythos, rejecting the patriarchal Watchers' Council and trusting her own knowledge and skill, as well as consulting her loved ones in order to make informed and just decisions. As the Slayer, ultimately the course of action is up to her, but she continually utilizes and nurtures the gifts of those around her—even when it may be easier for her to do the job alone. Therefore, it is because of her Bodhisattva, or compassionate, example that individuals are inspired to make the choice to realize their full potential as well as to nurture the potential of others.

Yet Buffy is often unaware of the trickle-down effect of her selfless acts. Fortunately, she is occasionally bolstered by profound expressions of sentiment as in the Season 3 episode "The Prom," when she is given a "Class Protector" award by her peers. They tell her:

> We're not good friends. Most of us never found the time to get to know you, but that doesn't mean we haven't noticed you. We don't talk about it much, but it's no secret that Sunnydale High isn't really like other high schools. A lot of weird stuff happens here. But, whenever there was a problem or something creepy happened, you seemed to show up and stop it. Most of the people here have been saved by you, or helped by you at one time or another.[48]

This recognition of Buffy's compassionate heroism inspires the students to recognize their own heroic nature two episodes later, when she asks them to risk their lives to save the world from yet another apocalyptic threat.[49]

Heroisms for the Twenty-First Century

The Bodhisattva of compassion is also useful for illustrating a gender-inclusive model of heroism. This particular Bodhisattva, Avalokiteshvara, is manifested in both female and male forms, just as heroic action born out of compassion is exhibited by both men and women in the *Buffy, the Vampire*

Slayer series—and for that matter, in the Whedonverse (The tagline of Angel Investigations, the detective agency of *Buffy* spin-off *Angel*, was a humorous, and accurate, "We help the helpless"). Compassionate heroism and its ability to inspire is not a phenomenon specific to superwomen, or limited to the works of Joss Whedon. Kevin Sorbo's Hercules goes from village to village helping those in need, while the late 1970s television version of *The Incredible Hulk* consistently showed David Bruce Banner (Bill Bixby) aiding everyday people. In another mid-1970s television series, *Kung Fu*, Kwai Chang Caine (David Carradine) was also compelled to help others, even if it jeopardized his own safety. In *The Lord of the Rings*, the ultimate destruction of the One Ring was made possible by Sam Gangee's love for Frodo Baggins.

But to illustrate the heroic values of loving compassion, friendship, and redemption as the values of a gender-inclusive form of heroism made possible by the modern superwoman, it's useful to revisit *Buffy the Vampire Slayer*. In the climactic scene from Season 6's finale, "Grave" (6.22), Willow has gone on a murderous rampage after the death of Tara and intends to destroy the world to stop the pain and suffering of humanity. But Xander—who has no "mystic" or "super" powers—stops her and saves the world through an act of love.[50]

As the scene begins, Willow stands atop a bluff overlooking Sunnydale. She intends to resurrect the buried temple of a powerful female demon in order to end the world. As Xander approaches, Willow tells him:

Willow: You can't stop this.

Xander: Yeah, I get that. It's just, where else am I gonna go? You've been my best friend my whole life. World gonna end, where else would I want to be?

Willow: (mockingly) Is this the master plan? You're going to stop me by telling me you love me?

Xander: Well, I was going to walk you off a cliff and hand you an anvil, but it seemed kinda cartoony.

Willow: Still making jokes.

Xander: I'm not joking. I know you're in pain. I can't imagine the pain you're in. And I know you're about to do something apocalyptically evil and stupid, and hey, I still want to hang. You're Willow.

Willow: Don't call me that.

Xander: First day of kindergarten. You cried because you broke the yellow crayon, and you were too afraid to tell anyone. You've come pretty far, ending the world, not a terrific notion. But the thing is, yeah. I love you. I loved crayon-breaky Willow and I love scary veiny Willow. So if I'm going out, it's here. If you wanna kill the world well, then start with me. I've earned that.

Willow: You think I won't?

Xander: It doesn't matter. I'll still love you.[51]

The scene continues with Willow physically attacking Xander, wounding him with her powerful magic. Xander stays strong throughout the attacks—after every painful electric bolt he is hit with, he repeats his devotion to his best friend by saying, "I love you." Willow succumbs to the profound power of loving friendship and human compassion as she returns to her true self.

This beautiful and intimate sequence shows us that *a compassionate act is a heroic act.* Though Willow initially mocks Xander's heroic intention by asking him, "Is this the master plan? You're going to stop me by telling me you love me?," his action has a successful outcome—the day is saved, as is his friend.[52]

In her essay "Love Saves the World," Jean Lorrah notes that it shouldn't surprise us that "only Xander, often considered the weakest of Buffy's cohorts, can reach and persuade Willow" because he and Willow share a lifelong bond of loving friendship.[53] His unexpected heroic deed is partly inspired by his deep affection for Willow, but it's important to note that Xander gets his courage from Buffy. (He's told her that "when it's dark and I'm all alone and I'm scared or freaked out or whatever, I always think, 'What would Buffy do?' You're my hero.")[54] Xander has great respect for female power, and he's not afraid to incorporate traditionally feminine traits into his behavior and actions—no matter how much he may make deflective jokes to the contrary.

As Lorna Jowett points out in her book *Sex and the Slayer: A Gender Studies Primer for the Buffy Fan,* Xander's expressions of "emotion, love, and friendship is part of [Whedon and Company's] project of dissociating gender and behavior." Invoking the group ritual in "Primeval," she points out that more conventionally the "heart" of a superfamily would be female.[55] Stephanie Zacharek echoes this sentiment in an article for *Salon* when she writes that Xander's actions "might be Whedon's way of saying that the best traits of men are sometimes those we associate with women."[56]

Compassionate collaboration leads to a realization of potential in the self and in others. The Buffyverse in particular provides a model of heroism that is gender inclusive because the Scoobies show us a world in which men and women work successfully together. Reiss notes that

> For Xander, Angel, Buffy, and other characters, self-sacrifice is not a sign of weakness but of strength: their altruism extends from a desire to see justice accomplished

for others as well as themselves. It's not a heroism that is out of reach but an every-day heroism born of compassion.[57]

Kathleen D. Noble envisioned a hero such as Buffy when she wrote in her book, *The Sound of a Silver Horn: Reclaiming the Heroism in Contemporary Women's Lives*, that "the female hero must fuse the best attributes of femininity and masculinity and so create a new archetype of heroism that speaks to both women and men."[58] Buffy's influence on Xander is proof that the Scoobies are this new archetype. The message of an episode such as "Grave" is that heroes act from a place of compassion and that compassion is a heroic act, regardless of sex or gender.

Generosity, kindness, and tolerance, especially when enhanced by love, transcend stereotypically gendered motivations to offer up twenty-first-century models of inclusive and resonant heroisms.

Love: Redemption, Collaboration, and Compassion

The early *Wonder Woman* showed women that they didn't need the love or protection of a man in order to live successful and fulfilling lives—but it also emphasized that women *should act lovingly* in the world. William Marston's concept of "love" is problematic as a feminist ideology because his work advocated a reversal of the existing gender hierarchy rather than an egalitarian society. Additionally, his belief that there are essential sex characteristics is a controversial and unproductive dogma. In his utopian fantasy world, men were expected to lovingly submit to a compassionate feminine authority rather than make sacrifices and work with women on equal footing.[59] bell hooks rightly stresses that such

> sexist thinking obscures the fact that these women [who make everyday sacrifices for others] make a choice to serve [and] give from the space of free will and not because of biological destiny ... When anyone thinks a woman who serves 'gives 'cause that's what mothers or real women do,' they deny her full humanity and thus fail to see the generosity inherent in her acts.[60]

As the superwomen in this chapter have shown, selfless compassion, and a giving of self to others, do not necessitate loss of identity or confinement to a biologically determined persona.

Love, as both concept and action in the Whedonverse, Xena's ancient Greece, and Max Guevara's Freak Nation, is much more egalitarian. The heroisms—for truly there are many ways to be heroic—of Buffy, Xena, and Max are reciprocal; the superwoman inspires others, who in turn inspire her. And love, when motivated by a spiritual interdependency, can show us how an act of compassion—regardless of who acts and who receives—can change lives, heal past wounds, and even save the world.

6

Who's Your Daddy?

On Fathers and Their Superdaughters

I'm not just any woman. I'm Jim Gordon's little girl.

—Batgirl: Year One[1]

My dad raised me to be independent and self-sufficient.

—Smallville[2]

A consistent theme in stories about the female super, or action, hero is that she is reared or mentored by a man rather than a woman. Some of the strongest, most complex, and independent superwomen in modern mythology are raised by a single father, while their mother is almost always physically absent, and at least emotionally unavailable—addicted, mentally ill, or outright clueless.

The morbid evidence: In her most recent incarnations, Lois Lane was trained in military combat by her father, General Sam Lane. Her mother is dead.[3] In an episode of the television series *Smallville*, Lois (Erica Durance) notes that it was her *father* who raised her to be independent and self-sufficient. On that same series, Chloe Sullivan (Allison Mack) was also raised by her single father. Her mother is in a mental institution. Sydney Bristow (Jennifer Garner) was molded into a spy without her knowledge or consent by her father, Jack—a man desperate to protect his little girl from a dangerous world. She was raised to believe that her mother, Laura, died in a car crash when she was six. Veronica Mars (Kristen Bell) lives with her dad, Keith. Her alcoholic and adulterous mother abandoned the family. On

Joss Whedon's *Buffy the Vampire Slayer*, the title character may live with her mother, Joyce, but it is her male mentor, Rupert Giles, who has the most influence over her development. The list goes on and on.

Marvelverse characters Araña Corazon and Elektra Natchios were raised by single fathers after the deaths of their mothers. Honey West, Ms. Tree, Nancy Drew, and Veronica Mars all followed in their fathers' footsteps to become private eyes; in the case of Joanna Dark, a bounty hunter. In *The Long Kiss Goodnight* (1996), Charly Baltimore's (Geena Davis) father was a Royal Irish Ranger. After his death she was adopted/recruited by his best friend, Mr. Perkins, to be an assassin for the US government. Her mother's whereabouts, and the reasons why she was adopted by a male government agent rather than a family, are never addressed. In the movie *Lara Croft: Tomb Raider* (2001), the title character is guided throughout the film by the spirit of her deceased father. He asks her to complete his work, and dutifully she complies, but all she wants is to get back the time that was stolen from them when he died. This wish does not extend to her mother, who doesn't appear to have a memorial plaque next to her husband's and is only mentioned once—in a dream sequence that serves to reinforce Lara's relationship with her father. In the dream he shows her a picture of her mother and says he wishes she could remember her. Little Lara says, "I wish I could remember her too," and then throws her arms around her father with an emphatic, "I still have *you* Daddy!"[4] Her mother is altogether irrelevant.

There are also a number of daughters with single fathers in law enforcement. The aforementioned Keith Mars; but also Barbara Gordon, a.k.a. the crime-fighting vigilante Batgirl, and daughter of the more traditionally law-enforcing Commissioner Gordon; and also Zoe Carter (Jordan Hinson) who lives with her father, Jack, the sheriff of a scientific community in the Pacific Northwest known as Eureka—also the name of the show. The Sci Fi channel's webpage for this series describes Zoe as: "Jack Carter's defiant, delinquent, and also terribly intelligent daughter. Though Zoe tries to keep up her 'riot grrrl' image, behind her attitude and piercings she's just another young woman who wants her absentee father to pay her some attention."[5] She loves her mother, but it's *his* attention she craves and his life she chooses to be a constant and meaningful part of. Max Guevara was created in a lab by a man named Sandeman, birthed by a surrogate mother she never knew, and reared and trained by Donald Lydecker. The Powerpuff Girls were born without the need for a mother at all: Bubbles, Blossom, and Buttercup were concocted in a lab by their single father, with sugar, spice, and everything nice, to be "the perfect little girls."

While it's wonderful to see depictions of fathers who take an active role in their daughters' lives, when we don't see women teaching women, the message an audience receives is that these virtual Athenas, whether sprung from their fathers heads or mentored by sage men, can only be as independent as they are because they lack a mother's womanly—almost always implied as passive—influence.[6]

From biological fathers to adoptive dads, father figures to institutionalized patriarchy, even dead fathers and ancient prophets guiding from the ether, the favoring of the father–daughter relationship over the mother–daughter bond begs questions. Why are men presented as teachers, and women as students? Where are depictions of women mentoring women? Why are mothers almost always absent? And why the pervasive spotlight on fathers?

Possible answers are few and frustrating. For one, men have traditionally held authoritative positions in the public sphere, while women have worked as homemakers or in ancillary positions supporting men in power as secretaries, nurses, etc. But with the strides gained by the second wave of feminism, one would assume that perhaps when we see more female role models in popular culture, as a result of seeing them in the real world, this would include stories featuring healthy relationships between mothers and daughters. Maybe there is a lack of imagination on the part of male writers, who continue to dominate the mainstream film and comic book industries. (And perhaps they are working out their own "Daddy Issues" through the perspective of a female protagonist.) But this trope also extends back in time to fairy tales, which Marina Warner notes is a female storytelling tradition. In *From the Beast to the Blonde: On Fairy Tales and Their Tellers*, she writes that "The raveled sleeve of these braided strands of male and female experience and wishes and fears can never wholly be combed out" and goes on to ask, "Above all, if and when women are narrating, why are the female characters so cruel and the mother so often dead at the start of the story?"[7] She provides a reasonable answer: "The absent mother can be read literally as exactly that: a feature of the family before our modern era, when death in childbirth was the most common cause of female mortality, and surviving orphans would find themselves brought up by their mother's successor."[8]

Yet what purpose does this serve today? What might it say about the needs of contemporary audiences? Is the narrative choice even a conscious one, or is it just that we are so used to not seeing the mother that we accept the situation as normal and without question? Maybe it's a result of the increase in the number of single fathers raising daughters after death or divorce? And at this point can we say anything about superwomen as motherless daughters other than they are almost always motherless?

As Carol Pearson and Katherine Pope note in their study *The Female Hero in American and British Literature*, in traditional stories of the hero "both men and women dissociate themselves from the mother at the beginning of the[ir] heroic quest." They point out that "The traditional quest is a search for the father, who will initiate the hero into the world"[9] and that "In works that make the patriarchal assumptions of traditional heroic theory, the mother–daughter bond is notable by its absence or by its subordinate position relative to the father–daughter relationship."[10]

In *The Power of Myth*, Bill Moyers also makes note of the father quest and asks Joseph Campbell, "But why no mother quest?"

Campbell answers, "the mother's right there. You're born from your mother, and she's the one who nurses you and instructs you and brings you up to the age when you must find your father." But this presumes that the mother is *always right there* (which clearly, she isn't) and that the hero is, by default, male. Campbell goes on to say that:

> [T]he finding of the father has to do with finding your own character and destiny. There's a notion that the character is inherited from the father, and the body and very often the mind from the mother. But it's your character that is the mystery, and your character is your destiny.[11]

Notably, there are a handful of superwomen, who, though they follow the spirit of the journey, do so in a moderately progressive way— meaning that, for them, it is the quest for the *mother* that is the key to their identity. The foregrounding of the father–daughter relationship may reinforce narrative tropes, but the search for the mother is a reimagining of the journey of the hero.

Spy Daddy: Jack Bristow

You know, some people go miniature golfing with their parents. We go to India and look for nukes. (*Alias*)[12]

Sydney Bristow's dynamic, tempestuous, and often moving relationship with her father forms the basis of *Alias* (2001–6)—a spy-fi television show that combined elements of *Mission Impossible*,[13] James Bond, and *The Avengers* with family drama. Sydney Bristow is a woman in her mid-20s attending grad school by day and fighting for the safety of her country by night. Sydney's mother, Laura, died when she was six years old, and she's estranged from her emotionally distant father, Jack (Victor Garber). Her friends Will (Bradley Cooper) and Francie (Merrie Dungey) and her finance, Danny (Edward Atterton), falsely believe Sydney works as a banker for Credit Dauphine. The company is merely a cover for SD-6, what Sydney and most of her co-workers believe is a secret subsection of the Central Intelligence Agency (CIA), but is actually part of a global terrorist organization.

When Sydney betrays protocol by telling Danny she's not a banker but a spy, SD-6's leader Arvin Sloan (Ron Rifkin) finds out and has Danny brutally murdered. Sloan's punishment of Sydney's disobedience leads to a series of startling discoveries about her career, recruitment, and family. When Sydney refuses to return to work, Sloan puts a hit out on her as well. But while being pursued by the men sent to kill her, Sydney's life is saved by an unexpected agent—her father.[14]

In a riveting scene, Jack pulls up in a black vehicle and tells his daughter to get in. She does, and having believed her father was a salesman, remarks with shock, "Dad, you have a *gun!*" As he drives, backwards, shooting at the enemy, and reminding his daughter to buckle her seatbelt no less, he explains, with what will become a trademark combination of crypticism and to-the-pointness:

Jack: You're going to have to accept that there are many things you won't understand tonight. The one thing you must understand is that the agency doesn't trust you anymore. And they're going to kill you unless you do as I say. I work for SD-6, just like you. Undercover at Genis Aerospace. You leave tonight. I've arranged a flight to France with a connection to Switzerland. You'll be red flagged at customs. I've given you new papers.

Sydney: I thought you sold airplane parts!

Jack: I don't sell airplane parts. I never sold airplane parts.

(They stop in a parking lot. A nearby car is parked with its headlights on.)

Jack: That car is taking you to the airport. I have to get back so they're not going to know.

Sydney: Who *are* you?[15]

Sydney later applies to the real CIA with the intention of serving as a double agent to bring down SD-6. In doing so she receives one more shock—her father is also a double agent, working toward the same end.

Finding out *who* Jack *is* will be important in finding out who *she* is, but so will revelations about her mother. As Abrams has stated, *"Alias* is a show about identity."[16]

Abrams conceived of the show in jest during a writer's meeting for his series *Felicity* (1998–2002), thinking it would be "incredibly cool if Felicity were recruited by the CIA, because she could go on incredible missions and have kick-ass fights and stunts!" As he told Mark Cotta Vaz for the series companion guide *Alias Declassified,*

> I wrote down these ideas about a grad school student who lived a double life and had trouble with Dad. I kept thinking about these characters and what their secrets and emotional lives would be. Any story about a family where there are secrets, and what happens when those truths emerge, was fascinating to me ... It's a spy show, but at its core is the relationship between this young woman and her father. I got excited about what happens to her, what that person would be like.[17]

Once Sydney becomes aware of Jack's true allegiances, the revelations snowball. She discovers that her mother, Laura Bristow, was actually Irina Derevko—a KGB spy responsible for the gruesome murders of over a dozen CIA agents, including the father of Sydney's handler and love interest, Michael Vaughn (Michael Vartan). Jack has kept this secret truth about Laura/Irina from his daughter to keep her from experiencing the pain of betrayal that emotionally crippled him. As a trained game theorist, this withholding of information, as well as his emotional distance, is a tactic intended to keep his daughter physically and emotionally safe. As Hope Edelman writes in her book, *Motherless Daughters: The Legacy of Loss,* some fathers use a

> relentless forward motion as a defense against [their] own emotional pain and a means of avoiding [their] children's grief. [This type of man] rarely speaks about his deceased wife out of a reluctance that may stem from his commitment to be the protector of his family, a job he believes involves shielding his children from emotional pain.[18]

And this is, of course, hyper-realized on *Alias* through secrets and espionage, the latter providing tools that aid Sydney on her quest.

But Irina (Lena Olin) is not dead, and when she resurfaces to turn herself into CIA custody, Jack goes into protective overdrive. Sydney has approached her mother, the prisoner, with trepidation, hoping to secure her cooperation in providing intel that will help the CIA dismantle the terrorist SD-6 organization. Jack, ever the tactician, visits the CIA's resident psychologist (Dr. Barnett) for assistance with "devising a strategy to persuade Sydney not to interact with her mother."

Dr. Barnett: But have you considered that the more you'll keep her from her mother, the more you're going to spark her interest?

Jack: Of course I have! Which is why I'm hoping to devise a strategy with the necessary subtlety.

Dr. Barnett: Well, I'm sorry, but I am not in the habit of helping a father manipulate his daughter. No matter how good his intentions may be.[19]

Jack truly believes his manipulations will protect his daughter, though his actions will have the very effect that Dr. Barnett predicts. He'll tell Sydney that he trusts her judgment with Irina and that she's "doing just fine" in what he recognizes is a difficult situation for her. But as a spy, a game theorist, and mostly a daddy, he will also assume that *he* knows what's best for *her* and will justify morally questionable steps to ensure her safety by stating that "There's *no one else* to do this job"—willfully ignoring the fact that Sydney is an adult woman and a highly trained agent.[20] Jack will initially claim Sydney as *his* daughter, telling Irina that her "motherhood is a biological fact with no substantive value in Sydney's life"[21] and "if Sydney in any way becomes victim to your endgame, I will kill you. She spent most of her life believing you were dead, she'll get used to it again. No matter what *bond* you try to forge with her."[22]

Sydney is initially cautious with her mother (in their first meeting in over 20 years, Irina shot her daughter in the shoulder). Understandably, she's both angry and curious. Irina is curious too, asking for personal information about Sydney's life, sharing stories with her daughter about her childhood, and offering to teach her meditative techniques. She's temporarily released from imprisonment to accompany Jack and Sydney on a mission to Kashmir, and when their daughter is injured, both parents rush to bandage her wound. Throughout the mission, Sydney will watch her parents' interaction closely for clues to her own identity and she'll later tell her friend Will:

> When I found out my mother faked her death twenty years ago, after mourning her for most of my life, she was still alive. I tried to imagine what it would feel like to stand in a room with both of my parents again. It seemed impossible. That two people with so much ... deceit between them could ever find a way to breathe the same air. And all of a sudden there we were. Just the three of us ... walking down a dirt road in the middle of Kashmir. When we were out there, working as a team, it was comforting.[23]

Irina's ultimate intentions will be a question mark for the rest of the series, and though she was ordered by the KGB to have a child as a means to secure Jack's loyalty, what becomes clear is that she *does* care about her family—though her love for them is in constant conflict with her endgame. As she tells her husband, "I may have been under orders to fabricate a life with you, but there were times when the illusion of our marriage was as powerful to me as it was for you, especially when Sydney was born."[24]

Sydney's exploration of her relationship with her mother is also an exploration of herself, and she will continue to look to *both* her parents for hints of the past and clues to her identity. As Pope and Pearson note, "Unlike the classical, patriarchal hero, the [modern] female hero . . . often seeks reconciliation with both parents," adding that:

> In doing so, she integrates the best qualities associated with each sex role and rejects its life-denying aspects . . . she rejects those attributes of her parents that limit her growth, but she does not reject her parents . . . When she accepts their simple human frailty, she often learns that both their positive and negative examples help her to live a heroic life. She can love them and learn from them, without living her life in their shadow.[25]

Sydney's parents will continue to do what most parents do, nurture and frustrate. She will ultimately combine their best qualities in order to become a more heroic spy, agent, partner, mentor, and mother.

Hero Daddy: Keith Mars

Keith Mars, the world's greatest dad. (Seriously. Greatest. There should be a mug.) (Joss Whedon[26])

Veronica Mars also focuses on the main female protagonist's search for identity, but here detective tropes, rather than spy-fi conventions (though similar), are used for the process of exposing, or maintaining, secrets. And though Veronica searches for her mother, this series does not offer as much of a progressive read as *Alias*, perhaps because it's slightly more grounded in reality.

Veronica (Kristen Bell) and her father, former sheriff Keith Mars (Enrico Colantoni), have become outcasts in their town—the fictional Neptune, California (essentially San Diego). They had previously lived in middle-class comfort with Veronica's mother, Lianne, but when Veronica's best friend Lilly Kane is murdered and Keith mistakenly pins Lilly's billionaire father, Jake, as the killer, Keith loses his job as sheriff in a recall election. Keith begins work as a private eye, with Veronica often helping out at his agency, Mars Investigations. But the loss of a steady paycheck causes the Mars to lose their home and take up residence in a junky apartment complex. Lianne begins to drink heavily and is so ashamed by her family's ostracism that she begs Keith to move them out of town. When he refuses, Lianne abandons them and is seemingly nowhere to be found. As Hope Edelman notes:

> The mother who abandons her daughter leaves a pile of questions behind: Who was she? Who is she? Where is she? Why did she leave? Like the child whose mother dies, the abandoned daughter lives with a loss, but she also struggles with the knowledge that her mother is alive yet inaccessible and out of touch. Death has a finality to it that abandonment simply does not.[27]

For Veronica, who thrives on solving puzzles, these very questions plague her—though at first she's too devastated to think about them ("The best way to dull the pain of your best friend's murder is to have your mother abandon you as soon as possible. It's like hitting your thumb with a hammer, then when it's throbbing so badly you don't think you'll survive, you cut the damn thing off"[28]). Her father says he doesn't want Veronica to see her mother as the villain in their current living situation.

Veronica: Isn't she?

Keith: No, it's not that simple.

Veronica: Yeah, it is. The hero is the one that stays and the villain is the one that splits.

Keith: I don't think that's a healthy perspective.

Veronica: It's healthier than me pining away everyday, praying she'll come home.[29]

Veronica's defensiveness is to be expected. To quote Edelman again, "children often have trouble mourning a lost parent ... because they have difficulty letting go of the image of an idealized mother they hope will one day return."[30] In Veronica's flashbacks and dreams, Lianne is loving and attentive, talking about boys with her daughter while they make waffles for dessert. Veronica hopes her parents will reunite and is faced with the fact that they won't when Keith begins to date again. Wounds are reopened, and Veronica finally admits she needs her mother.

Veronica: Mom is still out there somewhere. Do you even care if she ever comes back?

Keith: You didn't care until I started dating. You've been hard on your mom for months.

Veronica: You can find anybody! If she were a criminal, you'd make a couple grand tracking her down and you'd have her back in a week.

Keith: Well, maybe I don't care to find her. Have you ever considered that?[31]

As Edelman notes,

> When a mother deserts her child ...family bitterness or shame may discourage a daughter from uncovering details of the past. If the marriage went sour ... the loss may not be as severe for the father as it is for the daughter, and her fact-finding efforts that require his help may dead-end.[32]

Keith is privy to information that his daughter hasn't—or doesn't have—access to, and like Jack Bristow, he wants to spare his child even more pain. But like Sydney, Veronica takes the situation into her own hands and begins to actively search for her mother. She sends out untraceable pre-paid cell phones to all of Lianne's friends and relatives in hopes that one will reach her mother, and through her investigations she discovers more about her mother than she bargained for. Edelman writes that "for an abandoned daughter the question 'Why did she leave?' always includes the appendix 'me,'"[33] and for Veronica this will at least be partially true. She learns that her mother had been having an affair with her former high school sweetheart, Jake Kane. Celeste Kane, desperate to put her husband's infidelities to rest, hires her husband's head of security to take surveillance photos of Veronica. In the photos, sniper rifle targets circle Veronica's head, and these were sent to Lianne. Veronica finds them in a safety deposit box.

Keith hoped to protect his daughter from information that would hurt her—in this case, Lianne's infidelity (particularly because it raises an issue of paternity). Though Keith repeatedly tells her to "leave it alone," Veronica is consumed by a desire to *know*, and his deflections fuel her curiosity. When Veronica finally finds her mother, their relationship only continues for a relatively short time (whereas Sydney's mother is more or less a consistent presence, if an ambiguous one, throughout the course of *Alias*).

After finding Lianne, Veronica, in a last ditch attempt to reunite her family, uses her college savings to send her mother to rehab. Lianne soon returns to Neptune pretending to be rehabilitated, but is actually drinking in secret. Veronica confronts her mother by saying,

> I know, Mom. I know you're not through drinking, I know you didn't even finish rehab. You checked yourself out and that was my college money. I bet on you, and I lost. I've been doing that my whole life. And I'm through.[34]

Just as *Buffy the Vampire Slayer* used the horror genre as a metaphor for adolescence, both *Alias* and *Veronica Mars* use the conventions of their respective genres to exaggerate their protagonist's search for identity—for Sydney and Veronica this comprises an exposure of family secrets, an understanding of personal history, and reconciling the parent–child relationships with *both the father and the mother*. As Roz Kaveney notes, these "tropes point out that the truth of who you are and how you got to be that person is at once a necessary discovery and a painful one."[35] The novel thing about the journeys of these two superwomen is that though they keep with the trend of superdaughters raised by single fathers, they actually do interact with their mothers. And though their mothers are villainized, they still go in search of them to better understand their own identity.[36]

Veronica Mars, and especially Sydney Bristow, offer a contrast to the stories of Lara Croft, Elektra Natchios, The Powerpuff Girls, and others, where the mother is deemed irrelevant. And perhaps, as we will see in the following chapter, the quest for the mother, and the female hero becoming a mother herself, is a promising sign of things to come.

The final superwoman that should be mentioned in this chapter does not take a mother quest, per se, but a revealed truth about the woman who carried her to term is a profound comfort to Max Guevara, the protagonist of *Dark Angel*.

Max finds Hannah, the woman responsible for rescuing her after her escape from Manticore[37] and a woman she saw only once, but who selflessly helped a scared child on a fateful night. She, like Sydney and Veronica, has questions about her mother—only a few of which Hannah is able to answer. Hannah tells Max that Manticore recruited young women who they then kept on the base. They were monitored and tended to throughout their pregnancies and subsequently paid for their labor. They were young girls, desperate for money, and once they delivered their genetically enhanced progeny, they were unceremoniously sent away. To Max's disappointment, Hannah claims she can't tell her anything about her mother specifically.

> *Max:* I always wondered about her. My mother. Who she was, what she was like. Now I know. Just another girl looking to get paid. But it's all good. I turned out all right with my strange little life.[38]

But later in the episode, as Hannah and Max are saying their goodbyes, Hannah confesses that she did in fact know the woman that gave birth to Max. She tells her that "She wasn't like the others. Seven months into her pregnancy, she tried to escape, because she didn't want to give you up. When she was full term, they had to strap her down when they induced. Finally, they had to put her under. She fought so hard."

The episode ends with Max perched atop the Space Needle. Her voice-over narration speaks volumes to the motherless daughter and quester:

> So, now I know. I had a mother who loved me and maybe she's still out there somewhere. Like that really changes anything in my life. Only, it changes everything.[39]

For a daughter it truly does.

7

Always the Mother, Never the Messiah

On Mothers, Daughters, and Women Mentoring Women

You don't know what it's like to really create something; to create a life; to feel it growing inside you.

— *Terminator 2: Judgment Day*[1]

The only challenge to a father's will is a mother's love.

—*Smallville*[2]

As we explored in the previous chapter, the mother is often an absent or a destructive character in stories about the female hero. In stories about the *male* hero, the mother, or mother figure, is close to power, but rarely the revered source of it—reinforcing the idea that behind every great man, there's a great woman. While maternal characters such as Dana Scully of *The X-Files*, Trinity of *The Matrix*, Martha Kent of *Smallville*, and Sarah Connor of the *Terminator* films are written and played as intelligent, compassionate, and tough, their main purpose is to birth, protect, or otherwise nurture the male "savior."[3]

This is further reinforced by images that play on religious symbolism. Take, for example, the *X-Files* Season 8 finale episode, "Existence," in which Dana Scully (Gillian Anderson) gives birth to her son. Scully and Agent Reyes (Annabeth Gish) travel to a remote location to protect Scully from people who are a threat to her and the child. She gives birth in an abandoned house, and in a sci-fi take on the Nativity, a group of uninvited alien–human hybrids come to witness the birth. Mulder initially stays behind, but when he becomes aware that supersoldiers are still in pursuit of Scully, he travels by helicopter to rescue her. He never receives specific coordinates to her location, but rather "followed a light," and indeed an extraordinarily bright star was shown lighting the night sky and guiding him to her. The final scene shows Scully wearing a light-blue robe, evoking Mary as she cradles her child. The Lone Gunmen stand in for the Three Wise Men, bearing gifts and telling Mulder that they had to see the miracle child (born to the formerly infertile Scully) with their own eyes. Scully, once a groundbreaking character, became increasingly disempowered through her pregnancy and motherhood. She eventually gives the child up for adoption, ostensibly to protect it, but which narratively took her away from mothering a child and resituated her focus on the nurturance of Mulder's quest.

So if it's fathers who most often are responsible for raising heroic daughters, where does this leave mothers, or even heroic women who become mothers themselves?

Mother figures like Scully reinforce Campbell's assertion that the woman is the mother of the hero, not the hero herself. But as we'll see, characters such as The Bride, Sydney Bristow, and Sarah Connor manage to be both heroic *and* maternal without sacrificing one for the other. The supermoms and mother figures in this chapter therefore challenge traditional ideas about femininity and sex roles, rather than reinforce them. They show us the possibilities of being a hero who doesn't deny her quest for identity, nor her responsibilities to humanity, *and* is capable of being a kick-ass mom. Literally. And while this may evoke a different myth of "the Superwoman," she with a high-powered career, who is an attentive partner *and* mother, and who has an athlete's body and an unnaturally clean house, it lacks the sexism of that unattainable, unrepresentative, and fallacious stereotype.

Warrior Moms

Hippolyta, the Amazon queen of ancient myth, was appropriated by William Moulton Marston for his *Wonder Woman* comic, so we can say that the first superwoman of modern myth definitely had a supermom. But over the years, writers have pitted mother and daughter against each other through competition and deception, shamefully disregarding Marston's message of sisterhood. Buffy Summers adopted the role of mother to her sister Dawn after the death of Joyce and would later go on to train an army of superpowered girls called "The Potentials"—made into Slayers themselves through an ancient ritual. Xena and Gabrielle gave birth to daughters, but both were prevented from actually raising them. (Although for a while we did get to see wonderfully choreographed fight scenes that had Xena taking on multiple attackers with babe in arms.[4]) Charly Baltimore was a reluctant mother; her daughter born while Charly had amnesia and was living under the spell of a previous alias. When her memory is recovered, she initially rejects the child, stating she didn't ask for the kid and that "Samantha" had the kid not her. But when the child is kidnapped, her oppositional identities as small-town schoolteacher and government spy merges into one complete personality, and Charly saves the kid—with witty dialogue no less:

Caitlin: Mommy, am I gonna die?

Charly: Oh, no, baby, no. You're not going to die. They are. Cover your ears. Hey, should we get a dog?[5]

Fighting to protect one's family or community is often the motivation for a superwoman's actions. Whether this is laudable—shunning the quest for a prize, the conquering of others, and focus on the self in favor of nurturing and fostering community—or it's a sexist and tired way of justifying women's acts of violence is clearly debatable, subjective, and contextual. But it should be noted that while protecting their immediate communities, Buffy, Charly, Xena, and Sarah Connor also fight to save the world.[6]

But *Kill Bill*'s The Bride, one of the most exhilarating of warrior mothers, is enormously self-indulgent, her only concerns being exacting revenge and reclaiming her daughter.

Entertainment Weekly called *Kill Bill* "a character-driven and visually sophisticated ode to one angry mother."[7] The four-hour saga of The Bride (Uma Thurman) is this and so much more. Existing in what Tarantino calls his "movie-movie universe, where movie conventions are embraced, almost fetishized, as opposed to the other universe where Pulp Fiction and Reservoir Dogs take place, in which reality and movie conventions collide,"[8] *Kill Bill* is an homage to nearly all of writer/director Quentin Tarantino's influences: Spaghetti Westerns, Hong Kong kung fu and Japanese Samurai films, anime and manga, Blaxploitation and Mobster movies, comic books, obscure pop culture references and music, revenge flicks, and incredibly kick-ass, tough-talking women.

The core of the story—an assassin who is left for dead by her former colleagues on her wedding day—was conceived by Tarantino and his leading lady, Uma Thurman, over drinks during the production of *Pulp Fiction*. Tarantino wrote a handful of pages about The Bride and her tale of vengeance, which were then set aside for several years. When Thurman asked about them, Tarantino promised her a script for her upcoming birthday. The written script arrived a year and a half later.

The Bride, also known as Beatrix Kiddo, was a member of the Deadly Viper Assassination Squad—a group led by the ruthless Bill (David Carradine). When she discovers she's pregnant with Bill's baby, Beatrix is determined to bring the child up with some sense of normalcy. She takes up residence in a nowhere town and gets engaged to a nice guy. But Bill and the rest of the Vipers (comprised of Bill's brother Bud, Vernita Green, Elle Driver, and O Ren Ishii) track her down. They murder the entire wedding party, leaving behind a gruesome scene at the chapel; only The Bride survives. Four years pass before she finally wakes up from a coma. Her baby is gone and she's out for blood.

The Bride's story begins as a quest for vengeance, but when it's revealed the infant miraculously survived the assassination attempt, it also becomes a search for her daughter.

Mothers and daughters are as central a theme in *Kill Bill* as revenge itself, as we see when The Bride confronts Vernita Green (Vivica Fox). Her former colleague is now living the pedestrian life Beatrix was denied; only instead of retiring to a dusty town, she has a suburban house, a doctor spouse, and a daughter of her own, Nikki—who is nearly the same age as Beatrix's would be. Vernita acknowledges that her former colleague has every right to get even. "No. No," says The Bride, "To get even? Even Steven? I would have to kill you, go up to Nikki's room, kill her, then wait for your husband, the good Dr. Bell, to come home and kill him. That would be even, Vernita. That'd be about square." Beatrix assures Vernita that she can relax for the moment and that "I'm not going to murder you in front of your daughter." But adds:

> Just because I have no wish to murder you before the eyes of your daughter does not mean parading her around in front of me is going to inspire sympathy. You and I have unfinished business. And not a goddamn fuckin' thing you've done in the subsequent four years, *including getting knocked up*, is going to change that.[9]

Without intending to, The Bride does kill Vernita in front of Nikki. She tells the young girl, "It was not my intention to do this in front of you. For that, I'm sorry. But you can take my word for it, your mother had it comin'. When you grow up, if you still feel raw about it, I'll be waiting."

Some feminist critics feel that while *Kill Bill: Vol. 1* presented The Bride as a skilled, determined, fierce, and resourceful warrior and avoided fetishized catfights in favor of downright brutal fist-fights, stylized martial arts, and modestly clothed superwomen who got dirty, bloody, and mussed their hair, the second half of the story focuses on the reclaiming of Beatrix's daughter, B.B., and thus normalizes Beatrix by shifting her role from warrior to mother.

Lisa Jervis, co-founder of *Bitch* magazine, wrote that while *Kill Bill* managed to avoid many of the gendered pitfalls that plague other ass-kicking babe vehicles (skimpy outfits, romance, etc.), "Unfortunately, Vol. 2 manages to turn The Bride into a different but equally overused feminine archetype—not porn star but fierce mama, fighting to protect her family."[10] The last words before The Bride slips into a coma, and her first words upon waking, *are* about her baby. And as she'll later explain to Bill:

The Bride: Before that [pregnancy test] strip turned blue, I was a woman. I was your woman. I was a killer who killed for you. Before that strip turned blue, I would have jumped a motorcycle onto a speeding train ... for you. But once that strip turned blue, I could no longer do any of those things. Not anymore. Because I was going to be a mother. Can you understand that?

Bill: Yes. But why didn't you tell me then instead of now?

The Bride: Because once I would have told you, you'd claim her, and I didn't want that.

Bill: Not your decision to make.

The Bride: Yes, but it was the right decision and I made it for my daughter. She deserved to be born with a clean slate. But with you, she would have been born in a world she shouldn't have. I had to choose. I chose her.[11]

Jervis concedes she wouldn't argue that "quitting the assassin game is somehow not feminist, but this plot twist is just one more message that maternity trumps personality, history, logic, and more."[12]

That pregnancy is what inspires her to pursue a life of domesticity harks back to the days of the presumably widowed Mrs. Peel of *The Avengers*, who quit her assistant spook job when Mr. Peel turned up alive. In *Kill Bill: Vol. 1*, Beatrix attempts to assume her culturally proper gender role, even if it means leaving a career she excels at (albeit a morally questionable one), as well as a life of luxury and excitement, for one of poverty in a go-nowhere town. She gives it all up to become "Mommy"—the name of the final role Beatrix assumes in the two-part film. Perhaps the difference between Emma Peel and The Bride is that for Beatrix it *is* a choice, rather than a cultural imperative. Mrs. Peel did what a good wife should do, and Mommy did what she wanted to.

Grace, a reviewer for the website *Heroine Content*, gives another reading of the mommy angle:

The Bride and Vernita are mothers, and motherhood The Bride's big motivating factor. However, this didn't bother me as much in these films as it normally does, if only because non-mommy figures are portrayed as well (O-Ren and Elle), and because Bill takes fatherhood pretty seriously, too.[13]

Reflecting on the theme of motherhood in *Kill Bill*, particularly Vol. 2, Tarantino told *Entertainment Weekly* that

> I can honestly say that all that baby stuff would not have been in *Kill Bill* if I hadn't written the part for Uma. We are best friends, and when I was writing the script it was a good excuse to hang out with her. And if you hang out with Uma, you're going to hang out with her kids. I had a wonderful connection with her daughter, Maya. Actually, the truthful answer is that Maya made me want to have kids. [She] showed me I'd be a good father.[14]

Reuniting Beatrix and her daughter B.B. was a chance for a happy ending. "I love The Bride," said Tarantino, "I love her, all right? I want her to be happy. I don't want to come up with screwed-up scenarios that she has to fight the whole rest of her life. I killed myself to put her in a good place at the end of this long journey." The final title card of the movie even reads: *The lioness has rejoined her cub, and all is right in the jungle.*

Various prequels and sequels to *Kill Bill* have been proposed by Tarantino—at least one of which would again focus on mothers and daughters.[15] "The star will be Vernita Green's daughter, Nikki," he told *Entertainment Weekly*, adding, "I've already got the whole mythology: Sofie Fatale [Julie Dreyfus] will get all of Bill's money. She'll raise Nikki, who'll take on The Bride. Nikki deserves her revenge every bit as much as The Bride deserved hers."[16]

Nikki would be following a tradition of vengeance and reprisal seen in ancient Greek myths, for example, The House of Atreus in *The Oresteia*, and in the Samurai tales that directly influenced *Kill Bill*, namely *Lady Snowblood*, a daughter born and bred to avenge the slaughter of her family, and *Lone Wolf and Cub*—both manga written by Kazuo Koike and later adapted into films. Tarantino, always the authority on movies, noted that

> When you're dealing in the genres of Hong Kong kung fu films and spaghetti Westerns, or even American Westerns . . . an absolute staple of those movies [is that] the child on the prairie sees his parents slaughtered and spends the rest of his life avenging the deaths. At that moment the child is dead and the warrior is born.[17]

Woman as Mentor: Buffy Summers, Sarah Jane Smith, and Elektra Natchios

Teach me something. I don't care what, but something that only you can do, something special like that. (*Elektra/Wolverine: The Redeemer*[18])

I saw amazing things, out there in space—but there is strangeness to be found, wherever you turn. Life on Earth can be an adventure too ... you just need to know where to look! (*The Sarah Jane Adventures*[19])

Over and over again, men have served as mentors to superwomen: Modesty Blaise was educated by the Hungarian Professor Lob; Elektra trained with Stick—her former lover's sensei; Araña was indoctrinated into the ways of the Spider Society by her mage Miguel; Buffy studied with Rupert Giles; and The Bride was molded through the cruel tutelage of both Bill and Pei Mei.

While it makes these heroes no less extraordinary, it is a concern that the example of *women* mentoring women is all too rare, and when present, it generally isn't allowed to thrive. *Buffy the Vampire Slayer's* techno-pagan Jenny Calendar could have provided beneficial and practical support along Willow Rosenberg's quest for identity, but she was murdered after a handful of episodes. Buffy adopted the role of mother to Dawn after their mother died, making sacrifices for her as well as acknowledging, encouraging, and respecting the power in the youngest Summers:

> *Buffy:* I want to see you grow up. The woman you're gonna become. Because she's gonna be beautiful. And she's going to be powerful. I got it so wrong. I don't want to protect you from the world. I want to show it to you. There's so much that I want to show you.[20]

Buffy and Willow also train The Potentials, now Slayers themselves, and this mentorship has extended beyond the television series into the *Buffy the Vampire Slayer* Season 8 comic book. But powerful women who have, or could have, mentored the two most powerful female heroes of the series were generally kept in behind-the-scenes roles.[21] The Coven of Witches in England who helped rehabilitate Willow after her journey to the Dark Side were only spoken about—never actually seen. The Guardians, an ancient sect of women who tasked themselves with watching the Watchers and claimed to be "Women who want to help and protect" Slayers, were revealed in the second to last episode of the entire series.[22] Not only is this entirely too late in the game; the final remaining Guardian is murdered minutes after meeting Buffy.

Wonder Woman, of course, comes from *a whole community* of women mentoring women, the females-only Paradise Island. Diana is the matriarchal island's only child and is therefore fostered by many mothers, women who also support each other. "Between adults, mutual mothering becomes 'sisterhood'," write Carol Pearson and Katherine Pope, adding that in sisterhood, "the hero discovers not only a positive mother but a whole female support system, and by association, a nurturing, joyous, and powerful female heritage."[23,24]

A delightful example of a female support system comes in *The Sarah Jane Adventures*, a television series produced by the British Broadcasting Company (BBC). The title character, Sarah Jane Smith (Elisabeth Sladen), was an investigative journalist and a companion to the third and fourth Doctors (Jon Pertwee and Tom Baker, respectively) in *Doctor Who* and appeared regularly over the years 1973–6.[25] Elisabeth Sladen has since revisited the character a number of times over the past 35 years—including in a pilot featuring Sarah Jane and the robot dog, K-9, as well as in a special feature-length episode of *Doctor Who* called "The Five Doctors."[26] Sladen has also reprised the role in the revitalized *Doctor Who* alongside David Tennant's Doctor (the tenth incarnation).

The Sarah Jane Adventures is a spin-off of *Doctor Who*, intended for children, but witty enough for adults. The series debuted in the UK with an hour-long special shown on New Year's Day, 2007, called "Invasion of the Bane." In it, we meet a 13-year-old girl named Maria Jackson (Yasmin Paige) who has just moved to West London with her dad after her parents' recent divorce. Dad is a stand-up guy, and while Mom is flighty, she frequently drops by for hellos, meals, and family time. Maria's living situation (a daughter with a single father) could have made her yet another victim of the female hero-sans-female mentor trope that has plagued myth from ancient through modern times, but her mother isn't dead, drunk, ill, or vindictive; she's just elsewhere and has kind of a difficult personality.

On her first night in her new home, Maria is awakened by a strange pinkish glowing light emanating from outside. She sneaks out of the house and across the street to spy on Sarah Jane conversing with a floaty, ethereal, otherwordly creature (who we later discover is a Star Poet who'd gotten lost on her journey and sought Sarah Jane's assistance with directions). Maria is understandably curious, but Sarah Jane is terse and standoffish with her neighbors, believing that others should not be subject to the danger involved in her investigative work.

Later, when Maria and her friend Kelsey take a tour of the Bubbleshock Soda Company, they run into Sarah Jane at the factory trying to expose the soda makers for who they really are—tentacled aliens whose mother bug secrets a substance marketed as the "organic!" additive "Bane"—actually an alien chemical used in the soda to turn humans into easily controlled zombies (fortunately, Sarah Jane and Maria prefer tea to soda pop and so have retained their autonomy). In the process of escaping the factory, they encounter a human boy called "The Archetype," who is genetically constructed out of the thoughts and wishes of over 10,000 people. Sarah Jane and Maria rescue the child and at first, when he asks if he can live with Sarah Jane, she says no, but she ultimately adopts him into her home.

Sarah Jane recognizes Maria's inner strength and sees her as a kindred spirit. While figuring a way to stop the Bane from taking over Planet Earth, she tells her new young friend, "Maria, there are two types of people in the world. Those who panic, and then there's us. Got it?" Maria understands and affirms, "Got it." Over the course of the episode, Sarah recognizes, *even respects*, the children's ability to make choices for themselves. And she's remarkably honest with them, telling Maria and the Archetype—who chooses the name "Luke"—that

> When I was your age, I used to think "Oh, when I'm grown up, I'll know what I want, I'll be sorted." But you never really know what you want. You never feel grown up, not really. You never sort it all out ... so I thought, I could handle life on my own. But after today ... I don't want to!

The series may tap into the lives and thoughts of children, but scenes like these can resonate with adults. Life *never* happens as you expect it to. You just have to stick to your values and go with the flow of the adventure. And as Sarah Jane proves, if things aren't working as they are, you can always change your mind and approach with new perspective.

While it could be bothersome that Sarah Jane was given a child to care for, and read as yet another attempt to restabilize a strong and independent character in a normative position as a traditionally gendered woman, the adoption of Luke was presented as simply a part of her journey rather than the sole motivation for it. What is of greater concern is that she can't or won't find a partner because after the Doctor, "No man could quite compare." Further, other characters tend to disrespect her single, childless status, as though this makes her less of a woman.

A reviewer for the *Chicago Tribune* praised both *The Sarah Jane Adventures* and Sladen saying that

> she projects an air of trustworthiness, courage and unapologetic independence, and though Sarah Jane's attitude is brisk and unsentimental, it leaves room for plenty of wonder at the stranger things in the universe. And by the way, how many series feature a middle-aged woman as the lead—and even let her battle many-tentacled aliens? Score one for the Brits.[27]

Variety, on the other hand, panned the series, calling it "modestly entertaining for the moppet crowd" but patience trying for adults."[28] (The reviewer also called Sarah Jane "a rather boring heroine"—perhaps because she doesn't play into ass-kicking babe stereotypes; she's modestly clothed and over 30.) Regarding its "maturity," *The Sarah Jane Adventures* is a children's show in the way that the early Harry Potter novels are children's books—they are ostensibly for children but have a self-consciousness and intelligence that appeals to adults. (*The Sarah Jane Adventures* does feature some farting aliens—justifiably suitable for a munchkin audience.)

What's wonderful to see are the scenes between Sarah Jane and Maria; they brainstorm and problem solve, they comfort and support one another, and they mirror each other. Sarah Jane is experienced and wise, while Maria is a smart, compassionate, and brave young woman. As Pearson and Pope write, "Usually, when the hero is at the nadir of despair, a nurturing, strong, and independent woman appears to her ... the female rescue figure tells the hero that she is capable of saving herself."[29] Maria cannot rely on this type of support from her mother, but gets it in abundance from Sarah Jane. When Maria's father is turned to stone in "Eyes of the Gorgon," Sarah Jane tells her, "Listen to me Maria. You are not going to lose it. You are not going to fall apart. Do you understand me? Whatever's happened to your father—there is one thing I've learned after all these years—there is *always* a chance. Do you hear me?"[30]

This voice is essential to the hero's ability to trust her own vision and abilities—which is why depictions of female heroes are so important for women's self-esteem and confidence.[31] It is because of this nurturance that *Maria* is able to save the day, Sarah Jane, her own father, and humanity itself. A character of compassion, justice, and hope, Maria even makes an extra effort when she returns a necklace to an elderly woman with Alzheimer's disease in hopes that it will restore her memory. Later, Maria reflects upon this woman who had traveled the universe with her husband as Sarah Jane had with the Doctor. She again brings up Sarah Jane's single status asking, "Don't you wish you had found someone special to share it with?" Sarah wraps her arm around her friend and says, "Oh, I think I have. For *the second time.*"[32]

While *The Sarah Jane Adventures* presents a delightfully positive example of women mentoring women, we find a more disturbing, if intriguing, one in Elektra.

Elektra Natchios could hardly be considered a role model, but in at least two instances, and as many mediums, the character shares a reciprocal identification with a tween-age girl, offering us another opportunity to analyze the profound experience of finding a mentor of one's own gender.

Elektra was introduced in *Daredevil* #168, the first issue to be written by Frank Miller. The college sweetheart of Daredevil's alter ego, Matt Murdock, Elektra's world was understandably shattered upon her father's murder. She left Matt, as well as her studies at Columbia University, and ultimately became a bounty hunter, assassin, and ninja. Elektra was murdered by a rival bounty hunter named Bullseye a mere 13 issues later, but has remained one of the most beloved, if dark, characters of the Marvelverse. She has continued to appear in story arcs over the years even though Miller has said, "She had to be cruelly and coldly murdered by the worst possible enemy Daredevil had ever had"; a disturbing sentiment artist Klaus Jansen echoed by saying that he and Miller were "intent on killing her and leaving her dead."[33]

Elektra Assassin and *Elektra Lives Again* were scripted by Miller, while others have made contributions to the mythos, almost all of which irreparably confuse canon. The most interesting of these for the purposes of this chapter is *Elektra/Wolverine: The Redeemer*, written by Greg Rucka and hauntingly illustrated by Yoshitaka Amano—the core of which was used as the basis for the 2005 film *Elektra*.

In *Redeemer*, Elektra is hired to assassinate a man named Daniel Connor. The job goes awry when Daniel's daughter Avery witnesses the murder and gets a good look at the face of her father's killer. Additionally, Keifer, the man who paid the ninja 6 million dollars to carry out this deed, has also manipulated Wolverine into protecting Avery. Elektra abducts the child, and a series of betrayals and secrets are revealed when Wolverine and the girl's mother, Dr. Veronica Connor, attempt to rescue Avery. In this story, the Conners were present when Wolverine had the metal alloy adamantium attached to his bones and created Avery using his mutant DNA. Once they realized Keifer wanted the meta-human child for his own, possibly military, purposes, they devised a plan for escape. Outsiders were led to believe that Veronica was having a series of extra-marital affairs, which lead to a separation of the couple. Avery had been living with her father and, unaware of the deception, was furious with her mother's suggested betrayal.

Meanwhile, Elektra is faced with this girl. Assassin logic dictates that she must kill her to protect her own identity. But Elektra has become fascinated with the child, a mirror of herself—disarmingly stoic, patient, and curious in what should be a terrifying experience. "And while Elektra wasn't entirely certain why it mattered so much to her that she have contact with the girl, the thought of that contact being denied her was unacceptable."[34] When the pair stop for a meal at a diner, Avery tells the assassin:

> "I don't understand. . . . Why I am here. Why you care what I think. Why you're buying me pie. I don't understand." Elektra sighed. "Because I look at you, Avery, and I see me." Avery blinked at her, and then stared at her plate some more. "See, that's funny," Avery said softly. "That's kinda funny, because I look at you, and I think maybe I could be looking at me, too."[35]

The fact that the waitress has mistaken them for mother and daughter further complicates already confused emotions.

Elektra tells herself that she abducted Avery out of self-pity: "... *to keep from Avery what happened to me. Guilt, because I took her father the way another man, long ago, took mine.*"[36] Rucka has said of his contribution to the Elektra mythos that the character has always willfully refused to look at the evil things she did or consider the consequences of her actions. Her job prevents sentimentality. But she cannot bring herself to put a knife in a child—especially one so like herself.[37]

But it's not just the tinge of morality Elektra feels. There's also a factor of loneliness—and the seductive pull of companionship that Avery offers her. The girl tells Elektra all she wants is to be empowered and to learn from the ninja: "All my life I've had people telling me what to do and how to act, testing me and ... and doing *things* to me, and I don't want it to be like that anymore. I want to do what *you* can do, I want to be like you. Free like you." She astutely points out that "You want this [too], you just haven't admitted it yet. If you didn't want me here, if you didn't want to teach me, you'd have killed me already."[38]

The temptation for both parties is clearly there, but for Elektra, there is an added element of adult responsibility. How *does* an assassin-for-hire confront moral responsibility?

> The girl was dangerous, Elektra realized, more dangerous than she'd thought at first, and again she felt the seductive pull first offered by the waitress. Whatever was going on inside Avery's head, whatever it was that made her erupt in sudden laughter instead of tears, she was willing to become her friend, her confidante, her daughter. Elektra could feel in herself the desire to let it happen, even though she knew she shouldn't.[39]

Clearly these are the wrong circumstances for a healthy mentorship, and the mother–daughter bond is outright inappropriate. Elektra recognizes this and struggles to sort out her feelings from the actions she should take. But when the two are together, "Avery spoke as if it were just she and Elektra, all alone, and with all the time in the world. She spoke as if there was nothing that the two of them couldn't handle, as long as they handled it together."[40]

The movie, which is not a direct adaptation of *Redeemer*, but borrows heavily from the Elektra–Avery relationship, presents a more altruistic Elektra—making her story a character journey from darkness to light.[41] "This particular story is about her not being able to deny her need for her own redemption, and it comes up and smacks her in the face, much like falling for Matt Murdock did," says Jennifer Garner of the character she portrayed, adding, "except I think this is much more of a surprise, and it's more of a twist, and it's something she fights a lot harder than she fought falling for Matt."[42]

In the film, Avery is now "Abby." Elektra is still hired for an assassination job, but here she is sent to an island a few days before her targets are revealed, and meanwhile, she becomes acquainted with the father and daughter who reside in the house next door.[43] When she discovers they are to be her victims, she finds she cannot follow through with the job and goes so far as to take them under her protection. Here, redemption comes from saving the child and forgiving herself. Reflecting on the story, Garner said,

> I wanted to do this movie because I so love this character and I so love that, as much as she fights against her own re-entry into the world—her heart opening up after years and years of just being completely closed off—she loses the battle with herself, and she falls for basically a younger version of herself, Abby, and ultimately ... opens herself.[44]

As Roz Kaveney has noted, redemption and sentimentality aren't necessarily true to the established character of Elektra, and she observes that the film "falls apart whenever it shows the softer side that the [comic book incarnation of the] character does not really have."[45] Nowhere is this more clear than at the very end of the film. Elektra says to no one in particular, "Please don't let her be like me," and her sensei Stick answers, "Why not? You didn't turn out so bad." The journey from darkness to light the producers envisioned is thus complete, if untrue to the spirit of Elektra.[46]

Making Motherhood Heroic: Sydney Bristow

Who'd think you could turn a pregnancy into an alias?

...and in Chinese. (*Alias*[47])

Season 5 of *Alias* brought us television's first Spy Mama, and as Ms. Bristow said herself, she's "not like other moms." Being from a family of double agents, how could she be?

Jennifer Garner's own pregnancy was written into the show, thankfully, as a natural pregnancy rather than the result of an immaculate conception à la Xena, or a possible alien abduction as with Dana Scully. *Alias* was, of course, not the first show to incorporate an actresses' pregnancy into the narrative, but it is one of the few genre shows where paternity is not in question. Sydney's partner Michael Vaughn *is* the father.[48]

Regardless, television has come a long way in its approach to babies. Back when Lucille Ball and Desi Arnaz wanted to write their pregnancy into *I Love Lucy*, CBS said they couldn't show a pregnant woman on TV (as if twin beds were enough to prevent a married couple from intimacy). When they managed to blend art and life, they did so on the condition that they would not say the word "pregnant" on air and substituted "expecting." That was 1951, but 40 years later, pop culture controversy struck again.

In 1991, Murphy Brown became pregnant, although the actress who played her, Candace Bergen, wasn't. Murphy's choice to be a single mother became political fodder for then Vice President Dan Quayle, who went on to publicly criticize Ms. Brown, as if she were a real person, for eschewing a more traditional lifestyle. The eponymous series brilliantly used Quayle's narrow-minded polemic against him by airing a show on the controversy that validated *Murphy Brown* as a series and alternative families as well.

Garner's pregnancy allowed *Alias* to return to its principal theme—Sydney's identity and evolution as a woman, a daughter, and an agent. And in a series where removing eyeballs via plastic sporks was the norm du jour, Sydney's pregnancy was handled with the same amount of matter-of-factness, irony, and playfulness as every other plot line. It didn't overwhelm the show, but it wasn't ignored either (though Garner did have to remind the crew that she was still coordinated and an athlete, and therefore capable of continuing to do stunts[49]). In fact, Season 5's tagline, "Expect more," channeled Lucy, Desi, and little Desi Jr. and reveals just how much American cultural ideas about women and morality have changed; pregnancy has gone from taboo to fashion statement. "I think women who are pregnant are very sexy," *Alias* executive producer, Jeff Pinker, told *USA Today*.[50] He later expanded on this in the *New York Times*: "Sydney has always used her sexuality as a tool to take down the bad guys."[51]

It's true that Sydney's femininity and sexuality were always embraced, but these things—as titillating, campy, powerful, and playful as they were—never defined her, and pregnancy was no exception. Her swollen belly was just another disguise, exaggerating her feminine exterior to conceal her actual strength. One of the most fun examples of Sydney using her pregnancy as an alias was when she distracted patrons in a Monte Carlo casino by rubbing dice on her stomach for good luck. When she's "caught" cheating, the Pit Boss tells her, "I have seen some despicable acts of cheating in my time. But a pregnant woman using her own baby to escape suspicion ... I don't know how you live with yourself." Sydney answers, "What can I say, sir? I'm not like other moms."[52]

Alias is first and foremost a show about family, and Sydney's pregnancy brought her closer to her father. Jack accompanied her to doctor appointments, gave her her own baby rattle, and put together the baby's crib (executive producer, Jeff Pinker, joked that it was likely "the first time in 20 years he's used a screwdriver for its actual intended purpose").[53] But her own mother, Irina, loomed ominously in the background. "The fear of identifying with one's mother as a mother is particularly profound," wrote Hope Edelman of poorly mothered women.[54] For Sydney, whose mother was a brutal KGB agent, a traitorous wife, and a person with generally ambiguous intentions, identifying with Irina is clearly a concern.[55]

When Sydney goes into labor on a mission and Irina serves as midwife, Mother warns daughter:

> *Irina:* You should know something, Sydney. I never wanted to have a child. The KGB demanded it. They knew it would ensure your father's allegiance to me. You were simply a means to an end. And then when the doctor put you in my arms and I looked at you? So fragile. All I could think was, How could I make such a terrible mistake? And at that moment I was sure of one thing: I couldn't be an agent and a mother. I'd either fail at one or both. And I chose to fail at being a mother. In time you'll learn. You can't do both.

Sydney's response is a defiant, "Watch me."[56]

Season 5 also gave Sydney a chance to be a mentor herself when Rachel Gibson (Rachel Nichols) was brought into the covert A.P.O. organization for which Sydney works. Nichols' managers approached her and said that *Alias* was looking for a new female role, someone who would show the audience essentially how Sydney became a super-agent.[57] Garner enjoyed playing the mentor, telling an *Alias* fan magazine, "That made sense to me—Sydney has done it for awhile, and now there's a new kid coming up [through the ranks] who's really hungry and eager and looking for a mentor. Also, because I like Rachel so much and think she's such a good actress, it made me enjoy it more."[58]

Gotta Make Way for the Mother Superior: The Sarah Connor Chronicles

This is a mother and son show. (David Nutter[59])

Sarah Connor is the mother of a messiah, a protective lioness burdened with the duty to save the world by giving birth to the savior of humanity. She may be Mother Mary, but she's armed with a machine gun.[60]

Terminator: Sarah Connor Chronicles (Fox Network, 2008) affords new and deeper readings of Sarah. She becomes more than a revolutionary action hero and more than a woman whose sole purpose it is to nurture the "true" leader—the male savior of humanity. *Sarah Connor Chronicles* is a story about Sarah, not John, not robots, not the dangerous misuse of technology, not even Arnold Schwarzenegger—and that makes it, and her, ever so much more interesting.

The great failure of *Terminator 3: Rise of the Machines* (2003) was that it lacked Sarah—and so far it's *her* story. Part of the project of *Sarah Connor Chronicles* is to correct the trilogy, and therefore, in the television branch of the *Terminator* mythology, the events of *T3* never happened.

The series begins in 1999, two years after the original date of Judgment Day and five years after the events of *T2*, but by the end of the pilot episode, we will be transported eight years into the future. The pilot begins with Sarah (Lena Headey)in the middle of a nightmare. Terminators are after her son, Judgment Day is breaking, and in an echo of a scene from *T2*, we see her shielding John (Thomas Dekker) with her body, maternal lioness in full force; flames wash over them, and humankind is incinerated. When Sarah awakes, we learn she's engaged to be married, a choice that seems out of character for the otherwise cautious Sarah, but one that will serve a narrative purpose.

Sarah sees the nightmare as a premonition and decides it's time to change location again. After she disappears with John, her fiancé goes to the police where he is confronted by an FBI agent named James Ellison (Richard T. Jones). Ellison explains who Sarah is, what she believes, and what she's done. It's *Terminator* mythos 101 for the uninitiated.

The Connors arrive in New Mexico, where at his new high school, John meets a friendly beauty named Cameron, played by Summer Glau, her name an homage to James Cameron. As soon as John starts his first class, a Terminator appears. Fortunately for the Conners, here, as in *T2*, there are both assassin and protector Terminators, and Cameron is the later—we think.[61]

It's hard to believe that the T-800 in *T2* was enough to convince Sarah and John to trust *any* Terminator that comes along and says it will help them. But John is still a child, and Sarah is clearly a woman on the edge, doing whatever she can to stay sane. Her son is still in denial and acts almost as if he just wishes hard enough, it will all go away. Sarah knows better.

John: I'm not who they think I am! I'm not some … *Messiah*!
Sarah: You don't know that.[62]

Sarah doesn't know for sure either—but it's irrelevant. She must prepare John regardless; no fate but what *she* makes.

To make the show about Sarah, the mother, not John, the messiah (as in *The John Connor Chronicles*) honors her place in the *Terminator* mythos. Elevating Sarah to her rightful position as the narrative impetus is actually pretty radical. "In fact," write Pearson and Pope,

> any author who chooses a woman as the *central* character in the story understands at some level that women are primary beings, and that they are not ultimately defined according to patriarchal assumptions in relation to fathers, husbands, or male gods. Whether explicitly feminist or not, therefore, works with female heroes challenge patriarchal assumptions.[63]

Heretofore, this mentorship and matriarchal lineage of heroism has been, for all practical purposes, tragically absent from popular culture. Hopefully, with this new generation of superwomen giving birth to daughters, and occasionally mentoring girls, we are seeing the beginnings of a progressive female heroic tradition.

SECTION III
The Mythmakers

8

Women Making Myth

It was strange to think that all the great women of fiction were ... not only seen by the other sex, but seen only in relation to the other sex ... Suppose, for instance, that men were only represented in literature as the lovers of women, and were never the friends of men, soldiers, thinkers, dreamers ...

—Virginia Woolf[1]

It's no secret that the entertainment industry, and thus modern mythmaking, has been dominated by men. While there certainly *are* many males who write wonderful, dynamic, and complex women—Greg Rucka, Peter O'Donnell, and Joss Whedon to name a few—it's reasonable to assume that *women* making myth will color the journey of the female hero with female experience and perhaps provide an even more authentic reflection of our lives.

A consideration of how female artists, producers, writers, and actors have presented, interpreted, approached, or embodied themes that dominate the female hero's journey is in order, as women are more apt than men to write about mothers and daughters *and* sisterhood *and* women mentoring women, simply because writers tend to write what they know. Women also form organizations to help raise consciousness about gender representation in the media, and as actresses, they embody iconic characters with responsibility, complexity, and verve.

Actresses and Social Responsibility and Activism

Actresses who play superwomen often have stories about women who have told them how the characters they played inspired them.

Actress and comedian Whoopi Goldberg famously told Nichelle Nichols how seeing Lt. Uhura on television as a little girl inspired her toward her own groundbreaking career—affirming Martin Luther King's prediction that the character would have a profound effect on children.[2] Astronaut Dr. Mae Jemison was also inspired by Uhura, joining National Aeronautics and Space Administration (NASA) to become the first Black woman to cross the final frontier.

Lucy Lawless, Lynda Carter, and Jennifer Garner have all been told by people of various ages, and sexual preferences, what Xena, Wonder Woman, and Sydney Bristow have meant to them. Sarah Michelle Gellar takes her Kid's Choice and Teen's Choice Awards very seriously and is conscious about the public persona she reflects. Feeling a responsibility toward the young women who see the characters she plays as role models, Gellar recognizes how important it is for them to have positive inspiration.[3] In her meetings with the writers of *Smallville*, Allison Mack has insisted that her character, Chloe Sullivan, a proto—Lois Lane introduced to the Superman mythos in the television series, remains a positive role model for young girls—who have too few visions of smart, ambitious women with integrity.

The characters these actresses have embodied have also had a heroic effect on the players themselves. Nichelle Nichols, tired of seeing all-White, all-male teams of astronauts that weren't representative of the future her friend Gene Roddenberry envisioned, used the iconic status of Lt. Uhura to help recruit women and minority persons to NASA. As she wrote in her autobiography, she

> could not reconcile the term "United States space program" with an endeavor that did not involve anyone except white males. No offense to those fine, brave men, but if we in America tell our children they can be all they dream, why weren't there women and minority astronauts? Thousands of fans wrote thanking me for Uhura's inspiration. Little Black girls and boys, Latino and Asian children had a legitimate right to share in that dream. Things had to change.[4]

In 1977, after having undertaken a number of government contracts through her consultant firm, Women in Motion, Inc., Nichols was appointed to the board of directors of the National Space Institute and became a deputy administrator of NASA. She gave a speech in Washington D.C. called "New Opportunities for the Humanization of Space" and began a recruitment campaign as a NASA contractor—under one condition. "If I put my name and my reputation on the line for NASA," she said,

> and I find qualified women and minority people to apply, and a year from now I still see a lily-white, all-male astronaut corps, I will personally file a class-action lawsuit against NASA. I will not be used to attract publicity and then later hear

you say, "Gee, we really tried, but there weren't any qualified women or minorities out there."[56]

As part of her mission, Nichols made a series of Public Service Announcements, appeared in national publications including *Newsweek* and *People*, and was on television programs such as *Good Morning America*. She also produced a half-hour orientation film for the education director of the National Air and Space Museum and founded a youth organization called "Space Cadets of America."[7]

While Uhura was the face of possibility in the final frontier and Nichols was the future of the space program, Jennifer Garner, in her role as Sydney Bristow, became the modern face of the Central Intelligence Agency (CIA). When the actual CIA recognized the character as the embodiment of their ideals, they procured Garner to star in a promotional video for their recruitment center.

Geena Davis—who has made a career out of playing remarkable women including an outlaw, a baseball player, a pirate, an assassin, and even the president of the USA—was struck by the alarming lack of female characters in children's television while watching cartoons with her daughter. The imbalance inspired her to create The Geena Davis Institute on Gender in Media—a nonprofit organization that researches and brings awareness to gender in children's entertainment. At its core, the institute believes that "Kids need to see entertainment where females are valued as much as males."[8]

That these organizations, promotional campaigns, and endorsements can be as successful as they are speaks to the talent and drive of the actresses involved. When an actress can truly embody an iconic character, she becomes associated with that character's values and actions in the public mind (although, on the less fortunate flipside, she may also face typecasting as a result).

An actress can also take a sidekick character and make her an icon of female empowerment—Margot Kidder's Lois Lane being a perfect example. The tenacious *Daily Planet* reporter had for too long been devalued, the rationale being she was created as a secondary character and is therefore *only* a secondary character. Before Kidder, Lois was, as over 100 titular comic book issues proved, quite literally, Superman's girlfriend. But Kidder's feisty femme in 1978's *Superman: The Movie* provided a new, more empowered version of Lois. The familiar Lois is there: the one who talks to her editor-in-chief as if he were her equal, rather than her boss, and the respected writer, who though established, is *still* forced to hand over her beat to the new guy on *his first day*.

But she takes the assignments she can get, her mantra being "A good reporter doesn't get great stories. A good reporter *makes* them great."[9]

She's a bit lonely—a skeptical city girl bemused by the small-town boy, Clark Kent, and focused on her writing career. When the mild-mannered reporter asks Lois if she'd be interested in having dinner with him, she declines his offer:

Lois: Sorry, Clark. I'm booked.

Clark: Oh.

Lois: Air Force One is landing at the airport tonight and this kid's going to be there to make sure you-know-who answers a few questions he'd rather duck.

Clark: Don't you ever let up?

Lois: For what? Oh, I've seen how the other half lives. My sister, for instance ... three kids, two cats, one mortgage ... I'd go bananas after a week.[10]

She's a modern woman, successful enough to have her own apartment in Manhattan—with a view and a private roof garden, no less. While interviewing Superman on her patio, she swoons a little, but still manages to ask the questions her readers will want answers to. And this is what makes Kidder's portrayal different from that of her filmic predecessors. Phyllis Coates and Noel Neill are remarkable actresses, and each provided a memorable embodiment of Lois Lane. But Kidder, a woman as notoriously outspoken as Ms. Lane, never wanted to play roles that were female stereotypes, or where the female protagonist was simply someone's girlfriend.[11] So rather than playing Lois as *only* a love interest, Kidder also made Lois Lane her own woman.

Kidder further explains that she played Lois as two distinct characters: one "Vis-à-vis Clark as an independent career woman" and the other as "Mushy in the middle around Superman."[12] Her method makes sense; Kal-El himself has two different identities, each demanding a different sort of portrayal and interaction. As a result, her Lois is more complex than the reporter of the 1940s film serials and 1950s television show, and more complicated than the love interest of the comics. She gets to be a woman *and* a journalist.[13]

While Kidder doesn't believe Lois is a feminist per se, she does note that the women's movement played into her characterization, as she came out of the last generation of women that were expected to be demure, quiet, and googly-eyed, and in the mid-1960s, "things changed in a BIG way." Women experienced the liberation of being allowed to be themselves and there was, as Kidder notes, an idea of "I can be who *I* want!" Additionally, because of the relative rarity of female reporters, "You could not NOT portray [Lois] as a feisty, independent woman," she says. But clearly, the values of the women's movement Kidder internalized, as well as what she calls the "witty and fabulous lines" *Superman* scripter Tom Mankiewicz wrote for her, took Lois Lane to the next possible level of independent womanhood. By portraying Lois as the feminist she can be—hardworking, talented, and dynamic—Kidder became *the* quintessential face of the character, just as Lynda Carter did for Wonder Woman.[14]

Kidder believes the time is right for an updated/modern version of Lois Lane, saying, "I'd love to see some version [of her] that represents how you young women are now." She believes that feminism has come a long way since the 1970s, "and it should be really reflected in these new characters."[15]

Women in Comics

While actresses of film and television have managed to utilize their visibility, women have had even less of a presence and an empowered voice as both creators and characters in mainstream superhero comics.[16]

Stan Lee once contemplated the lack of fictional superwomen in comics thusly:

> We know that there are more superheroes than superheroines in comic books today. We also know that more males than females read superhero comics. Okay then, here's the question—do less females read comics because they seem to be aimed at a male audience, or are they aimed at a male audience because less females read them? If you're expecting an answer, forget it. I've spent years waiting for someone to tell me![17]

Lee may have had the best of intentions—as did (and do) many others in the comic book industry—but the truth is women have long felt alienated from superhero stories. And whether they still manage to be fangirls or not, the treatment of women in mainstream comics as cranky girlfriend, mother figure, vixen, and victim has left women frustrated. Unfortunately for fangirls (and boys), 30 years later, Lee's questions regarding comics' readership remain poignantly relevant. The likely answer to Lee's query is twofold: there have been relatively few women voices producing accessible modern myth, and there is the fallacious assumption that girls don't read comics.[18] As Trina Robbins has repeatedly stated, girls will read comics when there are comics for girls to read—a fact proven by the popularity of manga in the USA.

The emergence of female writers and artists in the mainstream industry, including Devin Grayson (*Batman, Nightwing*), Nicola Scott (*Birds of Prey*),

Gail Simone (*Birds of Prey, Wonder Woman*), and Fiona Avery (*Araña*) to name a few, indicates that perhaps the tide is finally starting to turn.

The recent explosion of feminist fangirl bloggers and critics on the Internet suggests this as well. Women are finding community in Cyberspace by discovering that other women enjoy superhero comics, but are also troubled by the treatment of women in the genre. Combating sexism and promoting diversity, both in the comics industry and in comics themselves, are groups like Friends of Lulu, a national organization in the USA whose goals are to increase female readership of comics, to promote the work of women in comics, and to provide support and networking opportunities. There are also *Sequential Tart*, a webzine founded and written by women and dedicated to exploring the comics industry, and When Fangirls Attack, a linkblog that compiles articles on gender in superhero comics, manga, and fandom from across the Net.

Girl Wonder is a collection of websites dedicated to female creators, as well as characters in mainstream comics. Their mascot is Stephanie Brown, who spent a short time as a largely unknown and greatly underappreciated "Robin" to Batman.[19] She was introduced to the mythos in 1992 and began fighting crime as a means to spoil the misdeeds of her father, Arthur Brown, a.k.a. Cluemaster. She did so under the secret identity of "Spoiler," leaving behind clues for Batman that would enable him to foil and imprison her dad. She later works with the then current Robin, Tim Drake, and the pair become romantically involved.

When Tim Drake is asked by his family to give up crime fighting, Stephanie sews herself a "Robin" costume in the trademark red, yellow, and green of the sidekick. She breaks into the Batcave, and when a surprised Batman asks, "Stephanie?," she replies, "No. Not Stephanie. Not even Spoiler. From now on, you can call me Robin."[20]

Batman, believing Stephanie lacks skill and discipline, has never truly accepted her into the crime-fighting community (though she'd been a part of it for over 12 years of continuity). Yet impressed with her determination, he concedes to honor her with the title Robin and takes her on as a protégée. Whether he does so because he wants to give her a chance or because he's using her as a means to manipulate Tim back into his fold is unclear.

Stephanie undergoes intense training with Batman and the Birds of Prey, and patrols with the Cassandra Cain version of Batgirl.[21] In her short career as Robin, Batman alternately praises Stephanie for "innovating on the fly" and then punishes her for disobeying a direct order—the latter leading to her abrupt professional dismissal. Desperate to regain Batman's approval, Stephanie steals and attempts to implement one of his crime-fighting plans.

It ultimately backfires; many people end up killed as a result, and Stephanie herself is taken captive by the villain Black Mask who brutally tortures her with a power drill in gratuitous and highly sexualized images—an assault that is depicted over *several* issues of the "War Games" storyline. Stephanie manages to escape, only to die as a result of her injuries.

Female comic book fans felt slapped in the face.

One fan, named Mary Borsellino, had seen an interview with Dan DiDio, the senior vice president and executive editor of DC Comics, in which he said that Stephanie's death would have an ongoing impact on "our heroes and their lives" throughout the forthcoming year.[22] Borsellino told *Sequential Tart* that she responded by making "a snotty comment in ... [her] online journal about how ... [she] would believe that only when Stephanie had her own memorial case. The statement discounted everyone who'd had Stephanie as their hero, and that really bothered ... [her]." She adds, "The journal entry got one hundred comments, expressing the same rage and frustration and sadness that I was feeling. That same day, I registered the domain girl-wonder.org."[23]

The site became a resource for empowered feminist fangirls to come together as an organized community. Project Girl Wonder was launched— a campaign that demanded DC Comics honor Stephanie Brown's contribution to the Bat-mythos by acknowledging her in the way Batman had honored another Robin lost to tragedy—with a glass memorial case in the Batcave. Project Girl Wonder included a letter-writing campaign as well as orchestrated activism at comic conventions to ask the powers that be at DC when Steph would get her due. Dismissive answers included: "She's not getting one." "She's never getting one." And the cruelest of all, "It was her fault"—a sentiment echoed in an edition of the *Batgirl* comic; Cassandra Cain is drowning, and a hallucination of Stephanie appears to guide her back to consciousness. Stephanie, who is illustrated as decaying, tells her friend that she takes responsibility for her own torture and death at the hands of Black Mask. She says, *actually* says: "I screwed up. I paid the price. Simple."[24]

But it's not so simple. Her statement recalls not only Wonder Woman's comment about not liking women in the "Women's Liberation Issue" of *Wonder Woman*—a snarky response to feminist activists of the 1970s era who had protested that character's treatment—but it also speaks to other, more sexist thinking and insidious misogyny such as blaming a woman's sexual assault on her attire or on her being out alone after dark. It recalls a woman being beaten, maybe even to death, by her husband because—as he says—she made him angry.

Another response as to why the Girl Wonder did not deserve a memorial was that "Stephanie was never *really* a Robin," to which Katherine Keller, the editrix-in-chief of *Sequential Tart*, responded in an open letter to Dan DiDio,

> Because Steph's a girl and didn't happen to have the Robin costume on at the time she died her time as Robin doesn't count? Is that the message you want DC male and female fans to be receiving? Because, sir, it's the one you're delivering: the female doesn't count. . . . It's the *absence* of the memorial that speaks the loudest, and what that absence says is profound.[25]

Keller goes on to note that while Stephanie may not have been the best, the brightest, or even the most loved superhero in comics, she rose above her short stint as Robin to become a symbol to many women:

> See, Steph became *Robin*, not Batgirl. Robin is the *icon*. Robin is Batman's closest, most intimate relationship. Robin is the heir apparent. Robin (whether adopted or not) is Batman's child. And I was interested in how the dynamics would change now that a father-son relationship had become a father-daughter relationship. But, alas, it was not to be. However, stunt casting doesn't change the fact that a *girl* had become Robin.
>
> So, Steph doesn't matter to me that much a *character*, but she matters to me as a very powerful *symbol*. And unfortunately, that symbol is now one of how the contributions of women are systematically denied, ignored, explained away, and undercut in every way. Of how one standard exists for males (Jason Todd) and how another standard exists for women (Stephanie Brown).[26]

Stephanie's death was finally retconned in 2008. She appeared in a one-shot comic *Robin/Spoiler* that explained that Dr. Leslie Thompkins—the woman who had supposedly let Stephanie die to teach Batman a lesson about involving children in his vigilantism—had actually taken her to Africa. Stephanie has also appeared in at least two additional issues of *Robin*.

Girl Wonder continues to host message boards, webcomics, and blogs as well as posts scholarly papers, recommended sites, and a map of female-friendly comic book stores.

Stephanie Brown was not the first woman in comics to be sexually assaulted, and indeed, the rape, torture, kidnapping, and disempowerment of women in superhero comics is abhorrent and persistent. It's generally used for one of three narrative purposes: shock value, as the initial motivation for a superheroine's quest and/or vigilantism (i.e., Red Sonja's rape), or more commonly, as the driving force of a *superman's* rage. In two memorable examples, Spider-Man's girlfriend, Gwen Stacey, was tossed off the Brooklyn Bridge by his villainous nemesis, the Green Goblin, and Matt Murdock's former flame, Elektra, was stabbed through the heart by Bullseye with her own weapon. In one particularly gruesome case, the Green Lantern's girl-friend, Alexandra DeWitt, was strangled and stuffed in a refrigerator by Major Force.[27]

But it's not just wives and girlfriends who are victims. In 1999, roughly five years before the assault and death of Stephanie Brown, Gail Simone, a hairdresser and comics fan in Oregon, compiled a list of superheroines who had been raped, crippled, depowered, magically impregnated (without consent and therefore a form of rape), turned evil, given a life-threatening disease, or murdered. Because of extended continuity—made necessary by the longevity of medium—characters were often subject to a combination of the above atrocities. Black Canary has, for example, been tortured, made infertile, and depowered.

The trend Simone observed became known as "Women in Refrigerators"—after Alexandra DeWitt's demise—and the list was sent to several comics creators, along with a letter, asking what they thought about it. Cautious not to blame anyone, or otherwise appear antagonistic, Simone emphasized her genuine curiosity, noting that when she "realized that it was actually harder to list major female heroes who HADN'T been sliced up somehow," she felt she "might be on to something a bit ... well, creepy."[28]

The responses she received (catalogued online along with the original list) were naturally mixed. Some creators were defensive, while others were genuinely embarrassed once faced with how often these narrative devices were used. Some were convinced that this trend was indicative of larger issues of sexism and misogyny in our culture. Others pointed out that men in superhero comics suffer too. Simone responded that the issue isn't with the violence women would necessarily be expected to face as protagonists in an action/adventure story, but in the ways this violence was depicted; the issues arise when women are shown as *only* victims or hostages, when they are raped or murdered for cheap shock value, or for the effect their assault will have on the male character's story.

Overwhelmingly, women were generally humiliated and/or canonically tossed aside in ways that male superheroes weren't; male heroes tended to come back to life or be healed more often and more quickly, and the deaths of females were usually perverted or sexualized in some way. As Simone told Shaenon K. Garrity for *The Comics Journal*, "You rarely have guy heroes killed in ways that thrust their crotches forward and expose their asses through strategic rips in their super-undies."[29] Additionally, the disproportionate number of male superheroes to female characters makes what happens to women much more noticeable.

As a result of the attention the Women-in-Refrigerators list received, Simone went on to write a column called "You'll All Be Sorry" for the website Comic Book Resources. She later ventured into scripting comics, becoming one of the best-loved writers at DC. She took over duties on *Birds of Prey* and later *Wonder Woman*.[30]

Birds of Prey: Supersisters Doing It for Themselves

Birds of Prey was conceived for DC by Jordan B. Gorfinkel and scripted by Chuck Dixon. Though the title started as a one shot in 1996, called *Black Canary/Oracle: Birds of Prey*, the series is still running over a decade later.[31] It featured Barbara Gordon, formerly known as Batgirl in her new secret identity as "Oracle"—an alias adopted after she was shot in the spine by the Joker and paralyzed from the waist down in 1988's *The Killing Joke*.[32] Barbara, refusing to be limited by her wheelchair, continues to fight crime and injustice by providing intelligence to others in the superhero community with her mad computer-hacking skills. Few know Oracle's true identity, and Barbara remains one of the few superheroes in comics to have a disability. In *Birds of Prey* she befriends and teams up with the Black Canary, also known as Dinah Lance.

Riding the wave of television superwomen inspired by the success of *Buffy the Vampire* Slayer, a short-lived live action series loosely based on Dixon's *Birds of Prey* premiered in 2002.

Developed by Laeta Kalogridis, the series featured Ashley Scott as the Earth Two version of the Huntress, also known as Helena Wayne, and the daughter of Catwoman and Batman. Dina Meyer starred as Barbara Gordon/Oracle, and Rachel Skarsten played a modified version of Dinah Lance. Instead of being the adult Dinah was in the comics, she was reimagined as a teenage runaway in need of a mentor to avoid conflicting with Kalogridis's favored version of Huntress. A female villain was added in Mia Sara's wild-eyed take on Harley Quinn.

While *Birds of Prey* contained elements of Dixon's interpretation of the Batman mythos, it lacked the mythic resonance of the similarly superhero-themed live-action show, *Smallville* (based on the teenage Clark Kent), and so only one season was produced. But regardless of its distortion of canon, as well as its sub-par scripting and production, *Birds of Prey* still managed to explore themes relevant to the female hero, namely, the importance of female friend and mentorship (also discussed in Chapters 5 and 7). When Helena tells Barbara in frustration, "I can't be what you were," referring to the latter's tenure as Batgirl, Barbara replies, "Good. Just be yourself instead." She honors and nurtures her friend's particular skills instead of making her a clone or relegating her to sidekick. Barbara also expects that Dinah will be more that a mini-Babs, though she does encourage her young ward's unique potential by setting some household ground rules. Dinah is required to go to school and to work on her skills both mental *and* physical. Even the voice-over to the series emphasizes the theme of women mentoring women, calling Barbara "a mentor and trainer to heroes" and adds that "Together," these three women, the Birds of Prey, "are protectors of New Gotham."

The television series was an unfortunate failure, but the very fact that it focused on three female leads, one of which is in a wheelchair, *and* had a female villain is in itself revolutionary. *Birds of Prey*, the comic, on the other hand, fared much better—particularly under the direction of Gail Simone. When she took over writing duties in 2003, Simone asked if she could add the Huntress to *Birds of Prey*. She received some resistance, as DC was attempting to distance themselves from the recently canceled television series.[33] They eventually relented, however, and other characters were added too: Savant, an occasional villain and sometimes ally of the Birds of Prey, and his sidekick Creote, a ginormous, Russian muscleman (who is in love with a clueless Savant).

Simone also incorporated a plethora of bad-ass females to the narrative who frequently collaborate with the original core team of Barbara, Dinah, and Helena; a list that includes: Lady Blackhawk, Lady Shiva, Big Barda, Misfit, Judomaster, Gypsy, and Manhunter. Icons Lois Lane and Wonder Woman have made appearances, and Dinah adopted a child prodigy named Sin—a girl who was being trained as the next Lady Shiva but who may now enjoy a healthy and loving upbringing with a strong and positive mother. Of the superwomen, Simone told *Newsarama*:

> I'm extremely proud of the fact that this book often had an almost exclusively female cast, and yet, no two characters are the same. They all had distinctive voices and characters, from Misfit to Huntress to Barda to Oracle and on and on. It put the lie to the idea that male readers wouldn't read a book with a female cast, and it stayed one of DC's steadiest selling and most critically acclaimed books. It's drawn the attention of the national media many, many times, without a single a-list star in it, and almost no big stunt events. I think, if you look at how many supposedly girl-friendly superhero books have come and gone while *Birds of Prey* keeps going, it's pretty impressive.[34]

She's also noted that the women of *Birds of Prey* "don't apologize for being asskickers, nor for being smart, nor for being sexy, nor for being sexual, for that matter."[35] And they are fabulously fun females indeed. Simone's female characters talk about things that are important to women, but also about girly things, without being defined by, or confined to, their femininity: the joy of really good food, that a new flattering costume is the result of

700 sit-ups a day, and the difficulty of coming to terms with your mother's flaws. There is an emphasis on deep and meaningful female friendships and on how an act of compassion can have as much positive and life-enriching effect on ourselves as on others.

For example, when Dinah returns from Asia with Sin, Barbara is worried that their crime-fighting lifestyle will put the child in danger. Dinah reminds her friend: "Sometimes we have to take the family we're *given*, Babs. She has *no one* . . . She's *my* responsibility. And more than that, I think I could be a good, you know—mother-type thing."[36] While out at brunch with the Birds and Sin, Dinah contemplates her family:

> *I thought it'd be awkward. Coming back, I mean. After what I experienced in Asia. But like it or not, this is home, and these are my she-peeps. And god help me, I simply straight up adore them. While I was away, in between being beaten to a pulp and crippling a small army in the mud and filth . . . I acquired two of the best things ever to happen to me in my impulsive and inelegant life. First, I figured out who I AM, and who I want to BE. Or more accurately, maybe, who I do NOT want to be. And the other's sitting next to me having her first restaurant meal, wearing her first formal dress shoes. I know she's not really my daughter. The word 'Mother' means terrible things to her. But good LORD, she's captured me already. She had nothing, no family, no one. Not even a pair of underwear to her name. But now, she's got me.*[37]

Barbara too will take responsibility for a daughter—though one slightly older than Sin. The teenage Charlotte Gage-Radcliffe has the ability to teleport and attempts to adopt the mantle of Batgirl by appearing in Barbara's secret location dressed in a makeshift cape and cowl. Babs convinces the girl not to pursue a career as Batgirl—that it's too dangerous—and uses herself and Stephanie Brown as examples. The girl agrees, but later returns in her new identity, "Misfit."

When Barbara finds out that Misfit is without a family or a home, having lost both to an apartment fire, she reaches out to the teen. Perhaps the influence of her most compassionate friend, Dinah. As Barbara narrates:

> *I started this operation for a reason. It's not something I talk about—I almost lost Helena over it. I wanted to help people, people who needed the help. Starting with me. She hasn't asked for anything, but she has the look of someone who's gotten all too used to disappointment. If I can't help someone like her . . . . If I won't help someone like her . . . . then what, really, is the point? I'm not Spy Smasher. I never meant to be anything like her. I'm not Spy Smasher. I'm not Batman. It's not about fear. It's not about control. I'm Oracle. I help people. People who have no one. People in need. And that's good enough.*[38]

Birds of Prey presents sisterhood without getting bogged down in rhetoric about sisterhood—which has the potential to come off as insincere.

As Gail Simone has repeatedly said at panel question and answer sessions, as well as in interviews, she doesn't write female characters, just characters. But her *femaleness*, her femininity, compassion, motherhood, sisterhood, intellect, humor, and bravery, shines through her characters nevertheless.

Mothers and Daughters: *GoGirl!* and *Wonder Woman*

Trina Robbins created a healthy, functioning, and supportive relationship in her and Anne Timmons's female positive comic book series *GoGirl!* The title character is the teenage daughter of Go-Go Girl—a famous super-heroine back in the 1970s who had retired because her husband "was kinda threatened by having a wife who could fly" (though they eventually divorced anyway).[39] Mrs. Goldman doesn't like to talk about the past, but when she discovers that her daughter, Lindsay, inherited her ability to fly, she tells the young girl that if she wants to be a hero, she's going to have to learn how to protect herself. Mother and daughter hit the gym for lessons in self-defense and kick-boxing because, as the wise Mrs. Goldman says, "Being a superheroine takes more than just the ability to fly."[40]

GoGirl! was conceived out of an act of sisterhood and female empow-erment. Artist Timmons had approached Robbins at a comic book conven-tion where Robbins was doing a portfolio review. Robbins was immediately impressed. "This woman shows up, and she's so talented, she can draw any-thing, but she's not selling to Marvel or DC. They won't buy her stuff. Well, to me it was obvious ...," she says. Robbins' conclusion? Timmons draws like a girl.

"There's definitely a boy's style and a girl's style," says Robbins, who adds that she knows people will tell her differently.[41] But Timmons agrees, noting that "You know, there really *is*. There's a different way of how I think girls and guys view life."[42]

Timmons says the two women became friends and email pen pals when they found out they "both like comics about girls."[43] They decided to col-laborate on a project together—though were convinced that in an era of Women in Refrigerators and "Bad Girl" comics, it would *never* sell. "At that point, what was going on in comics were bad girl comics. Giant breasts. Things like 'Lady Death,' or whatever the hell her name was. That's what they did," says Robbins, who adds

> And I've always had so many different ideas floating around in my head, many of which I've suggested over the past 30 years to various mainstream editors, and they've said, well this is a very nice idea, but it's for girls, and girls don't read comics.

You know the story. And of course they can't say it anymore because of Manga, but they sure used to say it a lot.[44]

Through previous work as an associate at a studio based in Portland, Oregon, Timmons had made several local connections, including at Image Comics, which publishes creator-owned material. She asked Robbins if they wanted to submit something together, and they did. While Image was very supportive of *GoGirl!*, sales were low.

Robbins explains the issue was problems with distribution:

> Comic book stores wouldn't carry girls' comics. So girls couldn't find the comics, so of course the sales were low. You know, if you're not going to order the book, the sales are gonna be low. So we figured, the only way to get around this, was to do a graphic novel. Because then we could get it into libraries and bookstores.[45]

Dark Horse took up the chance, and the books sold very well indeed. "Librarians in particular love us," says Robbins, who adds, "They're always looking for graphic novels for girls."[46] And *GoGirl!* is great for girls. There is a strong mother–daughter relationship inspired by Robbins' close relationship with her own daughter. She says, "I am a mother, and I have a great relationship. I love my daughter so much," and adds that she didn't realize when she created *GoGirl!*, how much of that bond had been reflected in Lindsay and her mother:

> It was all subconscious—but one of the things that had been important to me in the original Wonder Woman is the relationship with Wonder Woman and her mother. She has a strong mother, who is completely supportive of her daughter going out to Man's world, even though at the beginning she doesn't want her to do it. Just like GoGirl!'s mother, at the beginning, didn't want to talk about her being a superheroine because it had kind of disappointed her. But when she found out her daughter was doing it, she became supportive.[47]

Unlike most of the male-drawn, mainstream female superheroes, GoGirl! is always modestly dressed—a result of all the portfolios Robbins had seen at conventions that claimed to have strong female leads she'd appreciate; "And," she says, "the 'strong female lead' has giant breasts bigger than her head, and [she's] wearing a tiny little outfit, and a thong bikini. . . . And of course, here's librarians looking for books for girls, and obviously they're not going to want to carry those books. So GoGirl! was always decently dressed."[48]

GoGirl! also features a diverse cast. Lindsay has friends that are Asian, African American, smart, and preppy, and it teaches valuable lessons about bravery, loyalty, and friendship. One of its strengths is that Robbins' and Timmons' affection for the characters shines through. "I love writing *GoGirl!*," says Robbins,

I mean, I *love* it. I think as a writer you really have to love your characters, and you really have to know your characters. And I mean, I look at some of these mainstream comics, and they don't love their characters—or know them. I think that most of the guys who have written Wonder Woman don't love her.[49,50]

Fortunately, Gail Simone, who is currently writing *Wonder Woman*, is similarly endeared to her characters. Even though her industry friends have told her not to get too attached to company-owned characters, as writers and artists are shifted from title to title according to editorial needs, she finds no other way of writing works for her at all.[51]

Simone took over writing duties on *Wonder Woman* in 2007 with Issue 14. Her first story arc titled, "The Circle," is an intriguing elaboration on the birth of Diana.[52]

In "The Circle" we are taken centuries back in time to when Queen Hippolyta asks the gods for a child. The queen's four closest and most trusted bodyguards, Alkyone, Myrto, Charis, and Philomela, are against this, fearing that for one woman to have a child and the rest to not will wreak havoc on Themyscira and break the bonds of Amazonian sisterhood rather than reinforce them. Captain of the guards, Alkyone, explains:

> We'd been on this island, our homeland, for ages beyond memory. And still, the ache of an eternally empty womb was almost unbearable for some. Many of our sisters carved infant-shaped totems out of sandalwood, and carried them about our person. "Whittle-babies," we named them. A bit of pretend hope, the foolish dream of a sterile race, perhaps. But for some, it was a receptacle, a forum for thoughts we no longer had any capacity to express, for a kind of love we had no space to fit. I put the thoughts aside. One child amongst an island of women who could never experience . . . it was inconceivable.[53]

When these four royal guards hear that a woman on the island has a daughter, they investigate, but what they find instead is a heartbreaking and frightening scene. The poor woman is not a new mother; rather she has gone mad, singing lullabies while cradling a doll she has convinced herself was a real child. Alkyone, fearing that such a madness could spread, orders that no dolls resembling children can ever be crafted on the island again and has the woman discretely executed.[54]

But when Hippolyta, the one woman they cannot control or intimidate, is determined to craft a child for all the sister Amazons to share, Alkyone instead begs her queen not to, believing that the others' initial joy would quickly turn to envy and hatred if their queen had a daughter while they remained barren. But when Hippolyta returns from the ritual that created Diana and presents her to her beloved sisters with a hearty, "I give you your Princess. I give you our Daughter!," they respond with sincere cheers.[55]

Unconvinced, Alkyone, Myrto, Charis, and Philomela enter the queen's bedchamber that night, intending to kill the child. They are stopped for a moment by the beauty of the sleeping princess, just long enough for Hippolyta to awake and see her betrayal. The four women are imprisoned in solitary confinement on opposite ends of Themyscira. One night a year, Hippolyta offers them the chance to repent. They always refuse, still filled with personal envy that did not, in fact, extend to their sisters.

In an-all female society, women *would* think about children. Not every sister on the island would necessarily feel either an intellectual desire or a biological urge to raise a child, but certainly some would, perhaps even many. Yet this aspect of a woman's life hadn't been explored in the *Wonder Woman* comic before Simone.[56]

Additionally, even with a societal emphasis on sisterhood, it's reasonable to assume there would remain the possibility that other Amazons might feel it's unjust for their queen to have a daughter when such a privilege is denied to them. For Alkyone, this is precisely the problem, for the Amazons are supposed to be a "race of equals, of sisters."[57]

But Diana, as we know, did not cause a rift. Rather, she is a child of Themyscira—a daughter of Amazons. As Hippolyta later explains, "All the Amazons became her mother, as one. She brought us *hope* and *love*. She *saved* us . . . She *saved* us *all*."[58]

Simone has made an effort to tap into what's great about Wonder Woman—Wonder Woman the Amazon, the Princess, the Ambassador, the Human, the Ass-Kicker, the Empathizer, the Goddess, the Friend, and the Daughter—and expanded on all of these by considering that Diana's future identity may be even further fleshed out by the roles of Mother and Lover.

For example, when Wonder Woman begins courting a man named Thomas Tresser (the partner of her alter ego Diana Prince), she takes him to Themyscira to meet her mother. The queen intimidates the hell out of the man before giving her approval. She also gives him a spear crafted by her own hand, a title (Guardsman, Sir Thomas of Cleveland), and her allegiance: "You are an Amazon now, Thomas. No matter what happens from now on, you must never forget that. You must be true to your sisters. For any of us would give our life for you without a moment's hesitation." As Diana and Thomas prepare to leave the island, Hippolyta adds, "I only want one more thing from you. . . . Babies . . . As many as you can provide for, as quickly as you may produce them. Babies, babies, babies."[59]

Hippolyta is a warrior and a queen, but she is also a mother, longing for grandchildren. The issue is not belabored; there is no pressure placed on Diana, and no concern that she would ever be forced to choose between motherhood and heroism.

Just one issue later, Diana, after spending time with two young sisters, thinks to herself: "Children. Their joy is so infectious, they laugh completely and without reserve. My life is changing so much lately. I can imagine things duty would not allow, previously. Children. I *wonder*."[60]

Women Writing Women in Espionage: *D.E.B.S.*

Influenced by the Charlie's Angels redux, and therefore a spoof of a spoof, *D.E.B.S.* (2004) is a silly, spy-fi gem clothed in a teenage love story. Or perhaps, it's the other way around.

Originally an independent short film written and directed by Angela Robinson, and funded by a grant from Power Up—an organization that promotes the visibility and integration of gay women in entertainment, the arts, and all forms of media,[61] Robinson described the short as "a story about a trio of super spies who are all chicks." It was based on a comic book she'd written, as she says, "I love all the comic book characters: Charlie's Angels, Batman, Josie & the Pussycats. . . . But I always wanted them to be gay and they never were, so I wrote my own."[62]

After winning several film festival awards for *D.E.B.S.*, Robinson was approached by Sony's Screen Gems Pictures to turn the short into a feature-length film. The movie, also called *D.E.B.S.*, centers on the mysterious return of one Lucy Diamond (Jordana Brewster), a criminal mastermind who once tried to sink Australia. The D.E.B.S. (an acronym for discipline, energy, beauty, and strength) are an elite group of spies in training chosen for admission to their academy through secret questions on the scholastic aptitude tests (SATs)—sort of a test within a test.[63] D.E.B.S., Amy (Sara Foster), Max (Meagan Good), Janet (Jill Ritchie), and Dominique (Devon Aoki), are sent to surveil Lucy at a local restaurant, where she appears to be meeting with the Russian assassin Ninotchka (Jessica Cauffiel).

The girls are surprised to discover that Lucy is not planning something nefarious, but rather is attempting to excuse herself from a painfully bad blind date. (Lucy's sidekick Scud (Jimmi Simpson) had set up the date to try and get her back into the dating game after having been dumped by her girlfriend.) A firefight breaks out, and while in pursuit of Lucy, Amy literally runs into her. The two are instantly smitten. In fact, as it turns out, Amy is writing a paper on Lucy, "It's a Man's World: Lucy Diamond and the Psychology of Cultural Criminality" for her class Capes and Capers: Gender

Reconstruction and the Criminal Mastermind. Apparently the discovery of Lucy's sexual preference blows Amy's whole thesis.

The film is full of goofy spy gadgets; Lucy uses suction cups to scale a building, and the D.E.B.S's house is secured by a plaid force field that matches the girls' pseudo–Catholic School Girl microminis. Innuendo and entendre are clever and abundant. According to the secret test, Amy is the perfect spy, and is thus referred to as The Perfect Score, evoking themes of theft and sex. And a "deb" is of course short for a "Debutante"—a young woman who of a certain age has a "coming-out" party. Yet while lesbianism is present in the movie, it's truly a minor theme. When Amy and Lucy are discovered in the midst of an intimate encounter, the disappointment, betrayal, and anger of Amy's peers come not from the discovery that their friend is a lesbian, but from the fact that she was literally sleeping with the enemy.

D.E.B.S. is cheery-good fun—a sweet and endearing, playful movie about young love and self-discovery. Just because Lucy has always been a villain doesn't mean she can't change her ways. And just because Amy is The Perfect Score doesn't mean she is destined to be a spy.

At the end of the film, the couple drives off into the sunset together, but many mainstream reviewers did not give the movie the credit it deserves, and so it remains obscure. Owen Gleiberman wrote in *Entertainment Weekly*, "Hottie crime fighters in short skirts. How not exciting," and, "Did the director, Angela Robinson, realize that it's a fool's game to try and parody the Charlie's Angels movies, since they're cheeky parodies to begin with, or did she hoodwink herself into thinking she was doing something original?"[64] Peter Travers of *Rolling Stone* reduced the plot to "a thief who recruits D.E.B.S. star Amy for some hot lesbo action ... You might think there's no downside to a movie that peeks up the skirts of babes in microminis, but writer-director Angela Robinson's dimwitted satire is libido-killing proof to the contrary."[65] Stephen Holden of the *New York Times* called it a "heat-free pseudo-lesbian spoof of 'Charlie's Angels' by way of 'Heathers,' [that] offers an hour and a half of [an] empty tease" unjustly adding that "the love scenes are as erotically charged as a home movie of a little girl hugging her Barbie doll."[66]

The conceit of Gleiberman, Travers, and Holden is that lesbians in mainstream films (or porn) are meant to provide titillation to a heterosexual male audience—especially when they are dressed as schoolgirls. Not only are they completely blind to their sexist bias, but they forget that they aren't likely to know what may be appealing to a lesbian, and/or feminist, audience. Lastly forgotten is the fact that *D.E.B.S.* is a teenage love story, not an adult-centric erotic film such as *Bound* (1996) or *Basic Instinct* (1992).[67]

Superwomen Making Myth

Women don't automatically approach the journey of the female hero better or worse than men do simply because they are women. But they may approach it differently, perhaps even more authentically, because of the unique and specific experiences women encounter because they are women.

The women of *Ms.* magazine and Girl Wonder reclaimed the female symbols that were important to them, and Nichelle Nichols used her experience of sexism and racism to change the face of NASA. Trina Robbins's bond with her daughter was echoed in the pages of *GoGirl!* Angela Robinson, an African American lesbian, made a movie with lesbian teenagers and an ethnically diverse cast. And Gail Simone works to write inclusive comics by "actively not trying to *exclude* people, as so many comics do,"[68] because "It's not just more good female characters we need—it's more good gay characters, more good Asian characters, more good African American characters, and on and on."[69]

Sex and gender do not and should not define us or what we do, but a combination of nature and nurture colors our lives, regardless. Who we are influences the stories we tell and the stories we want to hear.

Conclusion
"Where Do We Go from Here?"

Throughout this book we have looked at the ways in which gender is represented in modern mythologies and how this is connected to contemporary social values; as Danny Fingeroth wrote, "Every generation makes the fictional characters it needs. What should inspire—or terrify—us are not the hero's power or gender, but what the heroes represent about our needs, our fears, and our attitudes."[1]

In the 1940s, Wonder Woman fought Nazis alongside Superman and Batman, and real Allied women were called upon to participate on the home front during the Second World War. British entertainment in the 1960s played with gender and modernity—particularly in the spy-fi genre—and American television and comics in the 1970s incorporated feminist themes with varying degrees of success. Blaxploitation and other B-movie genres featured some of the first action heroines in film. While in the Reagan era, men were presented as making the best mommies, career women were shown as *really* wanting to be at home being mommy instead of trying to "have it all"—with the exception of a few notable warriors. Grrrl Power in the 1990s, and adult mythmakers influenced by second wave parents, helped create some of the most complex women of popular culture to date.

So, as Buffy and the Scoobies famously joined hands and asked, "Where do we go from here?" Answering that question requires we take a look at where we are, so that we get a better idea of where we need to go.

The television series *Heroes* (2006–?) serves as a good example to explore, having a deeply layered mythology that viscerally captivates and intellectually challenges. Like *Lost* (2004–?) and *Battlestar Galactica* (2004–9)—shows with similarly complex canons—it also features some of the most ethnically diverse casts ever to grace television screens, and while these shows may lack the explicit feminist mission with which Joss Whedon infused Buffy, a commitment to diversity is inherently feminist.

Like *Buffy*, *Dark Angel*, and *Star Trek*, the characters and stories of *Heroes* and *Battlestar Galactica* are adept at reflecting contemporary concerns through innovative use of myth and archetype. *Battlestar Galactica* uses thinly veiled metaphor to explore issues of morality, abuse of power, and survival in a post-9/11 world and the conservative politics of the Bush era. *Heroes*—a series inspired by both *The Incredibles* and *Eternal Sunshine of the Spotless Mind*[2]—is an exploration of evolution in a time of global warming, terrorism, and diminishing natural resources. Series creator Tim Kring has said,

> The world is a big, scary place right now, with huge issues . . . that seem really out of control. The wish-fulfillment aspect of the show is that ordinary people like you or me may be coming along with special powers, and can ultimately do something about these larger issues.[3]

Heroes, though not a superhero show per se, is, as the title claims, a show about superpowered people and is thus a particularly useful gauge of superheroic representation. Some, like Hiro Nakamura (Masi Oka) and Peter Petrelli (Milo Ventimiglia), immediately recognize their responsibility to use these gifts to help humanity. Some, such as Sylar (Zachary Quinto), use them for self-gain. Many are confused, even afraid, and trying to make sense of what is happening to them.

Heroes has shown us marvelous individuals from all over the globe: from New York and Japan to India, California, Ireland, and Central America. Kring posits a theory in the show that "nature is somehow populating the world with people who will take us to the next evolutionary level"[4]—and what the possibilities and dangers of this might be. The global reach of the show, and the diversity of race and locale, ensures Kring's mission that audiences can "see themselves or their neighbors in these characters."[5] The unspoken implication being that audiences can take inspiration in this time of unusual need.

As progressive as *Heroes* is in its ethnic diversity, with a cast that includes people of South Asian, African American, European, Haitian, and Japanese descent, it still has work to do when it comes to making visible gays and lesbians, who at the time of writing have yet to be officially included on the show.[6] Additionally, to the frustration of fans, while male characters have most often been the ones to embark on journeys that take them across time and space in order to heroically heal the world as they learn about themselves and their moral responsibilities, many of the female characters have fallen victim to various elements of the Women-in-Refrigerator syndrome (discussed in Chapter 8). This includes Niki Sanders, who couldn't control her power and was placed in a mental institution but ultimately died a heroic death; Eden McCain, a shady agent who also sacrificed herself with a dramatic last act; Simone Deveaux, whose death created tension between her two male love interests; and Charlie Andrews, Yaeko, and Caitlin, one of whom died, while one was left in the past, and another in the future.

But Claire Bennett (Hayden Panettiere) and Monica Dawson (Dana Davis) prove that the series is capable of creating laudable female characters. Independently of each other, these two superwomen set out to test the limits of their abilities with the same admirable courage and inquisitiveness as the series' male characters. They are also pragmatic about their powers' potential to help other people and actively find ways to do so.

Claire has featured from the very first episode as one of the integral heroes of the show. When we are introduced to her, she is testing out her ability to spontaneously heal by various gruesome means—diving off a scaffolding, dashing into the wreckage of a burning train, and shoving her hand down a running garbage disposal—each time breaking bones, charring skin, or grating phalanges, only to fully recover with near immediacy.

Claire's adoptive father Noah Bennett (Jack Coleman) works for The Company, a secret organization that tracks, and occasionally recruits or studies, people with abilities—people like his daughter Claire. Noah is a morally ambiguous figure, to say the least. In not-so-subtle metaphor, flashback scenes of his past are even filmed in gray. Yet when he discovers Claire has manifested abilities, and is thus required to turn her over to The Company, he utilizes all his resources to protect her from his superiors including the frequent mind-wiping of his otherwise sharp and intelligent wife, Sandra (Ashley Crow).

At first, Claire is unaware that her father knows about her power and takes it upon herself to find answers about how she became nigh invincible. But she is not completely alone. With the help of her friend Zack, Claire finds her birth mother Meredith (Jessalyn Gilsig), presumed dead but living in secret in a small Texan town. Her birth father, Nathan Petrelli (Adrian Pasdar), is a politician in New York. Both biological parents, like Claire, have unusual abilities.

Claire's search for the truth about herself supersedes normal teenage pursuits like boys, shopping, and even the cheerleading squad she'd once thought she needed to join as a way to cement her high school identity. As she documents her injuries and recoveries on film for posterity, one assumes Claire will also study the videos for insight into her ability.

Fascinatingly, Claire isn't disgusted with her body as so many teenage girls and adult women are. She explores her body and what it allows her to be capable of; she never panics over a dislocated shoulder, or even her own autopsied chest cavity. She simply puts everything back in place and moves on. As Hayden Panettiere told *Sci Fi Wire*, teenagers are "constantly trying to test the limits of their freedom and how far they can push things . . . [Claire's] just doing it in a different way."[7]

Aside from her physical gift, Claire also shows strength and resolve in other ways. For example, when Noah finds videotapes of her testing her ability, he destroys them and mind-wipes Zack (Thomas Dekker) in an effort to protect his daughter. But as a result, the latter not only has no knowledge of Claire's power but also no memories of their friendship at all. As Claire's best friend, Zack was the only person she could trust with her secret. Rather than lose her confidant, she begins their friendship anew, reintroducing herself and re-filming her death-defying jumps.

Other examples of Claire's strength of will and sense of justice occur when she takes vengeance on a classmate who tried to rape and kill her, and when she escapes from the newly discovered grandmother who is holding her hostage by jumping out of a several stories high window.

Claire is centered in Season 1's major story arc. Propelled by the cryptic message, "Save the Cheerleader, Save the World," Peter Petrelli, later revealed to be Claire's uncle, seeks Claire out to save her from a murderous villain. This could have relegated Claire to a damsel-in-distress stereotype, but she actively makes efforts to protect herself and others rather than play the girly victim.[8] Her intelligence allows her to make logical connections, such as if her skin can regenerate after "boiling it with the eggs," perhaps her blood has the potential to heal people as well.[9] She's compassionate, reserving judgment for those labeled "villainous," and instead chooses to trust her gut and weigh the facts that she herself finds. She even goes so far as to try to reunite a person, whose chaotic and uncontrolled abilities accidentally hurt someone else, with his family rather than blindly turn him over to The Company for imprisonment. In another instance, she absorbs a character's erratic powers to relieve the woman of pain.

Claire began as her daddy Noah's "Claire Bear" and as the cheerleader who needed saving, but she quickly moved beyond her role as daughter and out of the shadows of both her adoptive and biological fathers. In fact, in Season 3 it is her adoptive and biological *mothers* she turns to for guidance and for assistance—as well as always to herself. The ability to be independent *and* connected to others is a crucial part of redefining heroism, as Kathleen Noble wrote: "To live heroically a woman must belong to herself and herself alone; she must be the center of her own life. She must pursue a wholeness of integrity that is fluid, inclusive, and interconnected and that does not preclude relationships." Noble adds that "the female hero must *insist* upon herself, something that most women are neither taught nor encouraged to do."[10] But Claire is no longer her daddy's little girl——she's a young woman, a heroic woman.

I had great love for the plucky Monica Dawson, cousin to Micah Sanders (Noah Gray-Cabey) and hero-in-discovery. The character came across, as Monica herself put it, "like a woman with a future." I was ecstatic to see such a determined woman on the series; Monica worked double shifts at a fast food establishment to financially support her extended family in the post-Katrina South, but had dreams of going back to college.

When she discovered her ability allowed her to instantaneously learn new skills simply by watching someone else perform them, her younger cousin used a comic book to explain what was happening to her. The title was about a muscle mimic, or copy-cat, named "St. Joan"—of course a nod to that tragic savior of her people, Jeanne D'Arc, who like Monica had a close relationship with God.

Like Claire, Monica explores her powers, learning Jeet Kune Do by watching a Bruce Lee film and going in for some Double Dutch (jump rope). Unfortunately, she was only in a handful of episodes. At the time of writing, Season 3 is well underway; Monica has not made an appearance, nor even been mentioned.[11] And it's a tragedy to lose such an interesting female character, a woman of color too, on a series that aims to represent difference in the world but still favors blonde women (Meredith, Elle, Claire, Niki/Tracy, Sandra, Daphne, etc.).

Men on *Heroes* were initially depicted more progressively than women. Claire's father Noah Bennett comes off more like a Sarah Connor–esque lioness rather than a traditional patriarch, and Peter Petrelli was a professional caregiver, praised for his ability to love unconditionally. He was even told that his love would save the world—recalling Xander Harris, the "heart" of the Scoobies on *Buffy the Vampire Slayer*. In Season 2 little Molly Walker had two daddies—two straight men living together to raise and protect an orphaned child while lacking the de-threatening humor of a sitcom.

So where *do* we go from here?

It appears that gender lines are beginning to blur as women and men continue to embrace both traditionally labeled "male" and "female" characteristics. Carol Pearson and Katherine Pope have stressed the importance of this, arguing, "Freeing the heroic journey from the limiting assumptions about appropriate female and male behavior, then, is an important step in defining a truly human—and humane—pattern of heroic action."[12] They add that "Until the heroic experience of all people—racial minorities and the poor as well as women—has been thoroughly explored, the myth of the hero will always be incomplete and inaccurate."[13]

Our stories will continue to evolve as humanity does. Increased acceptance of gay marriage, the first ever campaigns by serious Black and female US presidential candidates, and the presence of more women and other minorities in entertainment industry positions means that we will see an ever-increasing diversity in our heroes. We must, because wish fulfillment, fantasy, identification, and inspiration belong to all of us. There is no one way to be heroic, and there shouldn't be limited or conformative representations of a "hero." What we need are *heroes* and *heroisms*: Black, White, Asian, Hispanic, Aboriginal, Middle Eastern, gay, straight, male, female, transgender, fat, skinny, somewhere-in-the-middle, athletic, disabled, with the ability to fly, run faster than a speeding bullet, write, parent, kick-ass, grow, and make the world we live in a better place.

I began this book with an anecdote and I'd like to end it with one. When I was a little girl, my pantheon of inspirational female heroes grew when I fell in love with Dorothy Gale and Princess Ozma of L. Frank Baum's magical Oz series. I loved them so much that I even had my mother sew me an original Ozma-of-Oz costume for Halloween based on drawings and descriptions from the books. We also redecorated my room with a Wizard of Oz theme. In the books, when Dorothy wished to visit Oz she would just ask Ozma, who would see Dorothy in her magic mirror and transport her to Oz. I so wanted to visit that marvelous land and share in their adventures, and I would sit in my room and ask Ozma to bring me there too—If Dorothy could go, why couldn't I? Dorothy and Ozma helped me believe in magic and know that I could be a part of something splendid. When I shared this story with Trina Robbins over afternoon tea in San Francisco's Yerba Buena Gardens, she said,

> OK—then you understand, why, in the privacy of my bedroom, I used to go "SHAZAM? SHAZAM!" *hoping* that it would work. I love the idea of a magic word. It's so great, and so good for kids to think that if they can find their magic word, maybe they could be super too and it's good to give girls hope. Because maybe they can find their own way to Oz. You know what I mean? Or maybe their own magic word. Because we do—we all have a way to Oz, our own personal Oz, and we all have that magic word.[14]

We may not yet all have a hero that represents us as unique and varied individuals, but *we all have that magic word*. And we find it through the stories and the heroes that inspire us. For Trina, that word was Mary Marvel's "SHAZAM." For the Potentials of *Buffy the Vampire Slayer*, it was a simple, yet profound, "*Yes*," in answer to the question, "Are you ready to be strong?" For Hiro Nakamura, and fans of *Heroes*, it's a joyous "Yatta!"

My hope is that through the evolution of mythic stories we will all be able to find our magic word, heroes to relate to, and ways to live heroically.[15]

From (A)eon to (Z)oë

A Select Glossary of Superwomen in Modern Mythology

Aeon Flux: A lawless assassin of the fictional society of Monica. Created by Peter Chung in conjunction with Colossal Pictures for MTV's groundbreaking series *Liquid Television*. Later embodied by Charlize Theron in a 2005 film adaptation directed by Karyn Kusama.

Anyanka: A 1,000-year-old former vengeance demon, better known as Anya, on *Buffy the Vampire Slayer*. A member of the Scoobies, terrified of bunnies, once engaged to Xander, and best friend of Andrew. Portrayed by Emma Caulfield.

Araña Corazon: (Marvel) A meta-human who lives with her single father—an investigative journalist. Was allied with the Spider Society, and after the Superhero Registration Act, became associated with Ms. Marvel. The first Latina superhero in the Marvelverse.

Barbarella: A sexually adventurous space agent created by Jean-Claude Forest in 1962. Later immortalized in 1968 by Jane Fonda in the movie directed by Roger Vadim and produced by Dino de Laurentiis. (At the time of writing, Robert Rodriguez has been rumored to do a remake of the film.)

Batgirl/Barbara Gordon/Oracle: (DC) Daughter of Commissioner Gordon and protégée of Batman. Barbara Gordon debuted in 1966 in the comics and the *Batman* television series where she was played by Yvonne Craig. Later she was played by Alicia Silverstone in the movie *Batman and Robin* and by Dina Meyer in the television series *Birds of Prey*. Barbara was paralyzed from the waist down when The Joker shot her in the spine in Alan Moore's *The Killing Joke* (1988). She was later reintroduced in *The Suicide Squad* title as Oracle—a computer hacker who provided intelligence to the superhero community. She would go on to form the Birds of Prey. Barbara is one of the rare few superheroes with a disability.

Batwoman: (DC) Kathy Kane appeared as Batwoman in the *Batman* line during the late 1950s and early 1960s. She was reintroduced in 2006 as Katy Kane and is one of the rare examples of a gay superhero in mainstream comics. Katy is also Jewish.

Bionic Woman/Jamie Sommers: After being injured in a skydiving accident, Jaime's right arm, right ear, and both of her legs are replaced with bionics in this 1970s spin-off of *The Six Million Dollar Man*. The Bionic Woman was played by Lindsay Wagner.

Black Canary: (DC) A martial arts expert with a meta-human sonic scream called the "Canary Cry." Former member of the Justice Society of America and the Birds of Prey, and current member of the Justice League of America. Has appeared in television series *Birds of Prey* and *Smallville*. Dinah is the daughter of a police detective and the previous Black Canary—also named Dinah Lance.

The Bride/Black Mamba/Beatrix Kiddo/Mommy: The protagonist of *Kill Bill*. A former member of the Deadly Viper Assassination Squad. Defected after discovering she was pregnant, but was shot to near-death on her wedding day by her former colleagues, including Bill, the father of the child. Spent four years in a coma. Upon waking, she set out for revenge and to reclaim her daughter. Portrayed and co-created by Uma Thurman.

Buffy Summers: (Dark Horse/Mutant Enemy) Chosen as The Slayer, the one girl in all the world tasked with fighting the demons and the forces of darkness. Buffy, played in the film by Kristy Swanson and in the television series by Sarah Michelle Gellar, is a petite blonde whose calling has given her super-strength, advanced healing capabilities, and prophetic dreams. Changed the mythos with the aid of Willow Rosenberg when they called all Potentials into Slayerhood, and is currently the leader of their army.

Callisto: After Xena's army killed her family, Callisto became a warlord herself. She worked for many years to thwart Xena's path to redemption and to destroy her and Gabrielle's happiness and friendship. With an act of compassion, Xena saves Callisto's soul and Callisto chooses to be reincarnated through Xena in the form of a miracle child. Xena names the baby Eve. Played by Hudson Leick.

Cameron: A Terminator reprogrammed by John Connor and sent back to protect a younger version of himself and his mother, Sarah. Played by

Summer Glau, Cameron is partly a meditation on what it means to be female and partly on what it means to be human. She is one of the first Terminators to override her programming and thus exhibit independent thought.

Carrie Kelly/Robin/Catgirl: (DC) The first female Robin (although not canonically). When Batman comes out of retirement in Frank Miller's comic mini-series *The Dark Knight Returns*, Carrie takes it upon herself to fill the role of Robin—because Batman needs a Robin. She becomes Catgirl in *The Dark Knight Strikes Again*.

Catherine Gale: John Steed's first female partner in the television series *The Avengers*. Played by Honor Blackman and relatively unknown to American audiences. Cathy was an anthropologist and a photographer who lived in Kenya until her husband was killed in the Mau Mau uprisings. She met Steed while curating at The British Museum.

Catwoman: (DC) A burglar, and love interest/nemesis to Batman, she has alternately been portrayed as a femme fatale, a villainess, and an antihero. Has appeared in comics since 1940 and in television and film. She has been played by Julie Newmar, Lee Meriwether, Eartha Kitt, Michelle Pfeiffer, and Halle Berry.

Charlie's Angels: (Original & Redux) A group of three intelligent, sexy, and capable women who fought crime on the 1970s American television show of the same name. Reimagined for the twenty-first century in two campy films starring Dew Barrymore, Lucy Liu, and Cameron Diaz as the lead trio.

Charly Baltimore: An assassin for the CIA who lives as an amnesiac for eight years after an assignment goes awry. Her memory is recovered, and she goes on to stop a terrorist plot. Played by Geena Davis. Charly is one of the few action heroines who is also a mother.

Cherry Darling: Go-Go dancer played by Rose McGowan in *Grindhouse: Planet Terror*. After her leg is eaten by zombies, a.k.a. "Sickos," Cherry's boyfriend, El Wray, fashions her a prosthetic one out of a functional machine gun. Becomes the leader of those who survived the zombie outbreak.

Chloe Sullivan: (DC) Added to the Superman mythos on the series *Smallville*. Like Fox Mulder of the *X-Files*, Chloe pursues the paranormal, and as a proto–Lois Lane, she writes first for her high school newspaper and later for the *Daily Planet*. Chloe is one of the most intriguing characters on the series, and to date the most remarkable female character—a testament to actress Allison Mack and her insistence on maintaining the integrity of Chloe. Later revealed to be Lois Lane's cousin and a "meteor freak."

Christie Love: *Get Christie Love* was originally a made-for-television movie starring Teresa Graves as the title character, based on a novel called *The Ledger*, written by Dorothy Uhnak, who herself had worked with the NYPD. *Get Christie Love* aired as a series during the 1974–5 season.

Claire Bennett: A seemingly average teenage cheerleader who discovers that she has the ability to spontaneously heal due to advanced cellular regeneration. Claire, played by Hayden Panettiere on the television series *Heroes*, is one of the bravest, most complex female heroes to date.

Coffy: A nurse, played by Pam Grier, who independently takes revenge on drug pushers and mobsters in her community after her sister becomes a victim of drug addiction.

Dana Scully: Played by Gillian Anderson in the *X-Files* franchise and influenced by Clarice Starling of *The Silence of the Lambs*, Dana Scully is a scientist, a medical doctor, and an FBI agent. As the skeptic half of the famous Mulder and Scully duo, she always kept her partner honest.

Dawn Summers: (Dark Horse/Mutant Enemy) Younger sister of Buffy Summers, played by Michelle Trachtenberg. Formerly a ball of energy called "The Key" and fashioned into a human by monks who believed she would be loved and protected from evil by the Slayer.

Doll Squad: An undercover group of female commandoes under the leadership of Sabrina Kincaid. Sabrina, played by Francine York, recruits the ladies from a dojo, a library, a laboratory, a swim club, and a burlesque club. Possibly the inspiration for Aaron Spelling's *Charlie's Angels*.

Dorothy Gale: The protagonist of L. Frank Baum's *Oz* series. Has appeared in various media, most famously in the 1939 film starring Judy Garland; in 1978's *The Wiz*, in which Dorothy was portrayed by Diana Ross; and most recently in the Sci-Fi channel original mini-series *Tin Man*— a story that loosely plays with elements of the original myth and that reunites the protagonist "D.G." (played by Zooey Deschanel as a descendent of Dorothy Gale) with her mother and sister. Though oddly, the series is named after another, male, character.

Elektra Natchios: (Marvel) Bounty hunter, assassin, and ninja—Elektra Natchios is one of the darkest characters of the Marvelverse. Once the lover of Daredevil's alter ego, Matt Murdock, Elektra turned to crime for pay after the murder of her beloved father. She was ultimately murdered herself, but has died and been reborn several times. In *Elektra/Wolverine: The Redeemer*, and the subsequent film "adaptation," she is faced with her humanity when she is compelled to mentor a young girl reminiscent of herself. Played by Jennifer Garner.

Ellen Ripley: A pilot for The Company in the *Alien* franchise. Played by Sigourney Weaver in the film series. One of the few memorable female action heroes of the 1980s.

Emma Peel: John Steed's second female partner in the long-running television series *The Avengers*. The very epitome of British 1960s modish spy-fi cool. Played by Diana Rigg.

Faith: (Dark Horse/Mutant Enemy) A Slayer called after the death of Kendra (who was accidentally called after the temporary death of Buffy). Faith was formerly Buffy's nemesis, but is now striving for redemption. Played by Eliza Dushku.

Foxy Brown: An action heroine infused with Pam Grier's trademark ferocity and sass, Foxy takes down "The Man," while helping women in her community. The title character of this famous Blaxploitation flick went on to inspire other strong and independent female characters, including one who was an homage to Grier herself in Quentin Tarantino's *Jackie Brown*.

Gabrielle: A former farm girl in Potidaea who becomes Xena's traveling companion, friend, and lover, as well as a bard. Many see Gabrielle as the true hero of the series, and she's certainly the one who undergoes the most spiritual growth. Played by Renée O'Connor.

GoGirl!: (Dark Horse) Heroine of Trina Robbins' and Anne Timmons' eponymous comic, Lindsay Goldman is the teenaged daughter of former superheroine Go-Go-Girl. When Mrs. Goldman discovers her daughter has inherited her ability to fly, she takes it upon herself to train the girl in self-defense and crime fighting. One of the few mother–daughter mentorships in British and American modern mythology.

Greer Nelson/The Cat: (Marvel) Greer Nelson is a young widow rediscovering her identity during the second wave of feminism. Through an experimental procedure, she becomes The Cat.

Heroic Trio: Michelle Yeoh, Maggie Cheung, and Anita Mui starred as the heroines in this dark, 1993 Hong Kong action picture—one of the many influences for *Xena, Warrior Princess*.

Holliday Girls: (DC) A group of sorority girls, originally led by Etta Candy, who aid Wonder Woman.

Honey West: One of the first female protagonists of detective fiction, this vivacious and busty blonde jumped into the PI business head first after her beloved father, Hank, was murdered in a Hollywood alley. Appeared in 11 novels and a short-lived television series in which she was portrayed by Anne Francis.

Huntress/Helena Wayne: (DC) Pre-Crisis, Earth-Two version of the Huntress. Helena Wayne is the daughter of Bruce Wayne/Batman and Selina Kyle/Catwoman. She was also a core character of the short-lived *Birds of Prey* television series and was played by Ashley Scott.

Huntress/Helena Bertinelli: (DC) The Post-Crisis version of the Huntress and daughter of a mob boss in Gotham City. Brought into the *Birds of Prey* comic by Gail Simone.

Jane Moneypenny: Personal secretary to M—head of the British Secret Service in Ian Fleming's James Bond series. Moneypenny is the focus of a trilogy of novels, and two short stories, written by Samantha Weinberg under the pseudonym Kate Westbrook. Variously played by actresses Lois Maxwell, Caroline Bliss, and Samantha Bond.

Jane Tennison: Helen Mirren plays this Detective Chief Inspector on the British police procedural *Prime Suspect*—a show primarily produced by women.

Jean Grey/Marvel Girl/Phoenix/Dark Phoenix: (Marvel) An original member of The X-Men under the tutelage of Professor Charles Xavier. Began as a shallow character, to eventually anchor the series at a height of critical acclaim, as the omnipotent Phoenix/Dark Phoenix. Portrayed in film by Famke Janssen.

Jenette Vasquez: The tough, muscular, Latina marine of *Aliens*. Played by Jenette Goldstein, Vasquez is argued to be as revolutionary a depiction of female heroism as her co-crew member Ripley.

Joanna Dark: The protagonist of the video game *Perfect Dark*, developed by the UK-based studio Rare. She has also appeared in two novels written by Greg Rucka and a graphic novel by Eric S. Trautmann.

Kathryn Janeway: The captain of the starship *Voyager*. Played by Kate Mulgrew, Janeway was the first, and so far only, female captain in the Star Trek franchise to lead a television series. Was shown to be an admiral in the movie *Star Trek: Nemesis*.

Kitty Pryde/Sprite/Shadowcat: (Marvel) A member of the X-Men and protégée of Storm. Kitty is one of a handful of Jewish superheroines and is a mutant that can phase through solid objects. She also provided inspiration for the creation of Buffy Summers. The character was portrayed by Ellen Page in *X-Men: The Last Stand*.

Lady Snowblood: A child born and bred to exact vengeance against those who murdered her father and brother and raped her mother. Originally a manga written by Kazuo Koike and illustrated by Kazuo Kamimura, and later adapted into a film starring Meiko Kaji.

Lara Croft: A video game character created by Toby Gard, Lara is a British archeologist who has also appeared in novels, comics, and films (where she was played by Angelina Jolie). She also featured in an animated short called *Pre-Teen Raider* written by Gail Simone for GameTap.

Lois Lane: (DC) Star reporter for Metropolis' *Daily Planet* newspaper. Once rival to Clark Kent, and romantic interest to Superman, she and Kal-El married in the 1990s. Lois is tenacious, ambitious, and clever. She is also an award-winning journalist, but is often thought of as merely "Superman's Girlfriend." Various actresses have played Lois over the years: Phyllis Coates, Noel Neill, Margot Kidder, Teri Hatcher, Kate Bosworth, and Erica Durance.

Luna Moth: (Dark Horse) A comic book character created by Josef Kavalier in Michael Chabon's Pulitzer-Prize-winning novel *The Amazing Adventures of Kavalier and Clay*. The Luna Moth was based on Kavalier's girlfriend, Rosa Sacks. Later immortalized further in Dark Horse's *Escapist* comic.

Mary Marvel: (Fawcett/DC) Introduced in 1942 as a female counterpart and twin sister to Billy Batson, alter ego of Fawcett's successful Captain Marvel character. Upon uttering the magic word, "SHAZAM," Mary was granted superhuman abilities, equal to those of the male Captain Marvel. Part of the so-called "Marvel Family," she went on to anchor *Wow Comics*, as well as her own *Mary Marvel* comic.

Max Guevara: A genetically engineered super-soldier living in Seattle and protagonist of television's *Dark Angel*. Formerly a cat burglar who becomes leader of a group of transgenics in what she calls her "Freak Nation." Played by Jessica Alba.

Mighty Isis: The alter ego of science teacher Andrea Thomas. Has a magic amulet that allows her to have power over animals and the elements. JoAnna Cameron played the title character in the television series *The Secrets of Isis*, which was part of CBS's Saturday morning *Shazam/Isis* Hour. *Isis* featured the first weekly American live-action television series starring a female superhero.

Modesty Blaise: An orphaned child who became the leader of a global crime syndicate called "The Network." Appeared in a series of comic strips in England's *Evening Standard* newspaper, as well as 11 novels and 2 collections of short stories—all written by Peter O'Donnell. Retired from crime at the age of 26 to live a life of leisure, punctuated by capers with her best friend and soul mate, Willie Garvin. She continued to have adventures until well into her 50s when she and Willie undergo one last brave mission to help their dear friends. Additionally featured in two films, portrayed by Monica Vitti in 1966 and by Alexandra Staden in 2003.

Monica Dawson: A woman in her 20s working to support her family in post-Katrina New Orleans on the television series *Heroes*. Has photographic reflexes that allow her to instantly learn anything she sees. Played by Dana Davis.

Ms. Michael Tree: A private eye created by Max Allan Collins and Terry Beatty. Ms. Tree is part Mickey Spillane's Velda and part Peter O'Donnell's Modesty Blaise. Her husband is murdered on their wedding night, and Michael takes over their detective agency. Her first case is to find out who killed her husband. *Ms. Tree* ran for over 15 years, making it the longest-running detective comic book series of all time.

Nancy Drew: Daughter of attorney Carson Drew, Nancy is an independent and curious-minded girl sleuth. She first debuted in a 1930s novel and has consistently appeared in various media since then, including a series of video games produced by the Bellevue, Washington based company, HerInteractive.

Newt/Rebecca Jorden: Newt is the last surviving member of the terraforming colony of LV-426 in the movie *Aliens*. Though clearly much younger than Ripley, and as a child in a traditionally vulnerable position, Newt has just as much internal strength as the story's adult hero.

Nikita: Protagonist of film and TV series *La Femme Nikita*. Formerly a delinquent, drug addict and criminal who after arrest is given the choice to work as an assassin for the French Secret Service or be killed herself. Nikita is a classic example of a femme fatale, and at least in Luc Besson's film version, where she was played by Anne Parillaud, little more than a skilled tool. In the television series that starred Peta Wilson as the title character, Nikita was still a prisoner to her government—here, not a criminal but a street kid in a tragic case of mistaken identity—and so also practiced everyday acts of rebellion and compassion.

Nyota Uhura: Chief Communications Officer of the USS Enterprise and a native of the United States of Africa, on *Star Trek*. Nichelle Nichols starred as one of the first major black characters in an American television series. While the role was limited by the racist and sexist thinking of some powerful television producers, Uhura nevertheless became an inspiration and a role model to many viewers including Dr. Martin Luther King Jr.,

Whoopi Goldberg, and Dr. Mae Jemison. The character will be reprised in a 2009 movie by Zoë Saldaña.

O-Ren Ishii: In the *Kill Bill* movies, O-Ren is a Chinese-Japanese-American, a former member of the Deadly Viper Assassination Squad, and the current leader of the Tokyo Yakuza. Played by Lucy Liu, the character's backstory is loosely based on Lady Snowblood.

Pippi Longstocking: The assertive, eccentric, independent, and emotionally and physically strong hero of a series of children's novels by Swedish author Astrid Lindgren. The motherless daughter of the seafaring Captain Longstocking, Pippi chooses to live on land in her house, Villa Villekulla, with her monkey, Mr. Nelson, and her horse, Alfonso.

Powerpuff Girls: Bubbles, Blossom, and Buttercup first appeared in an animated short by Craig McCracken called *The Whoopass Girls*. The trio of little girls, made by Professor Utonium out of sugar, spice, and everything nice, as well as the accidental addition of Chemical X, made it their mission to fight crime before bedtime.

Princess Leia Organa: Leia is a member of the Senate and a leader in the Rebel Alliance against the Galactic Empire. The daughter of Anakin Skywalker and Padme Amidala, Leia has the potential to become a Jedi like her twin brother, Luke. Played by Carrie Fisher.

Promethea: (America's Best Comics) Created by Alan Moore, Promethea is a feminine persona adopted generationally by artists and writers. She is part superhero, part goddess.

Pussy Galore: The infamous lesbian leader of an all-female Harlem crime gang in the 007 film and novel *Goldfinger*. Played by Honor Blackman in the 1964 film adaptation.

Rachel Gibson: Sydney Bristow's protégée—brought in for Season 5 of *Alias*. Serves as one of the few examples in American modern mythology of a woman being mentored by a woman and portrayed by Rachel Nichols.

Red Sonja: (Marvel) In 1985, the film *Red Sonja* (starring Brigitte Nielsen) became the final installment in an increasingly disappointing trilogy, the characters of which had been loosely based on the 1930s pulp writings of Robert E. Howard. Red *Sonya* had appeared in only one of his stories, "The Shadow of the Vulture," as a pistol-wielding Russian in the sixteenth century. In the 1970s, the character was adapted by Roy Thomas and Barry Windsor-Smith for Marvel comics as a supporting character in their *Conan* title. The spelling of her name was changed from Sonya to *Sonja*, and her origins were moved from Russia to Conan's fictional prehistoric "Hyborian Age." Her deftness with a pistol was changed to mastery of the sword.

Reggie and Sam Belmont: Valley Girl sisters that survive a near-apocalypse when the Earth passes through the tail of a comet killing most humans, while turning others into zombies in *Night of the Comet*. The girls, played by Catherine Mary Stewart and Kelli Maroney, were taught self-defense techniques by their father and fight off monsters in between trying on clothes and dancing to Cyndi Lauper's hit song, "Girls Just Wanna Have Fun." One of the many inspirations for *Buffy the Vampire Slayer*.

Sarah Connor: The iconic "Mother/Warrior" of the *Terminator* franchise. Linda Hamilton's physical evolution of Sarah in 1991's *Terminator 2: Judgment Day* was one of the most progressive depictions of a female hero in modern myth. Lena Headey has taken her own approach to the character on *Terminator: The Sarah Connor Chronicles*.

Sarah Jane Smith: An investigative journalist and a companion to the third and fourth Doctors on *Doctor Who*, played by Elisabeth Sladen. Currently mentoring a group of teenagers as they keep the Earth safe from Alien invasion.

Scoobies: (Dark Horse/Mutant Enemy) Buffy's core group of allies. Includes: Xander Harris, Willow Rosenberg, Rupert Giles, Dawn Summers, and at times Oz, Cordelia Chase, Anyanka, Andrew, Angel, and Spike.

Senorita Rio Rita: A beautiful spy in comics of the 1940s.

Stephanie Brown/Spoiler/Robin: (DC) Introduced to the Bat-mythos in 1992, Stephanie began fighting crime to "spoil" the misdeeds of her father. Became Batman's iconic sidekick, Robin, for a short time in 2004. Was tortured to death with a power drill by the villain Black Mask. A campaign, led by feminist comic book fans and called Project Girl Wonder, was launched demanding that Stephanie be honored with a memorial in the Batcave. She never officially received this, but her story was retconned in 2008. As a result, Stephanie did not in fact die, but was nurtured back to health in Africa.

Storm/Ororo Munroe: (Marvel) Ororo is the daughter of a Kenyan mother and an African American father. While the family is living in Egypt, Ororo's parents are killed during an air strike. Orphaned, the child spends time as a thief before wandering into the Serengeti. Ororo's mutant power allows her to control the weather and for a time she is worshipped in the desert as a goddess. That is, before Charles Xavier of the *X-Men* tells her who and what she really is and recruits her for his team. Storm has been the leader of the X-Men and a teacher for Xavier's School for the Gifted. In particular, she was a strong mentor to Kitty Pryde. She is currently married to the Black Panther. Played by Halle Berry in the *X-Men* movie trilogy.

Sue Storm/Invisible Girl/Invisible Woman: (Marvel) The only core female member of the Fantastic Four and often situated as the maternal force of the group. Her superpowers were originally limited to invisibility, but now include the ability to project force fields. Played by Jessica Alba in the film adaptations.

Supergirl: (DC) Kara Zor-El, a.k.a. Supergirl, is the teenaged cousin of Superman. When she is sent by her father to Earth, she takes on the secret identity of Linda Lee Danvers. Played by Helen Slater in the 1984 film *Supergirl* and by Laura Vandervoort on television's *Smallville*.

Sydney Bristow: The spy-fi heroine of television's *Alias*, played by Jennifer Garner. Sydney speaks nearly a dozen languages, practices several forms of self-defense, is an expert problem solver and undercover operative, and still manages to be a stand-up friend. In Season 5 she not only takes an inexperienced agent under her wing (one of the few examples in American modern myth of a woman mentoring a woman), but also fights global terrorism while pregnant.

Turanga Leela: Pilot of the Planet Express delivery spaceship on television's animated series *Futurama*. Leela grew up thinking she was the last of her species until she learned she was a mutant given up for adoption. Skilled in martial arts called Arcturan Kung-Fu, this Cyclops is voiced by Katey Sagal.

Valeria: A thief and lone warrior woman played by Sandahl Bergman in 1982's *Conan the Barbarian*. Valeria was lithe and statuesque, but also fierce, strong willed, and brave. A notable action heroine, and though she ultimately dies to further the hero's story of revenge, she is also given life after death as a Valkyrie.

Varla: Murderous, shrewd, and sensual leader of a girl gang comprised of three go-go dancers in Russ Meyer's *Faster, Pussycat! Kill! Kill!* A character made iconic by burlesque dancer Tura Satana.

Vernita Green: Along with The Bride, Vernita was a member of the Deadly Viper Assassination Squad in *Kill Bill.* Codenamed Copperhead and played by Vivica A. Fox.

Veronica Mars: The saucy teenage private eye of her eponymous television series. Played by Kristen Bell. Veronica Mars lives with her single father and with a passionate drive for justice, battles crime, and high school alike.

★

Willow Rosenberg: (Dark Horse/Mutant Enemy) Best friend of Buffy Summers, Willow is a skilled computer hacker and witch. She is also one of a handful of Jewish superheroines. Portrayed by Allyson Hannigan.

Wonder Woman: (DC) Likely the most recognizable female superhero in American popular culture. Wonder Woman, a.k.a. Diana Prince, was created in 1941 by a psychologist named William Moulton Marston. Having gone through many evolutions over the past 65 years from Princess to romance columnist, mortal to ambassador, even to goddess, she is now for the first time being consistently written by a woman— Gail Simone. Famously portrayed by Lynda Carter in the 1970s television series.

Xena, Warrior Princess: A former warlord on a quest for redemption. Xena, played by Lucy Lawless, is aided by her partner and lover Gabrielle.

Zoë Washburne: (Dark Horse/Mutant Enemy) Second-in-command of the spaceship *Serenity*, in Joss Whedon's *Firefly* series. Played by Gina Torres.

Endnotes

Introduction

1. *Archie* is a long-running American comic book, with several spin-offs featuring the fictional teenagers of a town called Riverdale.
2. Terms like "archetype" and "icon" are used more colloquially as being a person, concept, or thing that is recognized as a typical, representative, or even definitive symbol of something. For example, Judy Garland as a gay icon or Wonder Woman and Buffy as icons of female power.
3. Women have, and continue to have, starring roles in sitcoms, i.e., Lucille Ball, Mary Tyler Moore, Candice Bergen, Roseanne Barr, Queen Latifah, the women of *The Golden Girls* and *Friends*, and so on.
4. For instance, in my mind, George Perez's Wonder Woman is not William Moulton Marston's. Phil Jimenez's Wonder Woman is not Greg Rucka's, and Gail Simone's is none of the above—especially considering she is one of a handful of women to have written the Amazon Princess.
5. From witches, to sorceresses, to the pagan goddess, there is a long tradition of women with power being labeled "villainess." Often the only way to spot a superwoman is to look to the dark side. But when in the role of the femme fatale, the nemesis, or the love interest (usually all one and the same), the villainesses' potential power is diminished by her affection for the hero— after all, she's usually a supporting player in *his* story. Her threat is contained by the possibility of rehabilitation, usually through love, but occasionally through a self-sacrificial death. Supervillainesses deserve critical attention too, but in another book at another time.
6. Kaveney, Roz. *Superheroes!*. London/New York: I.B.Tauris, p. 4, 2008.
7. Nussbaum, Emily. "Must-See Metaphysics," in *The New York Times*, September 22, 2002.
8. Ross, Sharon. " 'Tough Enough': Female Friendship and Heroism in *Xena* and *Buffy*," in *Action Chicks: New Images of Tough Women in Popular Culture*, Edited by Sherrie A. Inness. New York: Palgrave Macmillan, p. 231, 2004.

9. Pam Grier is a notable exception and will be addressed in subsequent chapters.

10. It's important to note that there are many enlightened men who have written extraordinary and complex superwomen characters. Joss Whedon is one of the most lauded, but he has also surrounded himself with an abundance of real superwomen.

Chapter One

1. Portions of this chapter have previously appeared in *The Encyclopedia of Gender and Society*, SAGE Publications.

2. See Trina Robbins' *The Great Women Superheroes* for a discussion of undercover policewoman Peggy Allen, a.k.a. "The Woman in Red" from *Thrilling Comics*, and Robbins' *The Great Women Cartoonists* for a look at Tarpe Mills' "Miss Fury."

3. Captain America stood for American righteousness as he was depicted kayoing Adolf Hitler on the inaugural cover of his eponymous book—a bold nine months before the USA was forced to officially involve themselves in the war (March 1941).

4. This concern would arise again in subsequent decades with the introduction of other entertainment media, namely television, video games, and the Internet.

5. Later known as DC Comics.

6. Marston, William Moulton. "Why 100,000,000 Americans Read Comics" in *The American Scholar*. Vol. 13, No. 1, pp. 35–44, Winter 1943–4. The comic publisher Marston alludes to here is M.C. Gaines of DC.

7. Quoted in Daniels, Les. *Wonder Woman: The Complete History*. San Francisco, CA: Chronicle Books, p. 22, 2000. The text is from a letter written to comics historian Coulton Waugh explaining how he came to create Wonder Woman.

8. Modern superheroes were often endowed with gifts from the gods of classic mythology, or their talents were equated with those of the great heroes of literature.

9. Blundell, Sue. *Women in Ancient Greece*. Cambridge, MA: Harvard University Press, p. 58, 1995.

10. Some tales told of a gender role-reversal in which the men stayed at home to weave and rear, while the women tended to the public sphere.

11. Fantham, Elaine, Foley, Helene Peet, Kampen, Natalie Boymel, Pomeroy, Sarah B., and Shapiro, H. Alan. *Women in the Classical World*. New York: Oxford University Press, p. 131, 1994.

12. Blundell, *Women in Ancient Greece*, p. 59.

13. Blondell, Ruby. "How to Kill an Amazon," in *Helios.* Vol. 32, No. 2, p. 198, Fall 2005.
14. Moulton, Charles. "Introducing Wonder Woman." *All Star Comics* #8, December 1941–January 1942.
15. These bracelets were also inspired by the ones Marston's lover Olive Byrne wore.
16. Collins, Gail. *America's Women: 400 Years of Dolls, Drudges, Helpmates, and Heroines.* New York: William Morrow/HarperCollins, p. 384, 2003. Collins writes that "while married women were being criticized as unpatriotic for failing to work, they were being denounced as bad mothers if they did."
17. Robbins, Trina. "When Women Flew." Presented at the Comic Arts Conference, San Francisco, a component of WonderCon, March 2007. See also Collins, *America's Women*, pp. 376–8.
18. Collins, *America's Women*, pp. 369–70.
19. Siegel, Jerry and Shuster, Joe. *Action Comics* #1, 1938.
20. Daniels, Les. *Superman: The Complete History.* San Francisco, CA: Chronicle Books, p. 20, 1998.
21. Siegel, Jerry and Shuster, Joes. *Superman Archives Vol. 1*, New York: DC Comics, p. 169, 1989.
22. Ibid, p. 186.
23. Ibid, p. 187.
24. Daniels writes that "Siegel viewed Superman's disguise as Clark Kent as a joke on Lois Lane." See Daniels, *Superman*, p. 20.
25. Source unknown. But I'd like to thank the webmaster of http://www.redboots.net/—a Superman and Lois and Clark reference site—for aiding me in identifying other sources.
26. *Action Comics* #47, p. 8, panel 2, April 1942. In Daniels, *Superman.*
27. For more examples of Kal-El's brutishness, see the amusing web site, Superman is a Dick (http://www.superdickery.com).
28. Even *Jane Martin, War Nurse*, one of the premier flying women of the comics was transferred behind a desk. She had started the war as a nurse, became a full-time ace pilot and sometimes spy, and when the war ended she was a test pilot and salesperson at an aircraft company. Trina Robbins writes that "by 1948 she was demoted still farther, to girl reporter."
29. "War, Women, and Opportunity." Part of the Library of Congress Exhibit: Women Come to the Front: Journalists, Photographers, and Broadcasters During World War II. http://www.loc.gov/exhibits/wcf/wcf0001.html (Accessed 11/26/07). A special thanks to Sara W. Duke, Curator, Popular & Applied Graphic Art Prints & Photographs Division, Library of Congress, for pointing me to this exhibit.

30. Ibid.
31. Robinson, Lillian S. *Wonder Women: Feminisms and Superheroes.* New York, London: Routledge, p. 65, 2004.
32. Daniels, *Wonder Woman*, p. 93.
33. When Lucille Ball and Desi Arnaz were pregnant with their second child, they incorporated it into the show. But at that time they weren't allowed to say the words "pregnant" or "pregnancy" on air and instead used "expecting."
34. *Wonder Woman.* August #124.
35. In the 1960s, the spelling of the Amazon Queen's name was changed from Hippolyte to Hippolyta.
36. Robbins, Trina. *From Girls to Grrrlz.* San Francisco, CA: Chronicle Books, p. 55, 1999.
37. Robbins, Trina. *The Great Women Superheroes.* Northampton, MA: Kitchen Sink Press, pp. 102–3, 1996.
38. See Jones, Gerard. *Men of Tomorrow: Geeks, Gangsters and the Birth of the Comic Book.* Cambridge, MA: Basic Books, pp. 270–80, 2004.
39. Although one must naturally wonder what a rich recluse wants with a young boy in tights.
40. Moral complexity would return in comics of the 1980s. Notable examples include *The Killing Joke* and *Watchmen.*
41. The 58-minute film was later used as a two-part episode in Season One.
42. For more see *Women Scientists in Fifties Science Fiction Films*, by Bonnie Noonan. North Carolina: McFarland, 2005.
43. Binder, Otto. "How Lois Lane Got Her Job," in *Superman's Girl Friend Lois Lane.* Reprinted in *Superman: Daily Planet.* New York: DC Comics, p. 43, 2006.
44. Pandora alternately meaning "giver of all gifts" or "giver of all evil."
45. Daniels, *Superman*, p. 100.
46. Many of the stories in *Superman's Girl Friend Lois Lane* revolved around her rivalry with Lana Lang—a character taken out of the *Superboy* comic book. Lana grew up with Clark Kent and eventually came to work at the metropolitan newspaper. In the big city she competed with Lois for the affections of Superman, leading to a number of super powered battles, backstabbing, and in at least one case a ten-pace pistol duel counted off by Jimmy Olsen.

Chapter Two

1. Source unknown.
2. Chabon, Michael. "A Woman of Valor," Accessed online March 2005. Unfortunately, since then, Chabon has closed down his site.

3. Douglas, Susan J. *Where the Girls Are: Growing Up Female with the Mass Media.* New York: Three Rivers Press, p. 44, 1995.

4. Suffrage is considered the "First Wave."

5. "Charlie X," 1.2. *Star Trek.* Writer D.C. Fontana, director Lawrence Dobkin. Original air date: September 15, 1966.

6. Nichols, Nichelle. *Beyond Uhura: Star Trek and Other Memories.* New York: G. P. Putnam's Sons, p. 144, 1994.

7. Ibid, p. 138.

8. Ibid, p. 128.

9. Ibid, p. 164.

10. Ibid, p. 164.

11. Jemison opened each of her Space Shuttle flight shifts by saying Uhura's famous line: "Hailing frequencies open."

12. Lee, Stan. *The Superhero Women.* New York: Simon and Schuster, p. 8, 1977.

13. Robbins, Trina. *The Great Women Superheroes.* Northampton, MA: Kitchen Sink Press, p. 110, 1996.

14. Lee, *The Superhero Women*, Preface.

15. Ibid, p. 57.

16. Robbins, *The Great Women Superheroes*, p. 57.

17. Ibid, p. 57–8.

18. Sturm, James. *The Fantastic Four Unstable Molecules: The True Story of Comics' Greatest Foursome.* New York: Marvel Comics, 2005.

19. Robbins, *The Great Women Superheroes*, p. 110. Unfortunately, the depiction of women who can't physically contain or control their powers has survived to this day. Niki Sanders in *Heroes* and Sarah Connor in *Terminator 2* are both "contained" in mental institutions. In the current *Fantastic Four* films, Sue Storm exerts herself to the point of nosebleeds, as has Willow Rosenberg on *Buffy the Vampire Slayer*, Angela Petrelli on *Heroes*, Chloe Sullivan on *Smallville*, and Jaime Sommers on the quickly canceled 2007 version of the *Bionic Woman*. The nosebleed phenomenon has happened with the occasional male character (Harry Potter) but is disturbingly frequent in depictions of powerful women.

20. Ibid, p. 110.

21. She also appeared in two feature films. The character has influenced the creation of numerous American superwomen, including Ororo Munroe and The Bride. For more detail, see Stuller, Jennifer K. *The Princess of Spy-Fi: A Critical and Historical Overview of Peter O'Donnell's Modesty Blaise,* presented at the Comic Arts Conference in 2007 (San Diego) and 2008 (San Francisco).

22. Newman, Sydney, in Macnee, Patrick, with Rogers, Dave. *The Avengers: The Inside Story.* London: Titan Books, pp. 32–3, 2008.

23. Quoted in Rogers, Dave. *The Complete Avengers.* New York: St. Martin's Press, 1989.

24. Taylor, Charles. "Mrs. Peel, We're Needed," *Salon.* August 17, 1998. Accessed online: October 28, 2006. http://www.salon.com/ent/movies/reviews/1998/08/17review.html

25. Quoted in Rogers, *Complete Avengers,* p. 126. Additionally, clothing served to upset gender norms on *The Avengers.* Alongside attitude, style served to reinforce the proto-feminism of Cathy and Emma, yet fashion also made Steed a proto-metrosexual.

26. Macnee, who was raised by his mother and her partner (whom he called "Uncle Evelyn"), notes in *The Avengers: The Inside Story* that his upbringing made him the perfect actor to assume the role of Steed: "I was brought up surrounded by a lot of strange women, and this made me the ideal man to make a series with these *women,* because nothing they did surprised me. The most important aspect of the way I played Steed was in *reaction,* not action" (Macnee, p. 69).

   He delights in describing the subversiveness of the series: "I was the straight man to the women's role of activator. That's what made the show so entertaining, because you expected me, the man, to make the decisions and I didn't. The women did" (Macnee, p. 69).

27. Chapman, James. *Saints and Avengers: British Adventure Series of the 1960s.* London/New York: I.B.Tauris, p. 86, 2002.

28. Taylor, "Mrs. Peel."

29. Daniels, Les. *Wonder Woman: The Complete History.* San Francisco, California: Chronicle Books, 2000.

30. The *Avengers* had debuted in the States just two years before *Wonder Woman* was revamped.

31. In the dreadful "Women's Liberation Issue," she goes so far as to say that she's not sure she even likes women—likely meant as a slap to feminist Gloria Steinem who had criticized the direction taken with the character.

32. "Editorial: A Personal Report," in *Ms.,* July 1972, Vol. 1, No. 1, p. 4.

33. Ibid, p. 4.

34. Ibid, p. 6. According to this editorial, *Ms.* received over 50,000 subscription requests, according to Mary Thom's *Inside "Ms." 25 Years of the Magazine and the Feminist Movement,* this number was 26,000 (p. 50, "Feminist Ink: The Making of *Ms.*" by Mary Thom excerpted from *Ms.,* July/August 1997).

35. Ibid, p. 6.

36. Steinem, Gloria. "Introduction," *Wonder Woman* (Tiny Folios). New York/London/Paris: Abbeville Press, pp. 5–19, 1995.

37. Gloria. *Wonder Woman.* USA: Holt, Rinehart and Winston, 1972.

38. In *Wonder Woman: The Complete History*, Les Daniels notes that Steinem was friends with Steve Ross, then owner of DC Comics and of Warner Communications—which had financially backed *Ms.* Perhaps, Steinem's connections helped bring Wonder Woman back to her Amazonian roots.

39. On a side note, once again, while Wonder Woman represents women's highest aspirations, Lois Lane also could have been a remarkable choice for that now-famous cover. Wonder Woman promoted love, sisterhood, and peace—all feminist values, yes—but wouldn't Lois have more accurately reflected the actual lives of the journalists at *Ms.?* Perhaps Ms. Lane was in need of some conscious-raising, particularly in the misogynistic years of *Superman's Girlfriend*, but she was also headstrong, determined, fearless, and resourceful—all admirably feminist qualities. So why isn't she valorized as Wonder Woman is; was she not as deserving of "rescue" as Diana? What if the editors at *Ms.* had chosen to put Lois on their inaugural cover? Would *she* then be *the* symbol of women's empowerment? Interesting food for thought.

40. Lee, *The Superhero Women*, p. 105.

41. Ibid, p. 147.

42. Robbins, *The Great Women Superheroes*, p. 125. It bears noting that Marvel was one of the first companies to publish without the CCA Seal of Approval.

43. Fite, Linda. "Beware the Claws of the Cat!" New York: Marvel Comics, p. 10, panels 6–8, 1972.

44. Ibid, p. 11, panel 3.

45. Ibid, p. 17, panel 2.

46. Ibid, p. 18, panel 5. Greer is able to empathically feel the pain of an injured squirrel, "as if it were her own." Such depictions of feminine power walk a fine line between embracing the traditionally feminine—as many women did with Goddess and Pagan religions and Woman's spirituality during the second wave of feminism—and being repressive by virtue of stereotype, limiting women (and men) by deeming nurturing traits feminine.

47. "Cat Scratches: Letters Column," *Beware! The Claws of the Cat*, Issue 3. New York, NY: DC Comics, April 1973.

48. Ibid.

49. Ibid, Issue 4, June 1973.

50. Ibid.

51. Lee, *The Superhero Women of Marvel*, p. 148.

52. *The Secrets of Isis*, part of CBS's Saturday morning *Shazam/Isis* Hour, was actually the first weekly American live-action television series starring a female superhero, having started in September 1975.

53. Les Daniels notes that because the show continues to run in syndication today and "given the comparative power of TV over comics, this must be considered the version of Wonder Woman that made her a permanent part of popular culture for the average American."

54. "Revolutionizing a Classic: From Comic Book to Television - The Evolution of Wonder Woman from Page to Screen," Featurette included on *Wonder Woman* DVD. Released March 1, 2005.

55. "Beauty, Brawn, and Bulletproof Bracelets: A Wonder Woman Retrospective," Featurette included on *Wonder Woman* DVD. Released June 29, 2004.

56. Underoos are a brand of underwear for children developed in the late 1970s that featured a matching top and bottom combo and a superhero or other pop culture theme.

57. "Wonder Woman Meets the Baroness Von Gunther," 1.2. *Wonder Woman*. Writer Margaret Armen, director Barry Crane. Original air date: April 21, 1976.

58. Mangels, Andy. "Interview with Lynda Carter," in *Back Issue*, August 2004, No. 5. pp. 20–1.

59. Mangels, "Interview with Lynda Carter," p. 35.

60. Ibid.

61. Douglas, *Where the Girls Are*, p. 215.

62. Inness, *Tough Girls*, p. 38.

63. Ibid, p. 41.

64. Helford, Elyce Rae, ed. "Introduction," *Fantasy Girls: Gender in the New Universe of Science Fiction and Fantasy Television*. Maryland: Rowman & Littlefield, p. 2, 2000.

65. "Welcome Home, Jaime," 1.1, Writer Kenneth Johnson, director Alan Crosland Jr. Original air date: January 11, 1976.

66. Scholar Sherrie A. Inness notes that "Like the widow Mrs. Peel, [once all memories of her relationship with Steve Austin are wiped clean] Jaime is now free to perform missions for Oscar and the OSI," unencumbered by heteronormative expectations.

67. "Welcome Home Jaime," 1.1. *Bionic Woman*.

68. Ibid.

69. Parts of this section have previously appeared on my blog: http://www.ink-stainedamazon.com/blog/2007/08/superwomen-belted-buckled-and-booted.html#links

70. *Faster, Pussycat! Kill! Kill!* Director Russ Meyer. Starring Tura Satana, Haji, and Lori Williams, 1965.

71. *Showgirls*. Director Paul Verhoeven, writer Joe Eszterhas. Starring Gina Gershon and Elizabeth Berkley, 1995. Writer Joe EsVIP limited edition DVD, release date: July 27, 2004. Commentary by David Schmader.

72. Quoted in McDonough, Jimmy. *Big Bosoms and Square Jaws: The Biography of Russ Meyer, King of the Sex Film.* New York: Three Rivers Press, p. 157, 2005.

73. *The Doll Squad* is a clear precursor to Aaron Spelling's *Charlie's Angels,* which debuted three years later, though Spelling denies the influence.

74. http://www.imdb.com/title/tt0069986/usercomments

75. Clearly, they inspired Tarantino to nod them in Pulp Fiction—when Mia Wallace tells Vincent Vega about her role in the pilot for "Fox Force Five," and then again with Kill Bill's Deadly Viper Squad—a racially diverse group of female assassins.

76. Sims, Yvonne D. *Women of Blaxploitation: How the Black Action Film Heroine Changed American Popular Culture.* North Carolina: McFarland, 2006.

77. Ibid, p. 30.

78. Grier has noted that the original version of *Coffy* had more of an emphasis on the relationship between the sisters. In 1975 she told Jamaica Kincaid for *Ms.* magazine that when the movie was first screened, no one thought it would make any money because it was too depressing and that the character was "too strong and too serious." Grier says the solution was to "cut it up," and the tragedy was they took out some of the most important scenes—tender scenes between the sisters—so all that was left was "*bang, bang, bang,* shoot 'em up tits and ass."

79. Ebert, Alan. "Pam Grier: Coming into Focus," *Essence,* p. 43, January 1979.

80. Ibid, p. 43.

81. Kincaid, Jamaica. "Pam Grier, Super Sass," in *Ms.,* pp. 50–2, August 1975.

82. Ibid, p. 52.

83. Inness, *Tough Girls,* p. 48.

Chapter Three

1. *Red Sonja.* Director Robert Fleischer. Starring Brigitte Nielsen and Arnold Schwarzeneggar, 1985.

2. Faludi, Susan. *Backlash: The Undeclared War Against American Women.* New York: Crown Publishers, Inc., p. xviii, 1991.

3. Ibid, p. xix.

4. *TIME.* "People," Monday, February 21, 1972. http://www.time.com/time/magazine/article/0,9171,905793,00.html

5. *Star Wars: Return of the Jedi,* Director Richard Marquand. Starring Mark Hamill, Harrison Ford, and Carrie Fisher, 1983.

6. There were also instances of the less common, but still notable, Girly-Girl—a sweet, naive, and overtly feminine young woman—still tough, yet quite the physical opposite of the imposing Action Babe. An example of the Girly-Girl can be found in the 1984 film *Supergirl* starring a lovely Helen

Slater. Although intended to create another branch of the franchise, director Jeannot Szwarc (who worked with Christopher Reeves on *Somewhere in Time*, and would later direct episodes of *Smallville* and *Heroes*), wanted to create in *Supergirl* a mythology that would focus more on grace than he felt *Superman* did. Kara Zor-El's home world of Argo City was made to look ethereal, delicate, and serene; pastel colors and rounded edges emphasized nonviolence and harmony. Though Slater manages to shine, the script falls prey to two age-old stereotypes about women. One is that a beautiful aging woman will always feel threatened by a beautiful blossoming woman and therefore must destroy her. In the director's commentary, Szwarc even notes that elements of both *Snow White* and *The Wizard of Oz* were consciously evoked. The other stereotype is that women will inevitably fight over the affections of a man. As Andrew Kopkind noted in *The Nation*, "Unfortunately, the plot has [Faye] Dunaway and Slater fighting like two alley cats scratching over a tom, and that's a far cry from the mission of the supermale" (January 26, 1985).

7. *Conan the Barbarian*. Director John Milius, Writer John Milius and Oliver Stone. Starring Arnold Schwarzenegger and Sandahl Bergman, 1982. Collector's Edition DVD. Commentary with John Milius and Arnold Schwarzenegger. Universal Studios. Released: May 30, 2000.

8. DVD commentary for *Conan the Barbarian*. Collector's Edition DVD. Commentary with John Milius and Arnold Schwarzenegger. Universal Studios. Released: May 30, 2000.

9. It's notable that in the film's promotional poster, Valeria is foregrounded. Women are often depicted looking off to the side or toward the hero, but here she is defiantly crouched, ready for action, and focused straight ahead. Conan stands behind her looking above to the gods.

10. The Internet Movie Database lists the film's tagline as reading, "He conquered an empire with his sword. She conquered HIM with her bare hands."

11. In the DVD commentary for this pivotal scene, Arnold Schwarzenegger completely misses the significance of Valeria. Blinded by his own magnificence, he blurts out, "Look at me, in gladiator form." Milius points out that after the battle, Conan bows to Valeria's funeral pyre. He is grateful for her example and honors her.

12. Lee, Stan. *The Superhero Women*. New York: Simon and Schuster, p. 36, 1977. Lee's comment reflects an intention that will continually be addressed in this book. Regardless of the effectiveness rendered by the execution of a character like Sonja—what with her objectifying metal bikini—there exists the idea that societal attitudes can be influenced through entertainment.

13. Even children's television wasn't exempt. Filmation's *He-Man and the Masters of the Universe* and it's sister spin-off, *She-Ra: Princess of Power*.

14. Bergman, who had won a Golden Globe award for her role in *Conan*, was offered the chance to portray Sonja, but chose the part of Queen Gedren instead. She was subsequently nominated for a Razzie award. Ironically, that award went to Brigitte Nielson for her role in *Rocky IV*, in which she starred with her then husband Sylvester Stallone.

15. Tasker, Yvonne. *Spectacular Bodies: Gender, Genre, and the Action Cinema.* London and New York: Routledge, p. 30, 1993.

16. Bolen, Jean Shinoda. *Goddesses in Everywoman: A New Psychology of Women.* New York, Cambridge, Philadelphia, San Francisco, London, Mexico City, São Paulo, Singapore, Sydney: Harper & Row, p. 16, 1985.

17. Recall that at the beginning of the film, Queen Gedren wants the nubile Sonja for herself. Sonja resists and even manages to scar Gedren's face. After her assault and vision, Sonja trains as a warrior and becomes master of the sword—a weapon that is both offensive and defensive. Sonja's body has been attacked, and she will do everything in her power to protect it.

18. At the time of writing, a remake of *Red Sonja* is in pre-production, although I don't hold out much hope—films featuring superwomen don't tend to receive the creative attention they deserve. Additionally, an early publicity poster depicts Rose MacGowan as Sonja—licking blood off her sword.

19. Corliss, Richard. "The Years of Living Splendidly," *TIME*, Monday, July 28, 1986.

20. *Aliens.* Director James Cameron. Starring Sigourney Weaver, Michael Biehn, Jenette Goldstein, and Carrie Henn, 1986. Special Edition DVD 1999.

21. Inness, Sherrie A. *Tough Girls: Women Warriors and Wonder Women in Popular Culture.* Philadelphia: University of Pennsylvania Press, pp. 108–9, 1999.

22. Kaveney, Roz. *From Alien to The Matrix: Reading Science Fiction Film.* London/New York: I.B.Tauris, p. 151, 2005. She suggests that Cameron's frequent use of doubling and parallels makes it safe to assume that while Newt is an independent character, she also represents a part of Ripley. More specifically, that the Alien Queen, Ripley, and Newt can be read as the triple goddess (Crone, Mother, and Maiden).

23. Hurd, Gail Anne. As quoted in the *San Francisco Examiner Datebook*, p. 19, August 10, 1986.

24. Schickel, Richard. "Help! They're Back!" *TIME*, Monday, July 28, 1986.

25. Corliss, "The Years of Living Splendidly."

26. "Two Orphans: Sigourney Weaver and Carrie Henn," Featurette. *Aliens* Collector's Edition DVD. 20th Century Fox. Released: January 6, 2004.

27. The term "Final Girl" was coined by Carol J. Clover and used in her book *Men, Women and Chain Saws: Gender in the Modern Horror Film.* The final girl is usually the last woman alive in a horror film and the one to confront

the killer; for example, Jamie Lee Curtis as Laurie Strode in *Halloween* and Ellen Ripley in *Alien*.

28. Inness, *Tough Girls*, p. 125.
29. McCaughey, Martha and King, Neal, eds., *Reel Knockouts: Violent Women in the Movies*. Austin, TX: University of Texas Press, p. 21, 2001.
30. Tasker, *Spectacular Bodies*, p. 149. She notes that " 'Musculinity' indicates the way in which signifiers of strength are not limited to male characters."
31. Steinem, Gloria. "Introduction," in Walker, Rebecca, ed., *To Be Real: Telling the Truth and Changing the Face of Feminism*. New York: Anchor Books, Doubleday, 1995.

Chapter Four

1. "Faith, Hope & Trick," 3.3. Writer David Greenwalt, director James A. Contner. October 13, 1998.
2. "The Many Faces of Feminism," *Ms.*, Vol. V, No. 1, p. 60, July/August 1994.
3. http://www.empsfm.org/exhibitions/index.asp?categoryID=129&ccID =135
4. Karp, Marcelle and Stoller, Debbie. *The Bust Guide to the New Girl Order*. USA: Penguin Books, p. xiii, 1999.
5. *Sassy* was a girl's best friend. Cherished and a phenomenon, it changed the lives of many young women, influenced their careers, and has a place as one of the greatest, most loved magazines of all time. Modeled after *Dolly*, an Australian magazine for teenage girls, *Sassy's* mission was to treat adolescent girls with the respect and honesty they deserved. Rather than shill beauty products and talk about how to get a boyfriend, articles frankly addressed sex—one of the more mysterious and confusing topics for readers of any age. An early issue of the magazine (which debuted in March of 1988) featured a piece that detailed in gentle honesty what to expect from a first trip to the gynecologist. Later issues also empowered girls to be active and informed about their health care needs and addressed such taboo subjects as incest and rape—leading many readers to feel *Sassy* was a confidant.
6. Baumgardner, Jennifer and Richards, Amy. *Manifesta*. New York: Farrar, Straus and Giroux, p. 400, 2000.
7. Karp, Marcelle and Stoller, Debbie (eds.). *The Bust Guide to the New Girl Order*. USA: Penguin Books, p. 266, 1999.
8. Baumgardner, *Manifesta*, p. xx.
9. Stoller, *The Bust Guide to the New Girl Order*, p. 266.
10. Ibid, p. 266.
11. Ibid, p. 267.

12. Fudge, Rachel. "Buffy: A Tale of Cleavage and Marketing." Accessed online: http://bitchmagazine.org/article/buffy-effect

13. "Investigation: The History of Aeon Flux." Featurette. *Aeon Flux: The Complete Animated Collection*. Paramount/MTV. Released: November 22, 2005.

14. Ibid.

15. Robinson, Tasha. "AV Club Interview with Peter Chung." April 30, 2003. http://www.avclub.com/content/node/22517

16. "Investigation: The History of Aeon Flux." Featurette.

17. *Aeon* would later feature as a half-hour stand-alone series.

18. This is according to a graphic novel, *The Herodotus File* (1995/2005), which may or may not be canon.

19. Mars, Mark and Singer, Eric. *Aeon Flux: The Herodotus File*. New York: MTV Books/Pocket Books/Melcher Media, 2005. See also: Healy, Karen and Johnson, Terry D. "Comparative Sex-Specific Body Mass Index in the Marvel Universe and the 'Real' World," for a study of how women's bodies are misrepresented in Marvel Comics. Accessed online: http://girl-wonder.org/papers/bmi.html and http://www.karenhealey.com/papers/comparative-sex-specific-body-mass-index-in-the-marvel-universe-and-the-real-world/

20. http://community.livejournal.com/monican_spies/44607.html

21. And yet, one critique of Chung's philosophy is that when those perceptions/interpretations/experiences aren't in line with his agenda (or lack of), he's quick to point out who's got it wrong—as with the 2006 live-action film version of the character.

22. Epstein, Daniel Robert. "Aeon Flux Creator Peter Chung." *SuicideGirls.com*. December 20, 2005. http://suicidegirls.com/interviews/%20Aeon%20Flux%20creator%20Peter%20Chung/

23. Heinecken, Dawn. "Boundary Battles: Heroic Narrative, The Feminine, and MTV'S Aeon Flux," 24.1. *Studies in Popular Culture*, 2001.

24. Ibid.

25. "Investigation: The History of Aeon Flux." Featurette.

26. Ibid.

27. Ibid.

28. It also is an example of the idea that the female hero does not always follow the traditional Campbellian model of the Journey of the Hero, but rather repeats the archetypal milestones in a cyclic or spiral pattern.

29. "Hooves and Harlots," 1.10. *Xena, Warrior Princess*. Director Jace Alexander, writer Steven L. Sears. Original air date: November 20, 1995.

30. "Xena's Hong Kong Origins." Featurette. *Xena, Warrior Princess 10th Anniversary DVD Collection*. DVD. Starz/Anchor Bay. Released: July 26, 2005.

31. "Unchained Heart," 1.13. *Hercules, the Legendary Journeys.* Original air date: May 8, 1995.

32. The imagery and action sequences were religiously borrowed from Hong Kong cinema and relied heavily on complex and innovative wirework. Martial arts movies that served as inspiration included the aforementioned *A Chinese Ghost Story* (1987), as well as *Swordsmen 3* (1992), *The Bride with White Hair* (1993), and *The Heroic Trio* (1993)—itself a film that featured not one, but three, fabulous fighting females (played by Michelle Yeoh, Maggie Cheung, and Anita Mui).

33. When Xena was a young girl, her village was attacked by the warlord Cortese. Most people wanted to run for safety, but she encouraged them to fight back and many villagers died as a result—including her beloved younger brother Lyceus. Xena was shunned by her community as they blamed her for these deaths. She left to take revenge on Cortese, and a series of events led her to become a warlord herself.

34. "Sins of the Past," 1.1. *Xena, Warrior Princess.* Director Doug Lefler, writers Robert Tapert and R. J. Stewart. September 4, 1995.

35. Ibid.

36. Ibid.

37. Flaherty, M. "Xenaphilia." *Entertainment Weekly.* Online edition, pp. 1–6, March 7, 1997. http://www.ew.com/ew/article/0,,287017,00.html

38. D'Erasmo, Stacey. "Xenaphilia." *Village Voice.* Vol. 40, No. 52, p. 47, December 26, 1995.

39. "Never Kill a Boy on the First Date," 1.5, *Buffy, the Vampire Slayer.* Director David Semel, writers Rob Des Hotel and Dean Batali. Original air date: March 31, 1997.

40. Nussbaum, Emily. "Must-See Metaphysics," in *The New York Times.* September 22, 2002.

41. *Buffy, the Vampire Slayer, Angel,* and *Firefly.* A cartoon *Buffy, the Animated Series* has never been broadcast. Whedon was slated to write and direct a feature film on Wonder Woman, but when he and the producers didn't see eye-to-eye on the project, Whedon withdrew. At the time of writing, he is working on a series titled *Dollhouse,* starring *Buffy* alum, Eliza Dushku, for Fox.

42. Nussbaum, "Must-See Metaphysics."

43. Whedon, Joss. "Foreword," in *Fray.* Oregon: Dark Horse Books, 2003.

44. Ibid.

45. Golden, Christopher and Holder, Nancy. *The Watcher's Guide Vol. 1.* New York: Pocket Books, 1998.

46. Nussbaum, "Must-See Metaphysics."

47. Jensen, Jeff. "The Goodbye Girl," in *Entertainment Weekly,* p. 18, March 7, 2003.

48. Goodman, Tim. " 'Buffy's' demise puts a stake in our hearts," *San Francisco Chronicle*, Monday, May 19, 2003. AARP—-an American life-planning organization for persons over the age of 50. http://www.sfgate.com/cgi-bin/article.cgi?f=/c/a/2003/05/19/DD61367.DTL

49. http://uk.tv.ign.com/articles/425/425492p6.html. Accessed March 13, 2008.

50. Quote from Gottlieb, Allie. "Buffy's Angels." From the September 26–October 2, 2002, issue of *Metro*, Silicon Valley's weekly newspaper. Accessed online March 17, 2008. http://www.metroactive.com/papers/metro/09.26.02/buffy1-0239.html (Roz Kaveney's *Reading the Vampire Slayer* (I.B.Tauris) was the first published anthology of critical essays on the series. Since then a number of other texts have been published addressing a number of issues within the series including family, race, compassion, body issues, literary references, and linguistics—among others. Professors Rhonda Wilcox and David Lavery founded *Slayage: The Online International Journal of Buffy Studies* as well as the *Slayage* Conference on the Whedonverses. Other academic conferences devoted to "Buffy Studies" have taken place in Turkey, England, and Australia. *Slayage* has a sibling publication for undergraduates called *Watcher, Jr.*)

51. To be fair to Angel, he "went all evil" because he had been cursed by gypsies with a soul—if he ever experienced a moment of true happiness, he would lose his morality and return to his monstrosity. But most girls have likely had the experience of a man seemingly "changing" after intimacy—hopefully without the Vampire part.

52. "Welcome to the Hellmouth," 1.1. Writer Joss Whedon, director Charles Martin. March 10, 1997.

53. Ibid.

54. Though not sexually impotent, Spike is unable to harm humans. Whedon has said that even though they are the undead, "If vampires couldn't have erections, our show would have been 12 episodes long." From Jensen, Jeff. "A bloody good chat with 'Buffy's' creator," in *Entertainment Weekly*. June 11, 2002. Accessed online: http://www.ew.com/ew/article/0,,260274,00.html

55. Just as Liz Friedman believed the "subtext" of *Xena* could convey potentially challenging ideas about sexuality and sexual preference.

56. Nussbaum, "Must-See Metaphysics."

57. Shanker, Wendy. "He Slays Me: An Interview with Joss Whedon," in *BUST*, p. 68, Winter 2000.

58. "The I in Team," 4.13. *Buffy, the Vampire Slayer*. Writer David Fury, director James A. Contner. Original air date: February 8, 2000.

59. Fudge, Rachel. "Buffy: A Tale of Cleavage and Marketing," in *Bitch*. Accessed online: http://bitchmagazine.org/article/buffy-effect. And, as

someone who grew up in California, I feel compelled to point out that layers are not warm-weather attire.

60. Karras, Irene. "The Third Wave's Final Girl: *Buffy, the Vampire Slayer.*" *Thirdspace.* Vol. 1, Issue 2, March 2002. ISSN 1499-8513. Accessed online: http://www.thirdspace.ca/articles/karras.htm

61. Rosen, Lisa. "R.I.P. 'Buffy': You drove a stake through convention," LA Times. May 20, 2003. Accessed online: http://www.whedon.info/R-I-P-Buffy-You-drove-a-stake.html

62. "Pilot," 1.0. *Dark Angel.* Writer James Cameron and Charles H. Eglee, director David Nutter. Original air date: October 2, 2000.

63. Featurette on Season 1 DVD "Dark Angel Genesis."

64. "Art Attack," 1.12. *Dark Angel.* Director James Contner. Original air date: February 6, 2001.

65. ET Online Jessica Alba Interview. Accessed online on March 16, 2008: http://www.darkangelfan.com//news/18.shtml

66. http://www.scifi.com/sfw/interviews/sfw6101.html

67. "Dark Angel Genesis" and "Creating an X-5." Featurettes. *Dark Angel.* Series created by James Cameron and Charles Eglee. Starring Jessica Alba and Valarie Rae Miller. 2000–2. The complete first season. 20th Century Fox Home Entertainment. 2003.

68. http://www.scifi.com/sfw/interviews/sfw6101.html

69. Poniewozik, James. "2020 Vision." *TIME.* Monday, October 2, 2000. Accessed online: http://www.time.com/time/magazine/article/0,9171, 998083,00.html?promoid=googlep

70. See especially the Season 3 episodes, "Let That Be Your Last Battlefield" and "Plato's Stepchildren," the latter of which featured the first interracial kiss on television.

71. The core cast of *BTVS* was always White, with the occasional inclusion of a Black character. In Season 2, there was Kendra (Bianca Lawson), a vampire Slayer called after Buffy had temporarily died, Olivia was Giles' rarely seen love interest, Nikki Wood was a previous Slayer killed by Spike in the 1970s, and in the final season we have her son, Robin Wood, the principal of the rebuilt Sunnydale High School. Season 7 featured many potentials of color, but most of them remained nameless.

72. On some levels, Alba's beauty still conforms to normative standards in an American market. She is petite, sultry, and pouty. But her coloring and her status as the headliner of the series acknowledges that all beauty is not blue eyed and blonde. Her X-5 sisters, Jace, Brin, and Tinga, reinforce this through their mixed-race features. *Dark Angel* worked harder to address issues of difference than any other mythic or sci-fi series on television.

73. Jowett, Lorna. "To the Max: Embodying Intersections in Dark Angel," 5.4. *Reconstruction.* Fall 2005. Accessed online: http://reconstruction.eserver .org/054/jowett.shtml
74. Ibid.
75. Blythe, Teresa. "Dark Angel," 30.2. *Sojourners* magazine, p. 61, March 2001.
76. Grace. http://www.heroinecontent.net/archives/2008/03/charlies_angels .html
77. Stoller, *The Bust Guide to the New Girl Order*, p. 266.

Chapter Five

1. Edgar, Joanne. Quoting Marston, William M. "Wonder Woman Revisited," *Ms.* magazine, No. 1, pp. 53–4, 1972. (Emphasis in original.)
2. Portions of this chapter were previously presented at The University of Washington's Undergraduate Research Symposium and the Holy Men in Tights Conference at the University of Melbourne; both in 2005.
3. Reynolds, Richard. *Super Heroes: A Modern Mythology*, p. 18, USA: University Press of Mississippi, 1994. Reynolds defines the "Lone Wolf" hero of the 1940s as "The self-reliant individualist who stands aloof from many of the humdrum concerns of society, yet is able to operate according to his own code of honor, to take the world on his own terms, and win."
4. This domestication of the "naughty girl" could easily be read as just another example of popular culture working to put women back in their normative place. But it could also be interpreted as a simplistic approach to narrative typical of the black-and-white moral universe of Golden Age comics. Regardless, on Transformation Island, reformation—though well intended—is more forced rehabilitation than enlightened atonement.
5. Whedon, Joss. "10 Questions for Joss Whedon." *The New York Times.* May 16, 2003.
6. hooks, bell. *All About Love*, p. 88.
7. Ibid, p. 161.
8. "Friend in Need II," 6.22. *Xena, Warrior Princess.* Writer R. J. Stewart, director Robert G. Tapert. Original air date: June 18, 2001.
9. "The Way," 4.16. *Xena, Warrior Princess.* Writer R. J. Stewart, director John Fawcett. Original air date: February 22, 1999.
10. Kathleen Kennedy observes in "Love Is the Battlefield" that "Preserving the purity of Gabrielle's faith in 'the way of love' is one of the most important components of Xena's quest." Kennedy, Kathleen. *Athena's Daughters: Television's New Women Warriors.* New York: Syracuse University Press, p. 43, 2003.

11. "The Way," 4.16. *Xena, Warrior Princess.* Writer R. J. Stewart, director John Fawcett. Original air date: February 22, 1999.

12. "The Ides of March," 4.21. *Xena, Warrior Princess.* Writer R. J. Stewart, director Ken Girotti. Original air date: May 10, 1999.

13. Hlusko, Dana. "The Way of Friendship Defined." *Whoosh!* Issue 45. Accessed online on March 25, 2008: http://www.whoosh.org/issue45/hlusko7.html

14. Notably, James Cameron was at one time attached to a Spider-Man film project before *Dark Angel,* so it wouldn't be a stretch to assume there is an influence on Max.

15. Jowett, Lorna. "To the Max: Embodying Intersections in Dark Angel." *Reconstruction* 5.4. Fall 2005. Accessed online on March 27, 2008: http://reconstruction.eserver.org/054/jowett.shtml

16. This grassroots form of heroism is not specific to superwomen. The television version of Hercules (Kevin Sorbo) goes from village to village helping those in need. And the late-1970s–early-1980s television version of *The Incredible Hulk* consistently showed David Bruce Banner aiding everyday people including an alcoholic dancer, a young police woman, and a woman in labor. The tagline of Angel Investigations, the detective agency of *Buffy* spin-off *Angel,* was a humorous, if accurate, "We help the helpless."

17. "Pilot," 1.0. *Dark Angel.* Writer James Cameron and Charles H. Eglee, director David Nutter. Original air date: October 2, 2000.

18. Both quotes are from "Flushed," 1.2. *Dark Angel.* Writer Charles H. Eglee and René Echevarria, director Terrence O'Hara. Original air date: October 17, 2000.

19. "Pilot," 1.0. *Dark Angel.* Writer James Cameron and Charles H. Eglee, director David Nutter. Original air date: October 2, 2007.

20. Sara Crosby convincingly argues in "Female Heroes Snapped into Sacrificial Heroines" in the anthology *Action Chicks: New Images of Tough Women in Popular Culture* that Max takes on her "heroic identity only after she subordinates her physical power to his political goals and literally begins to work for [Logan]." She suggests that accepting Logan's moral judgment causes Max to help him "in his crusade for a renewal of patriarchal privilege" and though *Dark Angel* "sells itself as being all about choice, the choices it gives Max are between patriarchy A [the military] or patriarchy B [Logan's journalistic obsessions]." Crosby does note that the series had potential for the promotion of "feminist and democratic goals more radically and on more levels than any previous superhero show," including feminist social justice issues such as class, race, sexuality, and gender hierarchies.

21. "Flushed," 1.2. *Dark Angel.* Writer Charles H. Eglee and René Echevarria, director Terrence O'Hara. Original air date: October 17, 2000.

22. Ibid.

23. The amazing feats of a Batman or other traditional hero lead us to believe that there is a separation between heroes and the rest of us and that amazing feats are for those who are special. Modern superwomen show us that we all have the potential to be special with devotion and efforts; Like Wonder Woman before them, Buffy, Max, and Xena inspire small armies of people who accomplish feats they never thought they could. Additionally, rather than adopting mentor–ward relationships that illustrate a clear separation of power, superwomen champion the sharing of it, as well as a mutual exchange of knowledge.

24. See "Beware Greeks Bearing Gifts," "The Debt Parts I & II," "A Friend in Need Parts I & II," and "Destiny," respectively.

25. "Is There a Doctor in the House?" 1.24. *Xena, Warrior Princess*. Director T. J. Scott. Original air date: July 29, 1996.

26. Inness, *Tough Girls*, p. 168.

27. "Is There a Doctor in the House?" 1.24.

28. "10 Questions for Joss Whedon." *The New York Times*. May 16, 2003.

29. hooks, *All About Love*, p. 133.

30. Ibid, p. 134.

31. "Family," 5.6. *Buffy, the Vampire Slayer*. Writer Joss Whedon, director Joss Whedon. Original air date: November 7, 2000.

32. http://www.buffy-vs-angel.com/buffy_tran_84.shtml

33. Battis, Jes. *Blood Relations: Chosen Families in Buffy the Vampire Slayer and Angel*. North Carolina: McFarland & Company, p. 147, 2005.

34. Ibid, p. 147.

35. Ibid, pp. 147–8. The created family is a theme Whedon explores in his *Angel* and *Firefly/ Serenity* franchises as well.

36. Ross, Sharon. " 'Tough Enough': Female Friendship and Heroism in *Xena* and *Buffy*," in *Action Chicks: New Images of Tough Women in Popular Culture*. Edited by Sherrie A. Inness. New York: Palgrave Macmillan, p. 231, 2004.

37. Ibid, p. 232.

38. "Primeval," 4.21. Writer David Fury, director James A. Contner. Original air date: May 16, 2000.

39. http://uk.geocities.com/slayermagic/Scripts/Episode77Primeval.html

40. Reiss, Jana. *What Would Buffy Do? The Vampire Slayer as Spiritual Guide*. San Francisco: Jossey-Bass, pp. 53–4, 2004.

41. "Pilot," 1.0. *Dark Angel*. Writer James Cameron and Charles H. Eglee, director David Nutter. Original air date: October 2, 2000.

42. hooks, *All About Love*, p. 98.

43. Ibid, p. 217.

44. "Fallen Angel," 5.1. *Dark Angel*. Writer R. J. Stewart, director John Fawcett. Original air date: September 27, 1999.

45. For more detail, see Taigen Daniel Leighton's *Bodhisattva Archetypes*. New York: Penguin Group, 1998—particularly Chapter 7, which explores Avalokiteshvara in detail.

46. Buffy achieves enlightenment in the Season 5 finale, when she sacrifices her life for that of her sister, Dawn. Buffy's spirit guide had told her that "Love is your gift" and that "death will bring you to your gift." On one level, the gift is that of life to Dawn, but as we learn early in Season 6, it turned out to also be a gift to Buffy. She'd fulfilled her Slayer duty and was at peace in Heaven. When she is forced to return to the world, her enlightenment is again delayed. She walks through the world trying to lead and inspire as before, but for most of the season, she's "just going through the motions."

47. Steinem, Gloria. *Wonder Woman*. USA: Holt, Rinehart and Winston, 1972.

48. "The Prom," 3.20. Writer Marti Noxon, director David Solomon. Original air date: May 11, 1999.

49. And it is not just her peers who are motivated or inspired by her Bodhisattva example, but her enemies as well. From Season 4 through to the end of the series, we watch the metamorphosic struggle of the vampire, Spike, whose admiration for Buffy inspires him to become a better man, to seek a soul, and ultimately to sacrifice himself to save humanity.

50. "Grave," 6.22. Writer David Fury, director James A. Contner. Original air date: May 21, 2002.

51. Ibid.

52. Again, notice the cyclic nature of Bodhisattva inspiration. Each of the Scoobies is at one time or another a hero in their own right, but it is always because of each other. Some have pointed out the Christian allegory in this scene. Simply put, Xander, who is by now a carpenter, saves the world though his selfless love. Yet this scene also directly echoes Jean Grey's sacrifice of herself in Chris Claremont's *Dark Phoenix Saga*, as well as the climactic scene in *Return of the Jedi* when Luke Skywalker defeats the evil Darth Vader and restores his father Anakin's humanity with compassion rather than weaponry. The influence of both is evident. Willow is directly referred to as "Dark Phoenix" by another character on the show. And when *SFX* magazine asked Joss Whedon what movie he would have loved to have written, he answered "*Revenge* of the Jedi." Ironically, the climactic scene in the film *X-Men 3: The Last Stand* would cinematically echo the scene between Xander and Willow in "Grave," although the rewriting of the *Dark Phoenix Saga*—especially with Jean's murder rather than sacrifice—would negate all the emotional poignancy that inhabited both the original X-Men story arc, and Whedon's likely appropriation of it.

53. Lorrah, Jean. "Love Saves the World," in *Seven Seasons of Buffy: Science Fiction and Fantasy Writers Discuss Their Favorite Television Show*. Edited by Yeffeth, Glenn. Dallas, TX: BenBella Books, pp. 167–75 (p. 172), 2003.

54. "The Freshman," 4.1. *Buffy, the Vampire Slayer*. Writer Joss Whedon, director Joss Whedon. Original air date: October 5, 1999.

55. Jowett, Lorna. *Sex and the Slayer: A Gender Studies Primer for the Buffy Fan*. Connecticut: Wesleyan, p. 134, 2005.

56. Zacharek, Stephanie. "Willow, Destroyer of Worlds." *Salon*. May 22, 2002. Nancy Holder has written of Buffy that "what was perhaps more interesting than this *Wonder Woman* redux was the fact that *BTVS* redefined *male* power." She quotes Gail Berman, former president of FOX Entertainment who said, "We'll have more Buffys when we have more Xanders."

57. Reiss, *What Would Buffy Do?*, p. 11.

58. Noble, Kathleen D. *The Sound of a Silver Horn: Reclaiming the Heroism in Contemporary Women's Lives*. New York: Ballantine Books, p. 194, 1994.

59. According to Les Daniels, Marston gave an interview to the *New York Times* in November of 1937 where he stated that "the next one hundred years will see the beginning of an American matriarchy—a nation of Amazons in the psychological rather than physical sense." Daniels writes that Marston believed "women could and would use sexual enslavement to achieve [political and economical] domination over men, who would happily submit to their loving authority." *Wonder Woman: The Complete History*. p. 19.

60. hooks, *All About Love*, p. 142.

Chapter Six

1. Beatty, Scott and Dixon Chuck. *Batgirl: Year One*. New York: DC Comics, 2003.

2. "Crusade," 4.1. *Smallville*. Writer Alfred Gough and Miles Millar, director Greg Beeman. Original air date: September 22, 2004.

3. The female protagonists of the fantastic 1984 zombie/apocalypse movie *Night of the Comet* were also trained in army techniques by their widowed Daddy.

4. *Lara Croft: Tomb Raider*. Director Simon West. Starring Angelina Jolie. 2001.

5. http://www.scifi.com/eureka/cast/zoe/

6. Athena, the Greek goddess of wisdom and war, was born after her father Zeus swallowed her pregnant mother, Metis. Athena sprung forth from his head, fully grown and armed.

7. Warner, Maria. *From the Beast to the Blonde: On Fairy Tales and Their Tellers*. New York: Farrar, Strauss and Giroux, p. 209, 1994.

8. Ibid, p. 213.

9. Pearson, Carol and Pope, Katherine. *The Female Hero in American and British Literature*. New York: R.R. Bowker Company, p. 177, 1981.

10. Ibid, p. 178.

11. Campbell, Joseph and Moyers, Bill. *The Power of Myth*. New York: Doubleday, p. 166, 1988.

12. "Passage Part 2," 2.9. *Alias*. Writer Crystal Nix Hines, director Ken Olin. Original air date: December 8, 2002.

13. Both the original series, as well as the contemporary films—one of which *Alias* creator J. J. Abrams would go on to direct.

14. It should be noted that Sydney has a surrogate "bad" father in Arvin Sloan, whose discovery of his own fathered daughter (with Irina Derevko no less) will lead to many parallels between the "good" relationship of Jack and Sydney and the "bad" relationship of Sloan and Nadia throughout Season 4. She also has a "spirit" father in Milo Rambaldi, the fictional fifteenth-century prophet and inventor loosely based on a combination of Nostradamus and Leonardo da Vinci, whose works guide a good portion of the series mythology.

15. "Truth Be Told," 1.1. *Alias*. Writer J. J. Abrams, director J. J. Abrams. Original air date: September 30, 2001.

16. Abrams, J. J. "Preface," in Vaz, Mark Cotta. *Alias Declassified: The Official Companion*. New York: Bantam Books, 2002.

17. Vaz, Mark Cotta. *Alias Declassified: The Official Companion*. New York: Bantam Books, p. 19, 2002.

18. Edelman, Hope. *Motherless Daughters: The Legacy of Loss (Second Edition)*. USA: Da Capo Lifelong Books, p. 132, 2006.

19. "Cipher," 2.3. *Alias*. Writer Alex Kurtzman, director Daniel Attias. Original air date: October 13, 2002.

20. "Dead Drop," 2.4. *Alias*. Writer Jesse Alexander, director Guy Norman Bee. Original air date: October 20, 2002.

21. "Passage Part 2," 2.9. *Alias*.

22. "Cipher," 2.3. *Alias*.

23. "The Abduction," 2.10. *Alias*. Writer Alex Kurtzman, director Nelson McCormick. Original air date: December 15, 2002.

24. "Cipher," 2.3. *Alias*.

25. Pope and Pearson. *The Female Hero in American and British Literature*, p. 205.

26. Whedon, Joss. "Ace of Case," in *Entertainment Weekly*. Posted online October 7, 2005. Published in Issue 844–5, October 14, 2005. http://www .ew.com/ew/article/0,,1114734,00.html.

27. Edelman, *Motherless Daughters*, p. 95.
28. "You Think You Know Somebody," 1.5. *Veronica Mars*. Writer Dayna North, director Nick Gomez. Original air date: October 26, 2006.
29. "Meet John Smith," 1.3. Writer Jed Seidel, director Harry Winer. Original air date: October 12, 2004.
30. Edelman, *Motherless Daughters*, p. 96.
31. "You Think You Know Somebody," 1.5. *Veronica Mars*.
32. Edelman, *Motherless Daughters*, p. 97.
33. Ibid.
34. "Leave It to Beaver," 1.22. *Veronica Mars*. Writer Rob Thomas, director Michael Fields. Original air date: May 10, 2005.
35. Kaveney, Roz. *Teen Dreams: Reading Teen Film and Television From Heathers to Veronica Mars*. London/New York: I.B.Tauris, p. 180, 2006.
36. This is particularly resonant with women, like myself, who have in fact been raised by their fathers and whose mothers are physically absent. Seeing the journeys of superwomen helps us reconcile conflicting ideas about cultural representations of femininity with our personal experiences of humanity.
37. See Chapter 4.
38. "Heat," 1.1. *Dark Angel*. Writer Patrick Harbinson, director Michael Katleman. Original air date: October 10, 2000.
39. "Heat," 1.1. *Dark Angel*.

Chapter Seven

1. *Terminator 2: Judgment Day*. Director James Cameron. Starring Linda Hamilton, Arnold Schwarzenegger, and Edward Furlong. 1991. *T2* Extreme DVD (Special Edition DVD). Artisan Home Entertainment. Released: June 3, 2003.
2. "Crusade," 4.01. *Smallville*. Writer Alfred Gough and Mark Millar, director Greg Beeman. Original air date: September 22, 2004.
3. Paul "Muad'Dib" Atreides, of the Dune, series is an archetypal example. As holy and powerful as his mother is, the Bene Gesserit, Lady Jessica, cannot be the salvation of that universe—no woman can. If Frank Herbert intended to honor the phenomenal women in his own life, why did he put a limit on feminine power? Why is it only the masculine who can achieve ultimate Godhood by becoming the Kwisatz Haderach? Why is there a place that women cannot look?
4. Directly influenced by scenes in *The Heroic Trio*.
5. *The Long Kiss Goodnight*. Director Renny Harlin. Starring Geena Davis and Samuel Jackson. 1996.

6. Also recall Pam Grier's Coffy, who fought to protect her community—as discussed in Chapter 2.

7. Schilling, Mary Kaye. "The Second Coming." *Entertainment Weekly*. New York, Issue 760, p. 24, April 16, 2004.

8. Biskind, Peter. "The Return of Quentin Tarantino." *Vanity Fair*. New York, Issue 518, p. 296, October 2003.

9. Ironically, Beatrix had herself used her baby as an excuse to inspire sympathy and save herself from assassination.

10. Jervis, Lisa. "Hot Girl-On-Girl Action: The Peculiar Problem of Politics, Pornography and the Ass-Kicking Babe." July 15, 2004. Accessed online: http://
www.lipmagazine.org/articles/featjervis_girlongirl.htm

11. *Kill Bill: Vol. 2*.

12. Ibid.

13. Grace. "Review of Kill Bill." *Heroine Content*. http://www.heroinecontent
.net/archives/2007/12/kill_bill_vol_1_and_kill_bill.html

14. He's also praised his own mother, whom he described as "a single mom who came from white-trash beginnings" and yet "created a very nice career for herself as an executive–a legend in her own time in the HMO field." That she taught him an appreciation for women is clear when he says that "From the very beginning I never considered that there were boundaries, things a woman can and can't do. I had my mom as an example of someone who came from nothing, who paid her own way, had nice s_____, drove a Cadillac Seville. She was living the life." In Schilling, Mary Kaye. "The Second Coming." *Entertainment Weekly*. New York, Issue 760, pp. 7, 24, April 16, 2004.

15. Bloody-Disgusting.com reported that Quentin Tarantino said at the 2006 Comic Con that after the completion of *Grindhouse*, he wants to make two anime *Kill Bill* films. One will be an origin story about Bill and his mentors and the other will be an origin story starring The Bride. http://www.bloody-disgusting.com/news/6841

16. Schilling, Mary Kaye. "The Second Coming." *Entertainment Weekly*. New York, Issue 760, pp. 24, April 16, 2004.

17. Ibid.

18. Rucka, Greg and Amano, Yoshitaka. *Elektra/Wolverine: The Redeemer*. New York: Marvel Comics, 2002. Unpaginated, Chapter 2.

19. "Invasion of the Bane," 1.0. *The Sarah Jane Adventures*. Writer Russell T. Davies and Gareth Roberts, director Colin Teague. Original air date: January 1, 2007.

20. "Grave," 6.22. Writer David Fury, Director James A. Contner. Original air date: May 21, 2002.

21. See "Choosing Your Own Mother: Mother–Daughter Conflicts in *Buffy*," by J. P. Williams in *Fighting the Forces*, and Lorna Jowett's *Sex and the Slayer* for more details.

22. "End of Days," *Buffy the Vampire Slayer*. Writer Douglas Petrie, director Marita Grabiak. Original air date: May 13, 2003.

23. Pearson, Carol and Pope, Katherine. *The Female Hero in American and British Literature*. New York: R.R. Bowker Company, p. 202, 1981.

24. It should also be mentioned that Gail Simone's run on the comic series *Birds of Prey* features sisterhood, but this will be explored in Chapter 8.

25. Parts of this section have previously featured on my blog: http://www.inkstainedamazon.com/blog/2008/04/women-mentoring-women-and-introduction.html

26. *K-9 and Company* didn't evolve into a series but was released on DVD in 2008.

27. Ryan, Maureen. " 'Torchwood' Wraps Up a Fine Season as a New 'Doctor Who' Spinoff Debuts," in *Chicago Tribune*. April 10, 2008. http://featuresblogs.chicagotribune.com/entertainment_tv/2008/04/if-they-met-i-w.html

28. Lowry, Brian. "Review: The Sarah Jane Adventures," *Variety*. April 8, 2008. http://www.variety.com/review/VE1117936741.html?categoryid=32&cs=1

29. Pearson and Pope, *Female Hero*, p. 184.

30. "Eyes of the Gorgon, Pt 2," 1.4. *The Sarah Jane Adventures*. Writer Phil Ford, director Alice Troughton. Original air date: October 8, 2007.

31. Pearson and Pope, *Female Hero*, p. 185.

32. "Eyes of the Gorgon, Pt 2," 1.4. *The Sarah Jane Adventures*.

33. "Elektra Incarnations." Featurette. *Elektra*. Director's Cut—two-disc collector's edition. 20th Century Fox. Released: October 18, 2005.

34. Rucka, Greg and Amano, Yoshitaka. *Elektra/Wolverine: The Redeemer*. New York: Marvel Comics, 2002. Unpaginated, Chapter 2.

35. Rucka, *Redeemer*, Chapter 2.

36. Ibid.

37. "Elektra Incarnations." Featurette.

38. Rucka, *Redeemer*, Chapter 2.

39. Ibid.

40. Rucka, *Redeemer*, Chapter 3.

41. "Relentless: The Making of *Elektra*, Part 1." Production Documentary. *Elektra*. Director's Cut—two-disc Collector's Edition. 20th Century Fox. Released: October 18, 2005.

42. Lee, Patrick. "Better Red Than Dead." *Sci Fi* magazine, p. 32, February 2005.

43. In this version, the mother is already dead. Both Jennifer Garner and Fox studios said at the beginning of the film that Elektra should not be burdened with a romantic interest. But of course the strong mother character of "Redeemer" is replaced here by a father.

44. Lee, "Better Red Than Dead," p. 32.

45. Kaveney, Roz. *Superheroes! Capes and Crusaders in Comics and Films.* London/New York: I.B.Tauris, p. 265, 2008.

46. The ending of *Redeemer* is much more in line with Elektra's temperament; regardless, in both stories, she is protecting a part of herself, much as Ripley did with Newt.

47. "Solo," 5.6. *Alias.* Writer Jeffrey Bell, director Jeffrey Bell. Original air date: November 10, 2005.

48. Though the series could easily have gone in a ludicrous direction, Sydney's eggs were stolen from her in a previous season with the intent of creating a Sydney/Rambaldi child.

49. Terry, Paul. "This One Has a Kick ... Interview with Shauna Duggins." *Alias: The Official Magazine*, Issue 17, pp. 70–5, September/October 2006.

50. Oldenburg, Ann. "'Alias' Returns, Pregnant with Possibilities," in USA Today, September 28, 2005. http://www.usatoday.com/life/television/news/2005-09-28-alias_x.htm

51. Kantor, Jodi. "On 'Alias,' the Star Is Now Spying for Two." *New York Times.* October 6, 2005.

52. "Mockingbird," 5.4. *Alias.* Writer Drew Goddard, director Fred Toye. Original air date: October 20, 2005.

53. Kantor. "On 'Alias,' the Star Is Now Spying for Two."

54. Edelman, Hope. *Motherless Daughters: The Legacy of Loss* (Second Edition). USA: Da Capo Lifelong Books, p. 102, 2006.

55. When they first reencountered each other, Sydney told Irina, "Let's get something clear. You are not my mother. My mother was Laura Bristow. Laura Bristow died in a car accident twenty-one years ago. *You* are a traitor and a prisoner of the United States government" ("Trust Me," 2.2). But as Irina continually reminds Syd—she *is* her mother.

56. "Maternal Instinct," 5.11. *Alias.* Writer Breen Frazier, director Tucker Gates. Original air date: April 19, 2006.

57. "The New Recruit, Rachel Nichols." Featurette. *Alias :The Complete Fifth Season.* DVD. Buena Vista Home Entertainment/Touchstone. Released: November 21, 2006.

58. Terry, Paul. "There's Only One Sydney Bristow." *Alias: The Official Magazine*, Issue 17, pp. 10–15, September/October 2006. Garner is generous in her praise of all the female guest stars, and even associates different seasons with the different actresses who came on the show. In this interview, she

tells Terry: "The second season was about Lena [Olin], the third season was about Melissa [George], the fourth season was about Mia [Maestro], and the fifth season was about Rachel [Nichols] and Elodie [Bouchez]. So for me, I had a very different friendship and relationship with each of those women, and somehow in the miracle of casting, I love them all. I'm incredibly fond of them all, so I feel *so* lucky for that."

59. Dawidziak, Mark. "She's back! Fox Premieres 'Terminator: The Sarah Connor Chronicles'." *Cleveland.com.* Tuesday, January 8, 2008. http://www.cleveland.com/tv/index.ssf/2008/01/fox_premieres_sarah_connor_chr.html

60. Parts of this section have previously appeared on my blog: http://www.inkstainedamazon.com/blog/2007/08/gotta-make-way-for-mother-superior.html

61. Cameron is an interesting character as well. Much could easily be written about the construction of gender, and of humanity, though this chapter is about mothers and mentors, and at the time of writing, there have not been enough episodes of *SCC* to detect much mentoring or sisterhood between Cameron and Sarah.

62. "Pilot." *Terminator: The Sarah Connor Chronicles.* Writer Josh Friedman, director David Nutter. Original air date: January 13, 2008.

63. Pearson and Pope, *Female Hero*, p. 12.

Chapter Eight

1. Woolf, Virginia. *A Room of One's Own.* USA: Harcourt Brace Jovanovich, p. 83, 1989.

2. *Trekkies.* Director Roger Nygard. 1997. Also see *Beyond Uhura: Star Trek and Other Memories.* New York: G. P. Putnam's Sons, p. 13, 1994.

3. Jensen, Jeff. "The Goodbye Girl." *Entertainment Weekly.* March 7, 2003.

4. Nichols, *Beyond Uhura.* p. 211.

5. Ibid, p. 222.

6. Women had previously gone through the initial Mercury Astronaut Candidate Testing Program. Of the 25 women pilots selected to undergo the same testing as men, 13 candidates passed the same tests developed for the selection of male astronauts. But in 1961, NASA quickly and quietly canceled all further testing of women.

7. Female astronaut candidates were not considered again until 1978. Sally Ride joined NASA in 1978 and became the first American woman in space in 1983. Dr. Mae Jemison became the first African American woman in space in 1992. Guion Bluford became an astronaut in 1979 and the first African American man in space, also in 1983, but not on the same

mission as Ride. Robert Henry Lawrence, Jr., was the first African American astronaut, but died during a training accident and thus never made it into space. The first Asian American astronaut, Ellison Onizuka, was selected for the program in 1978. His first space mission was in 1985. He died one year later in the Challenger accident.

8. http://www.thegeenadavisinstitute.org/home.php

9. *Superman: The Movie.* Director Richard Donner. Starring Margot Kidder and Christopher Reeve. 1978.

10. Ibid.

11. Saba, Arn. "Kidder on Kidder." *Globe and Mail Weekend Magazine.* December 18, 1978, pp. 10–12. Accessed online: http://www.supermancinema.co .uk/superman1/general/media/index.shtml

12. Interview with author, July 7, 2008.

13. For those with an interest in Margot Kidder's Lois Lane, I highly recommend the Richard Donner cut of *Superman II*—the intended version of the movie. Donner was fired after having a falling out with *Superman's* producers and was replaced by Richard Lester—who took the film in a more comic direction. But in Donner's version (recut in 2006 and now available on DVD), Lois and Clark are shown as having the potential to have a more honest relationship—a partnership of equals, even. This version of Clark respects Lois' intellect enough to discontinue his charade with her and reveal his true identity. He makes a further effort toward equality between them by choosing to become mortal for her, giving up his godhood in exchange for humanity. And in this version of the film, when Superman must return to his duty, the pragmatic Lois is understanding, calmly telling him that "Those people need you. Do you think I don't understand that?" and assuring him that his secret is safe with her. Kidder too had had a falling out with the producers, and in Lester's revised movie, Lois is written as shrill, telling Clark how she's selfish when it comes to him (which in the original shoot she wasn't) and that she's "jealous of the *whole* world." Her role in *Superman III* was also drastically reduced.

14. With all due respect of course to Phyllis Coates, Noel Neill, Teri Hatcher, Erica Durance, and Kate Bosworth.

15. On a side note, Erica Durance's Lois Lane comes very close to Kidder's vision.

16. Underground, autobiographical, and "arty" comics, on the other hand, are filled with diverse female experience, but that is another book for another time.

17. Lee, Stan. *The Superhero Women.* 1977. If Stan Lee could have sold comics to girls, he would have been thrilled with both the converts to his four-color religion and the extra sales—Excelsior!

18. Meaning for one there simply aren't as many women in the entertainment industry as men, and secondly, comic book stores have, until recently, been male-dominated spaces.

19. Though she was not the first female Robin; that honor belongs to Carrie Kelly from Frank Miller's *Batman: The Dark Knight Returns*.

20. Willingham, Bill. *Robin*. Issue 126. New York: DC Comics, July 2004.

21. Willingham, *Robin*. Issue 127, August 2004. Also see Horrocks, Dylan. *The New Adventures of Batgirl and Robin*. Issue 53. New York: DC Comics, August 2004.

22. http://girl-wonder.org/robin/projectgirlwonder.html

23. Keller, Katherine. "Superheroes Are for Everyone: The Brains Behind Girl-Wonder." September 1, 2006. http://www.sequentialtart.com/article.php?id=239

24. Gabrych, Anderson. *Batgirl*. Issue 62. New York: DC Comics, May 2005.

25. Keller, Katherine. "An Open Letter: On the Topic of Stephanie Brown." *Sequential Tart*. April 1, 2007. http://www.sequentialtart.com/article.php?id=488

26. Ibid.

27. "Metrokitty" refers to this overused storytelling crutch as a "you-touched-my-stuff" story. On her blog, she breaks down the formula thusly, "Man + Dead/Violated Wife + Thirst for Violent Vengeance = Movie." She also notes that *Kill Bill* is one of the only examples of a "You-touched-my-stuff" film, Friday, November 14, 2003. http://www.metrokitty.com/?id=78.

28. http://www.unheardtaunts.com/wir/r-gsimone.html

29. Garrity, Shaenon. "The Gail Simone Interview." *The Comics Journal*. No. 286, pp. 68–91, November 2007.

30. Including stories for Bongo's *Simpsons* line, as well as Marvel's *Deadpool* (later *Agent X*) title.

31. As of November 2008, it was announced that the *Birds of Prey* title, along with *Robin* and *Nightwing*, has been canceled.

32. Many writers would attempt to emulate this powerful graphic novel, but while inspired by the story, they lacked Moore's skill to balance the gruesome details with the tragedy of humanity. Unfortunately, copying Moore without Moore's talent was one of the instigators of the Women-in-Refrigerators trend, and Moore himself has regretted the decision to paralyze Babs. While it seemed *The Killing Joke* had effectively written her out of continuity, Babs was soon reintroduced by Kim Yale and John Ostrander in the title *Suicide Squad*.

33. Garrity, Interview with Gail Simone. *The Comics Journal*. Issue 286, p. 84.

34. Brady, Matt. "Gail Simone Talks Birds of Prey Exit." April 6, 2007. http://forum.newsarama.com/showthread.php?t=107819

35. Brady, Matt. "The Simone Files I: Birds of Prey." http://forum.newsarama
.com/showthread.php?t=98825

36. Simone, Gail. *Birds of Prey: Perfect Pitch.* New York: DC Comics, p. 220,
2007.

37. Simone, Gail. *Birds of Prey: Blood & Circuits.* New York: DC Comics, pp. 8–
9, 2007.

38. Simone, Gail. *Birds of Prey: Dead of Winter.* New York: DC Comics, pp. 123–
4, 2008.

39. Robbins, Trina and Timmons, Anne. *Go Girl!.* Oregon: Dark Horse Comics,
2002. Unpaginated, Issue 1.

40. Ibid.

41. Trina Robbins' interview with author, February 22, 2008. Transcribed by
Ryan Wilkerson.

42. Anne Timmons' interview with author, June 2, 2008.

43. Timmons' interview.

44. Robbins' interview.

45. Ibid.

46. Ibid.

47. Ibid.

48. Ibid.

49. Ibid.

50. As one of the co-founders of the Wimmen's Comix Collective, the editor of the first all-female produced comic ever, "It A'int Me Babe," and a
renowned comics herstorian, Trina Robbins has long been active in wom-
en's issues. In 1998, she wrote a short graphic novel for DC Comics that
used a Wonder Woman story to address domestic violence. *Wonder Woman:
The Once and Future Story* is a perfect example of what can be accomplished
when someone uses an identifiable, yet fictional, character to champion
social justice. Whether or not Wonder Woman is considered a feminist
character today, she will always be a recognizable icon of women's issues,
and female empowerment. Robbins is justifiably very proud of the book,
which has Wonder Woman helping her friend Julia Kapatelis with translat-
ing ancient tablets uncovered in Ireland. They are accompanied by a couple,
James and Moira Kennealy, and James is clearly abusing his wife. The story
Wonder Woman translates from the tablet is the tale of a young woman
named Artemis. She has left her women's-only island to rescue her mother,
who has been kidnapped by the brutal Greek General Theseus to be his
wife. It's a story within a story, and the past is echoed in the present when
the Kennealy's daughter arrives to try to rescue her own mother from the
shame and brutality of abuse. Leaving her husband is a difficult decision

for Moira to make, but as circumstances escalate, it's one that she must, and does, confront. The back page of the book has facts about domestic violence and includes a list of resourceful phone numbers for assistance in both the USA and Great Britain.

51. Brady, Matt. "Gail Simone Talks Birds of Prey Exit." April 6, 2007. http://forum.newsarama.com/showthread.php?t=107819

52. Simone also wrote drafts of the direct-to-DVD animated feature *Wonder Woman* (March 2009).

53. Simone, Gail. *Wonder Woman: The Circle*. New York: DC Comics, p. 36, 2008.

54. Ibid, p. 37.

55. Ibid, pp. 57–62.

56. To my knowledge.

57. Simone, *Circle*, p. 85.

58. Ibid, p. 99.

59. Simone, Gail. *Wonder Woman*. Issue 24. New York: DC Comics, November 2008.

60. Simone, Gail. *Wonder Woman*. Issue 25. December 2008.

61. http://www.power-up.net

62. http://www.afterellen.com/archive/ellen/Movies/debs/picture.html

63. The Scholastic Aptitude Test, or SAT, is a standardized test taken by American teenagers.

64. Gleiberman, Owen. "D.E.B.S. Review." *Entertainment Weekly*. Issue 813, p. 49. New York. April 1, 2005.

65. Travers, Peter. "D.E.B.S. Review." *Rolling Stone*. Issue 971, p. 79. New York. April 7, 2005.

66. Holden, Stephen. "D.E.B.S. Review." *New York Times*. Late edition (East Coast), p. E.1:10. New York. March 25, 2005.

67. Gay-themed publications *The Advocate* and *After Ellen* gave more glowing reviews, and *Variety* praised the movie as "Lesbian teen fantasy [that] blends the infectious buoyancy of high school pics like 'Bring It On' with the comicstrip, girl-power action of 'Charlie's Angels' and the spy spoofery of the 'Austin Powers' franchise." The reviewer adds that "...the film's good-natured mirthfulness and the relative non-issue of its sexual agenda should make it inclusive to teenage girls regardless of their sexual persuasion." Rooney, David. "Film Review: D.E.B.S." *Variety*. p. 26. January 26–February 1, 2004, 393, 10. On a side note, *D.E.B.S.* should also be applauded for its ethnic diversity.

68. Oler, Tammy. "Gail Simone: DC's New Wonder Woman." *Geek Monthly*. p. 88, November 2008.

69. Cochran, Shannon. "The Cold Shoulder: Saving Superheroines from Comic Book Violence." *Bitch*. No. 35, p. 25, 2007.

Conclusion

1. Fingeroth, Danny. *Superman on the Couch: What Superheroes Really Tell Us About Ourselves and Our Society*. New York: Continuum, p. 95, 2004.
2. Mudhar, Raju. "*Heroes* Creator's Super Power His Fresh Eye for Epic Adventure; Tim Kring Admits He's No Geek or Comics Fan. Doesn't Make Him a Bad Guy." *Toronto Star*. Toronto, Ont.: p. C.4, January 21, 2007.
3. Armstrong, Stephen. "Heroes Don't Call Us Super ..." [Final 7 Edition] *Sunday Times*. London, UK: p. 21, February 18, 2007.
4. Elsworth, Catherine. "Ordinary People, Extraordinary Powers It's 'Desperate Housewives' Meets 'X-Men' – the Hit US Series 'Heroes' Mixes Sci-Fi and Soul to Dazzling Effect." *The Daily Telegraph*. London, UK: p. 16, July 21, 2007.
5. Ibid.
6. To be fair, the character of Zack was intended to be gay. His sexuality was overtly hinted at on the show and in promotional materials but later vigorously denied by Thomas Dekker's handlers.
7. White, Cindy. "*Heroes* Cheerleader to Test Self." *Sci Fi Wire*. August 13, 2007. http://www.scifi.com/scifiwire/print.php?id=43210
8. Although, on a side note, Claire is not an active agent in saving the world. In the climatic battle of Season 1, it is her position as a *daughter* that saves the day. Peter Petrelli's saving of the cheerleader was one of a series of events that led to the discovery that Claire is his niece. When Peter later inadvertently becomes the bomb that threatens to destroy Manhattan, it is his brother Nathan, Claire's biological father, who swoops in to save the day. The cheerleader did not save the world; it was the father who did—to prove to her, to his brother, and to himself that he was a worthy man.
9. Additionally, you'd *never* see Buffy Summers actually researching her abilities—that was a job for Giles or the Scoobies. But we know that when Claire received a copy of *Activating Evolution*, she read it.
10. Noble, Kathleen D. *The Sound of a Silver Horn: Reclaiming the Heroism in Contemporary Women's Lives*. New York: Ballantine Books, p. 193, 1994.
11. Additionally, in a bit of stunt casting, Nichelle Nichols featured as Monica's grandmother but only had a handful of throwaway lines—a waste of her talent.
12. Pearson, Carol and Pope, Katherine. *The Female Hero in American and British Literature*. New York: R.R. Bowker Company, p. 5, 1981.
13. Pope and Pearson, *Female Hero*, p. 5.

14. Interview with author, February 22, 2008.
15. This has been an ambitious project, though for me, an impassioned and rewarding undertaking. There is much I wish I could have included, but time and space would not allow. Regardless, the last chapter on this topic can never be written, and until superwomen, and a diverse range of *superpeople*, are commonplace, it's important to continue talking about them passionately, eloquently, critically, joyously, and incessantly. I invite you to do so on ink-stainedamazon.com.

Bibliography, Filmography, and Internet Sources

Bibliography

Abbot, Stacey and Brown, Simon, eds. *Investigating Alias: Secrets and Spies.* London: I.B.Tauris, 2007.

Abrams, J. J. "Preface." in Vaz, Mark Cotta, ed. *Alias Declassified: The Official Companion.* New York: Bantam Books, 2002.

Armstrong, Stephen. "Heroes Don't Call Us Super. . . ." [Final 7 Edition] *Sunday Times.* London, UK, p. 21, February 18, 2007.

Avery, Fiona Kai. *Araña: The Heart of the Spider.* New York: Marvel Comics, 2005.

———. *Araña: In the Beginning.* New York: Marvel Comics, 2005.

———. *Araña: Night of the Hunter.* New York: Marvel Comics, 2006.

Bartol, John. "Dead Men Defrosting." http://www.unheardtaunts.com/wir/r-jbartol2.html

Battis, Jes. *Blood Relations: Chosen Families in Buffy the Vampire Slayer and Angel.* North Carolina: McFarland & Company, 2005.

Baumgardner, Jennifer and Richards, Amy. *Manifesta.* New York: Farrar, Straus and Giroux, 2000.

Beatty, Scott and Dixon, Chuck. *Batgirl: Year One.* New York: DC Comics, 2003.

Beckett, Simon. "Review: Modesty Blaise: The Xanadu Talisman and The Silver Mistress." in *The Observer.* London, UK, p. 18, September 15, 2002.

Bernstein, Abbie. "Claire and Present Danger." in *Heroes: The Official Magazine.* Issue 3, pp. 16–23, April/May 2008.

Binelli, Mark. "Spy Girl." in *Rolling Stone.* Issue 889, pp. 36 (5 pages), New York, February 14, 2002.

Billson, Anne. *Buffy the Vampire Slayer: A Critical Reading of the Series.(bfi TV Classics).* London: British Film Institute, 2005.

Biskind, Peter. "The Return of Quentin Tarantino." in *Vanity Fair.* Issue 518, p. 296, New York, October 2003.

Blackmore, Lawrence. *The Modesty Blaise Companion.* London: Book Palace Books, 2005.

Blundell, Sue. *Women in Ancient Greece.* Cambridge, Massachusetts: Harvard University Press, 1995.

Blondell, Ruby. "How to Kill an Amazon." in Ruby Blondell and Mary-Kay Gamel,eds., *Ancient Mediterranean Women in Modern Mass Media.* pp. 73–103. in "Helios," 32.2, 2005.

Blythe, Teresa. "Dark Angel," *Sojourners* magazine, Vol. 30, No. 2, p. 61, March 2001.

Bolen, Jean Shinoda. *Goddesses in Everywoman: A New Psychology of Women.* New York, Cambridge, Philadelphia, San Francisco, London, Mexico City, São Paulo, Singapore, Sydney: Harper & Row, 1985.

Borsellino, Mary. "A Lot Like Robin if You Close Your Eyes: Displacement of Meaning in the Post-Modern Age." in *Girl Wonder.* http://girl-wonder.org/papers/borsellino.html

Brady, Matt. "The Simone Files I: Birds of Prey." http://forum.newsarama.com/showthread.php?t=98825

———. "Gail Simone Talks Birds of Prey Exit." April 6, 2007. http://forum.newsarama.com/showthread.php?t=107819

Britton, Piers D. and Barker, Simon J. *Reading Between Designs: Visual Imagery and the Generation of Meaning in The Avengers, The Prisoner, and Doctor Who.* Austin, TX: University of Texas Press, 2003.

Britton, Wesley A. *Beyond Bond: Spies in Fiction and Film.* Connecticut: Praeger Publishers, 2005.

Brode, Douglas. *Boys and Toys: Ultimate Action-Adventure Movies.* New York: Citadel Press, 2003.

Brown, Jeffrey A. "Gender and the Action Heroine: Hardbodies and the 'Point of No Return.' " *Cinema Journal,* spring 1996, Vol. 35, No. 3, pp. 52–71.

———. "Gender, Sexuality, and Toughness: The Bad Girls of Action Film and Comic Books." in Inness, Sherrie A, ed. *Action Chicks: New Images of Tough Women in Popular Culture.* New York: Palgrave Macmillan, pp. 47–74, 2004.

Bunche, Steve. "Giant-Size Mandingo: A Time for Modesty" *The Vault of Buncheness.* Sunday, December 3, 2006. http://buncheness.blogspot.com/2006/12/giant-size-mandingo-time-for-modesty.html

Burns, James H. "Sarah Douglas: The Human-Hating, Kryptonian Super-Villainess from 'Superman II.'" *Starlog.* June 1981. Accessed online: http://www.supermancinema.co.uk/superman2/general/media/starlog47_june81/index.htm

Byrne, John and Claremont, Chris. *The Uncanny X-Men: The Dark Phoenix Saga.* New York: Marvel Comics, 1991.

Cairns, Bryan. "Blond Ambitions." *Smallville: The Official Magazine.* Issue 16, pp. 22–9, September/October 2006.

———. "Fuller Ideas." in *TV Zone.* Inter-Special Issue 2./Cult Times Special 44, pp. 38–43, 2007.

Campbell, Joseph. *The Hero with a Thousand Faces.* New York: Barnes and Noble Books, original copyright 1949.

Campbell, Joseph and Moyers, Bill. *The Power of Myth.* New York: Doubleday, 1988.

Chabon, Michael. "A Woman of Valor"–Online Essay. No longer accessible.

———. *The Amazing Adventures of Kavalier and Clay.* New York: Picador, 2000.

Chapman, James. *Saints and Avengers: British Adventure Series of the 1960s.* London/New York: I.B.Tauris, 2002.

———. *License to Thrill: A Cultural History of the James Bond Films.* London/New York: I.B.Tauris, 2007.

Charyn, Jerome. *Raised by Wolves: The Turbulent Art and Times of Quentin Tarantino.* New York: Thunder's Mouth Press, 2006.

Claremont, Chris. *The Uncanny X-Men #102.* New York: Marvel Comics, December 1976.

———. *The Uncanny X-Men: From the Ashes.* New York: Marvel Comics, 1993.

Cochran, Shannon. "The Cold Shoulder: Saving Superheroines from Comic Book Violence." *Bitch.* No. 35, pp. 23–6.

Collins, Gail. *America's Women: 400 Years of Dolls, Drudges, Helpmates, and Heroines.* New York: William Morrow/HarperCollins, 2003.

Collins, Max Allan and Beatty, Terry. *The Files of Ms. Tree. Vol. 1.* Canada: Aardvark Vanaheim Inc, 1984.

———. *The Files of Ms. Tree. Vol. 2.* Canada: Renegade Press, 1985.

Collins, Max Allan. *Deadly Beloved.* New York: Dorchester Publishing Co., Inc., 2007.

Coogan, Peter. *Superhero: The Secret Origin of a Genre.* Austin, TX: Monkey Brain Books, 2006.

Corliss, Richard. "The Years of Living Splendidly." *TIME*. Monday, July 28, 1986.

Cox, John. The Samantha Weinberg CBn Interview." October 28, 2005. http://commanderbond.net/article/2983

Cunningham, John. "Saturday Review: Books: Paperbacks: Adventures in Old Fleet Street: A Life in Writing: John Cunningham Meets Peter O'Donnell, Creator of Modesty Blaise." *The Guardian*. London, UK, p. 11, September 16, 2000.

Daniels, Les. *Superman: The Complete History*. San Francisco, CA: Chronicle Books, 1998.

——. *Batman: The Complete History*. San Francisco, CA: Chronicle Books, 2004.

——. *Wonder Woman: The Complete History*. San Francisco, CA: Chronicle Books, 2000.

D'Erasmo, Stacey. "Xenaphilia." *Village Voice*. Vol. 40, No. 52, p. 47, December 26, 1995.

Desowitz, Bill. "Saving the World with Bond May Just Be the Start for Berry." *Los Angeles Times*. Los Angeles, CA, p. E.10, November 25, 2002.

Dixon, Chuck. *Batman: Huntress/Spoiler*. Issue 1. New York: DC Comics, May 1998.

——. *Birds of Prey*. New York: DC Comics, 2002.

——. *Birds of Prey: Old Friends New Enemies*. New York: DC Comics, 2003.

——. *Robin*. Issue 172, New York: DC Comics, May 2008.

——. *Robin/Spoiler Special*. Issue 1, New York: DC Comics, August 2008.

Douglas, Susan J. *Where the Girls Are: Growing Up Female with the Mass Media*. New York: Three Rivers Press, 1995.

Driscoll, Catherine. *Girls: Feminine Adolescence in Popular Culture and Cultural Theory*. New York: Columbia University Press, 2002.

Early, Francis and Kennedy, Kathleen. *Athena's Daughters: Television's New Women Warriors*. New York: Syracuse University Press, 2003.

Ebert, Alan. "Pam Grier: Coming into Focus." *Essence*. p. 43, January 1979.

Eby, Douglas. "Warrior Women on Screen." http://talentdevelop.com/articles/wwos.html

Edelman, Hope. *Motherless Daughters: The Legacy of Loss (Second Edition)*. USA: Da Capo Lifelong Books, 2006.

Edgar, Joanne. "Wonder Woman Revisited." *Ms.* magazine, No. 1, pp. 53–4, 1972.

Ehrenstein, David. "Spy Camp." *The Advocate.* Issue 871, p. 59, September 3, 2002.

Elsworth, Catherine. "Ordinary People, Extraordinary Powers It's 'Desperate Housewives' Meets 'X-Men' - the Hit US Series 'Heroes' Mixes Sci Fi and Soul to Dazzling Effect." *The Daily Telegraph.* London, UK, p. 16, July 21, 2007.

Epstein, Daniel Robert. "Aeon Flux Creator Peter Chung." *SuicideGirls.com.* December 20, 2005. http://suicidegirls.com/interviews/%20Aeon%20Flux%20creator%20Peter%20Chung/

Faludi, Susan. *Backlash: The Undeclared War Against American Women.* New York: Crown Publishers, Inc, 1991.

Fantham, Elaine, Foley, Helene Peet, Kampen, Natalie Boymel, Pomeroy, Sarah B. and Shapiro, H. Alan. *Women in the Classical World.* New York: Oxford University Press, 1994.

Fickling, G. G. *Honey West: A Kiss for a Killer.* New York and Woodstock: The Overlook Press, 2006.

———. *Honey West: This Girl for Hire.* New York and Woodstock: The Overlook Press, 2005.

Findlen, Barbara, ed. *Listen Up: Voices from the Next Feminist Generation.* Seattle: Seal Press, 1995.

Fingeroth, Danny. *Superman on the Couch: What Superheroes Really Tell Us About Ourselves and Our Society.* New York: Continuum, 2004.

Fite, Linda. *Beware! The Claws of the Cat.* Issue 1, New York: DC Comics, November 1972.

———. *Beware! The Claws of the Cat.* Issue 2, January 1973.

———. *Beware! The Claws of the Cat.* Issue 3, April 1973.

———. *Beware! The Claws of the Cat.* Issue 4, June 1973.

Flaherty, M. "Xenaphilia." *Entertainment Weekly.* Online edition 7, pp. 1–6, March 1997. http://www.ew.com/ew/article/0,,287017,00.html

Fleming, Ian. *From Russia with Love.* London: Penguin Books Ltd, 2002.

———. *Goldfinger.* London: Penguin Books Ltd, 2002.

———. *On Her Majesty's Secret Service.* London: Penguin Books Ltd, 2002.

———. *The Spy Who Loved Me.* London: Penguin Books Ltd, 2002.

Fudge, Rachel. "Buffy: A Tale of Cleavage and Marketing." *Bitch*. Accessed online: http://bitchmagazine.org/article/buffy-effect

Gabrych, Anderson. *Batgirl*. Issue 62, New York: DC Comics, May 2005.

Garrett, Susan M. "You've Come a Long Way, Baby: A Forty-Year Leap for the Spygirl from the Swingin' Sixties to the Naughty Oughties." in Weisman, Kevin and Yeffeth, Glenn, eds. *Alias Assumed: Sex, Lies, and SD-6*. Dallas, TX: Smart Pop/Benbella, pp. 191–7, 2005.

Garrity, Shaenon. "The Gail Simone Interview." *The Comics Journal*. No. 286, pp. 68–91, November 2007.

Gilbert, Matthew. "Claire: A Cheerleader but Also a Girl Who Refuses to Be Afraid." Boston, MA: Boston Globe. p. N.8, November 12, 2006.

Gilchrist, Todd. "Interview: Angela Robinson *D.E.B.S.* Director Chats with IGN." March 25, 2005. http://movies.ign.com/articles/599/599139p1 .html

Gleiberman, Owen. "*D.E.B.S.* Review." *Entertainment Weekly*. Issue 813, p. 49, New York, April 1, 2005.

Goh, Robbie B. H. "Peter O'Donnell, Race Relations and National Identity: The Dynamics of Representation in 1960s and 1970s Britain." *Journal of Popular Culture*. Vol. 32, No. 4, p. 29, spring 1999, Research Library.

Golden, Christopher and Holder, Nancy. *The Watcher's Guide Vol. 1*. New York: Pocket Books, 1998.

Goodman, Tim. "'Buffy's' Demise Puts a Stake in our Hearts." *San Francisco Chronicle*. Monday, May 19, 2003. http://www.sfgate.com/cgi-bin/ article.cgi?f=/c/a/2003/05/19/DD61367.DTL

Gottlieb, Allie. "Buffy's Angels." From the September 26–October 2, 2002, issue of *Metro*, Silicon Valley's weekly newspaper. http://www.metroactive .com/papers/metro/09.26.02/buffy1-0239.html

Gravatt, Paul and Stanbury, Peter. *Great British Comics*. London: Aurum Press Limited, 2006.

Green, Phillip. *Cracks in the Pedestal: Ideology and Gender in Hollywood*. USA: The University of Massachusetts Press, 1998.

Gross, Edward. "Richard Donner Interview." *Starlog*, 1989. Accessed online: http://www.supermancinema.co.uk/superman2/general/media/s2media_ starlog89_donner_interview.htm

Harvey, R. C. "The Unforgettable Jane." *Rants and Raves*. Posted April 13, 2007. http://gocomics.typepad.com/rcharvey/2007/04/the_unforgettab .html

Healy, Karen and Johnson, Terry D. "Comparative Sex-Specific Body Mass Index in the Marvel Universe and the 'Real' World." Accessed online: http://girl-wonder.org/papers/bmi.html

Heinecken, Dawn. *The Warrior Women of Television: A Feminist Cultural Analysis of the New Female Body in Popular Media.* New York: Peter Lang Publishing, 2003.

———. "Boundary Battles: Heroic Narrative, The Feminine, and MTV'S Aeon Flux." *Studies in Popular Culture.* p. 24.1, 2001.

Helford, Elyce Rae, ed. *Fantasy Girls: Gender in the New Universe of Science Fiction and Fantasy Television.* Maryland: Rowman & Littlefield, 2000.

Holden, Stephen. *"D.E.B.S.* Review." *New York Times.* Late edition (East Coast) New York: p. E.1:10, March 25, 2005.

Holder, Nancy, Mariotte, Jeff and Hart, Maryelizabeth. *The Watcher's Guide Vol. 2.* New York: Pocket Books, 2000.

hooks, bell. *All About Love: New Visions.* New York: William Morrow & Company, 2000.

Horrocks, Dylan. *The New Adventures of Batgirl and Robin.* Issue 53, New York: DC Comics, August 2004.

Horwell, Veronica. "Saturday Review: Graphic Fiction: Modesty Ablaze: Veronica Horwell Enjoys a 60s Icon." *The Guardian.* London, UK, p. 23, July 24, 2004.

Howell, Kevin. "Modesty Blaise's Final Bow." *Publisher's Weekly.* Vol. 248, No. 14, p. 17, April 2, 2001, ABI/INFORM Global.

Inness, Sherrie A. *Tough Girls: Women Warriors and Wonder Women in Popular Culture.* Philadelphia: University of Pennsylvania Press, 1999.

———. ed. *Action Chicks: New Images of Tough Women in Popular Culture.* New York: Palgrave Macmillan, 2004.

Jensen, Jeff. "A Bloody Good Chat with 'Buffy's' Creator." *Entertainment Weekly.* June 11, 2002. Accessed online: http://www.ew.com/ew/article/0,260274,00.html

———. "The Goodbye Girl." *Entertainment Weekly.* p. 18, March 7, 2003.

Jervis, Lisa. "The Politics of Pornography and the Ass-Kicking Babe." Posted July 7, 2004. Accessed online: http://www.alternet.org/mediaculture/19166/

Johnson, Steven. *Everything Bad Is Good for You: How Today's Popular Culture Is Actually Making Us Smarter.* New York: Penguin Group, 2005.

Johnston, Maura. "Girl Power for Sale." *Ms.* Vol. X, No. 3, pp. 81–2, April/May 2000.

Jones, Gerard. *Men of Tomorrow: Geeks, Gangsters and the Birth of the Comic Book.* Cambridge, MA: Basic Books, 2004.

Jowett, Lorna. *Sex and the Slayer: A Gender Studies Primer for the Buffy Fan.* Connecticut: Wesleyan, 2005.

———. "To the Max: Embodying Intersections in *Dark Angel.*" *Reconstruction.* Vol. 5, No. 4, fall 2005. Accessed online: http://reconstruction.eserver.org/054/jowett.shtml

Kane, Bob and Andrae, Thomas. *Batman & Me.* California: Eclipse Books, 1989.

Kantor, Jodi. "On 'Alias,' the Star Is Now Spying for Two." *New York Times.* October 6, 2005.

Karras, Irene. "The Third Wave's Final Girl: *Buffy the Vampire Slayer.*" *Thirdspace.* Vol. 1, Issue 2, March 2002. ISSN 1499-8513. Accessed online: http://www.thirdspace.ca/articles/karras.htm

Karp, Marcelle, and Stoller, Debbie. *The Bust Guide to the New Girl Order.* USA: Penguin Books, 1999.

Kaveney, Roz. *From Alien to the Matrix: Reading Science Fiction Film.* London/New York: I.B.Tauris, 2005.

———. *Teen Dreams: Reading Teen Film and Television From Heathers to Veronica Mars.* London/New York: I.B.Tauris, 2006.

———. Kaveney,ed. *Reading the Vampire Slayer: The New, Updated Unauthorized Guide to Buffy and Angel.* London/New York: I.B.Tauris, 2004.

———. *Superheroes! Capes and Crusaders in Comics and Films.* London/New York: I.B.Tauris, 2008.

Keller, Katherine. "Superheroes Are for Everyone: The Brains Behind Girl-Wonder." September 1, 2006. http://www.sequentialtart.com/article.php?id=239

———. "An Open Letter: On the Topic of Stephanie Brown." *Sequential Tart.* April 1, 2007. http://www.sequentialtart.com/article.php?id=488

Kelly, Christina. "*Sassy* Postscript." *Ms.* Vol. VII, No. 4, p. 96, January/February 1997.

Kidder, Margot. Interview with author, July 7, 2008.

Kincaid, Jamaica. "Pam Grier, Super Sass." *Ms.* pp. 50–2, August 1975.

Koike, Kazuo. *Lady Snowblood: The Deep Seated Grudge Vol. 1 & 2.* Oregon: Dark Horse Comics, 2005.

Kopkind, Andrew. "Supergirl." *The Nation.* Vol. 240, p. 88, January 26, 1985.

Latchem, John. "A Donner Party." *Home Media Magazine.* November 3, 2006. Accessed online: http://homemediamagazine.com/news-donner-party-9890

Lavery, David, ed. *Deny All Knowledge: Reading the X-Files.* London: Faber and Faber, 1996.

Lawson, Corrina. "Why Spoiler Matters to Me: The Evolution of Stephanie Brown." *Sequential Tart.* July 7, 2008. http://www.sequentialtart.com/article.php?id=1021

Lee, Jim, ed. *Heroes Vol. One.* California: Wildstorm, 2007.

Lee, Patrick. "Better Red Than Dead." *Sci Fi* magazine. p. 32, February 2005.

Lee, Stan. *Marvel Romance.* New York: Marvel Comics, 2006.

———. *The Superhero Women.* New York: Simon and Schuster, 1977.

Leighton, Taigen Daniel. *Bodhisattva Archetypes.* New York: Penguin Group, 1998.

Lester, Peter. "'Tell Us It Ain't So, Superman! Margot Kidder Says She's Been Sacked and She's Found a New Role: As Mom." *People* magazine. August 24, 1981. Accessed online: http://www.supermancinema.co.uk/superman2/general/media/s2media_kidderfired_from3_peoplemag_Aug81.htm

Lewis, Jon. *Robin.* Issue 111. New York: DC Comics, April 2003.

Logan, Michael. "Heroes: The Next Generation." *TV Guide.* pp. 30–4, October 1–7, 2007.

Lorrah, Jean. "Love Saves the World." in Yeffeth, Glenn, ed. *Seven Seasons of Buffy: Science Fiction and Fantasy Writers Discuss Their Favorite Television Show.* Dallas, TX: BenBella Books, pp. 167–75.

Macnee, Patrick and Rogers, Dave. *The Avengers: The Inside Story.* London: Titan Books, 2008.

Mainon, Dominique and Ursini, James. *The Modern Amazons: Warrior Women on Screen.* New Jersey: Limelight Editions, 2006.

Mangels, Andy. "Interview with Lynda Carter." *Back Issue.* No. 5, pp. 17–35, August 2004.

Mars, Mark and Singer, Eric. *Aeon Flux: The Herodotus File.* New York: MTV Books/Pocket Books/Melcher Media, 2005.

Marston, William Moulton. "Why 100,000,000 Americans Read Comics." *The American Scholar.* Vol. 13, No. 1, pp. 35–44, winter 1943–44.

———. *Wonder Woman Archives Vol. 1.* New York: DC Comics, 1998.

Matthews, Richard. "Truth Bearer." *Smallville*: The Official Magazine. Issue 9, pp. 8–13, June 2005.

McCaughey, Martha and King, Neal, eds. *Reel Knockouts: Violent Women in the Movies*. Austin, TX: University of Texas Press, 2001.

McCullough, Joan. "The 13 Who Were Left Behind." *Ms*. pp. 41–5, September 1973.

McDonough, Jimmy. *Big Bosoms and Square Jaws: The Biography of Russ Meyer, King of the Sex Film*. New York: Three Rivers Press, 2005.

McKeever, Sean. *Elektra: The Official Movie Adaptation*. New York: Marvel Comics, 2005.

Mendez, A. E. "The Look of Love the Rise and Fall of the Photo-Realistic Newspaper Strip, 1946–1970." Accessed Online: http://profmendez.tripod.com/html/photo2.htm

Miller, Frank. *Daredevil*. Issue 168. New York: Marvel Comics, January 1981.

———. *Daredevil*. Issue 181. New York: Marvel Comics, April 1982.

Miller, Toby. *The Avengers*. London: British Film Institute, 1998.

Misiroglu, Gina and Roach, David A, eds. *The Superhero Book*. Canton, MO: Visible Ink Press, 2004.

Minkowitz, Donna. "Xena: She's Big, Tall, Strong - and Popular." *Ms*. Vol. VII, No. 1, pp. 74–7, July/August 1996. Accessed online: http://www.mirrorblue.com/annex/ms796/index.shtml

Mizejewski, Linda. *Hardboiled & High Heeled: The Woman Detective in Popular Culture*. Routledge. New York, 2004.

Moore, Alan. *Promethea Series: Issues 1-32*. Illustrated by J. H. Williams III., Mick Gray and Todd Klein. La Jolla, CA: America's Best Comics (a division of Wildstorm), 1999–2004.

Mudhar, Raju. "Heroes Creator's Super Power His Fresh Eye for Epic Adventure; Tim Kring Admits He's No Geek or Comics Fan. Doesn't Make Him a Bad Guy, writes Raju Mudhar." *Toronto Star*. Toronto, Ont., p. C.4, January 21, 2007.

Nichols, Nichelle. *Beyond Uhura: Star Trek and Other Memories*. New York: G. P. Putnam's Sons, 1994.

Noble, Kathleen D. *The Sound of a Silver Horn: Reclaiming the Heroism in Contemporary Women's Lives*. New York: Ballantine Books, 1994.

Nussbaum, Emily. "Must-See Metaphysics." *The New York Times*. September 22, 2002.

O'Donnell, Peter and Holdaway, Jim. *Top Traitor*. London: Titan Books, 2004.

———. *Bad Suki*. London: Titan Books, 2005.

———. *Mister Sun*. London: Titan Books, 1985.

———. *The Black Pearl*. London: Titan Books, 2004.

———. *The Gabriel Set-Up*. London: Titan Books, 2004.

O'Donnell, Peter, Holdaway, Jim and Badia, Enric Romero. *The Hell Makers*. London: Titan Books, 2005.

O'Donnell, Peter and Romero, Enric Badia. *Cry Wolf*. London: Titan Books, 2006.

———. *The Gallows Bird*. London: Titan Books, 2007.

———. *The Green-Eyed Monster*. London: Titan Books, 2005.

———. *The Inca Trail*. London: Titan Books, 2007.

———. *The Puppet Master*. London: Titan Books, 2006.

O'Donnell, Peter. *A Taste For Death*. Great Britain: Souvenir Press, 2006.

———. *Cobra Trap*. Great Britain: Souvenir Press, 2006.

———. *Dragon's Claw*. Great Britain: Souvenir Press, 2006.

———. *I, Lucifer*. New York: Fawcett Crest, 1969.

———. *Last Day in Limbo*. Great Britain: Souvenir Press, 2002.

———. *Modesty Blaise*. Great Britain: Souvenir Press, 2005.

———. *Sabre-Tooth*. Great Britain: Souvenir Press, 2003.

———. *The Silver Mistress*. Great Britain: Souvenir Press, 2003.

———. "Girl Walking: The Real Modesty Blaise." *Crime Time*. Accessed online: http://www.crimetime.co.uk/features/modestyblaise.php

Oldenburg, Ann. "'Alias' Returns, Pregnant with Possibilities." *USA Today*. September 28, 2005. http://www.usatoday.com/life/television/news/2005-09-28-alias_x.htm

Oler, Tammy. "Gail Simone: DC's New Wonder Woman." *Geek Monthly*. pp. 87–9, November 2008.

O'Neil, Denny and Sekowsky, Mike. *Wonder Woman*. Issues 178–204, New York: DC Comics.

Pearson, Carol and Pope, Katherine. *The Female Hero in American and British Literature*. New York: R.R. Bowker Company, 1981.

Pohl-Weary, Emily, ed. *Girls Who Bite Back: Witches, Mutants, Slayers and Freaks*. Toronto: Sumach Press, 2004.

Poniewozik, James. "2020 Vision." *TIME*. Monday, October 2, 2000. Accessed online: http://www.time.com/time/magazine/article/0,9171,998083,00.html?promoid=googlep

Pulver, Andrew. "Friday Review: Little Things We Like: Modesty Blaise." *The Guardian*. London, UK, p. 23, June 25, 2004.

Reiss, Jana. *What Would Buffy Do? The Vampire Slayer as Spiritual Guide*. San Francisco: Jossey-Bass, 2004.

Reynolds, Richard. *Super Heroes: A Modern Mythology*. USA: University Press of Mississippi, 1994.

Richards, Peter. " 'Real, Ice, Man': Joseph Losey's Modesty Blaise." *Film Comment*. Vol. 31, Issue 4, p. 60, New York, July 1995.

Robbins, Trina. *From Girls to Grrrlz*. San Francisco: Chronicle Books, 1999.

———. *The Great Women Superheroes*. Northampton, MA: Kitchen Sink Press, 1996.

———. Letter to Alan Moore. "Imaginary Lines." *Promethea #3*. La Jolla, CA: America's Best Comics, October 1999.

———. "Lily Renee." *The Comics Journal*. Wednesday, November 20, 2006. Accessed online: http://www.tcj.com/index.php?option=com_content&task=view&id=466&Itemid=48

———. "Wonder Woman: Lesbian or Dyke?: Paradise Island as a Woman's Community." Originally presented at WisCon, May 2006. Accessed online: http://girl-wonder.org/papers/robbins.html

———. *Wonder Woman: The Once and Future Story*. New York: DC Comics, 1998.

———. Interview with author, February 22, 2008.

Robbins, Trina and Timmons, Anne. *Go Girl!* Oregon: Dark Horse Comics, 2002.

———. *Go Girl! The Time Team*. Oregon: Dark Horse Books, 2004.

———. *Go Girl! Robots Gone Wild*. Oregon: Dark Horse Books, 2006.

Robinson, Lillian S. *Wonder Women: Feminisms and Superheroes*. New York/London: Routledge, 2004.

Robinson, Tasha. "AV Club Interview with Peter Chung." April 30, 2003. http://www.avclub.com/content/node/22517

Rogers, Dave. *The Complete Avengers*. New York: St. Martin's Press, 1989.

Rooney, David. "Film Review: *D.E.B.S.*" *Variety*. Vol. 393, No. 10, p. 26, January 26–February 1, 2004.

Rosen, Lisa. "R.I.P. 'Buffy': You Drove a Stake Through Convention." *The Los Angeles Times*. May 20, 2003.

Rossen, Jake. *Superman vs. Hollywood: How Fiendish Producers, Devious Directors, and Warring Writers Ground an American Icon*. Chicago: Chicago Review Press, 2008.

Ross, Sharon. "Tough Enough: Female Friendship and Heroism in *Xena* and *Buffy*." in Inness, Sherrie A., ed. *Action Chicks: New Images of Tough Women in Popular Culture.* New York: Palgrave Macmillan, pp. 231–55, 2004.

Rucka, Greg and Amano, Yoshitaka. *Elektra/Wolverine: The Redeemer.* New York: Marvel Comics, 2002.

——. *The Hiketeia.* New York: DC Comics, 2002.

——. *Queen and Country: Operation Broken Ground.* Portland, OR: Oni Press, 2002.

Rucka, Greg and Leiber, Steve. *Whiteout: Vols. 1–2.* Portland, OR: Oni Press, 2007.

——. *Whiteout Vol. 2: Melt.* Portland, OR: Oni Press, 2007.

Ryan, Maureen. "Torchwood" Wraps Up a Fine Season as a New 'Doctor Who' Spinoff Debuts." *Chicago Tribune.* April 10, 2008. http://featuresblogs. chicagotribune.com/entertainment_tv/2008/04/if-they-met-i-w.html

Saba, Arn. "Kidder on Kidder." *Globe and Mail Weekend Magazine.* pp. 10–2, December 18, 1978.

Sanderson, Peter. "The Perfect Storm." *Back Issue.* No. 8, pp. 61–76, February 2005.

Saunders, Andy. *Jane: A Pin-Up at War.* Great Britain: Leo Cooper, 2004.

Schickel, Richard. "Help! They're Back!" *TIME.* Monday, July 28, 1986.

Schilling, Mary Kaye. "The Second Coming." *Entertainment Weekly.* New York, Issue 760, p. 24 (7 pages), April 16, 2004.

Schubart, Rikke. *Super Bitches and Action Babes: The Female Hero in Popular Cinema, 1970–2006.* Jefferson, North Carolina, and London: McFarland & Company, Inc. 2007.

Shanker, Wendy. "He Slays Me: An Interview with Joss Whedon." *BUST.* p. 68, winter 2000.

Siegel, Jerry and Shuster, Joe. *Superman Archives Vol. 1.* New York: DC Comics, 1989.

Silva, Horatio. "Heroine Chic." *New York Times* magazine. p. 74, spring 2003; National Newspapers (27).

Simone, Gail. *Birds of Prey: Of Like Minds.* New York: DC Comics, 2004.

——. *Birds of Prey: Sensei & Student.* New York: DC Comics, 2005.

——. *Birds of Prey: Between Dark & Dawn.* New York: DC Comics, 2006.

——. *Birds of Prey: The Battle Within.* New York: DC Comics, 2006.

——. *Birds of Prey: Perfect Pitch.* New York: DC Comics, 2007.

——. *Birds of Prey: Blood & Circuits.* New York: DC Comics, 2007.

———. *Birds of Prey: Dead of Winter.* New York: DC Comics, 2008.

———. *Wonder Woman: The Circle.* New York: DC Comics, 2008.

———. *Wonder Woman.* Issue 22, New York: DC Comics, September 2008.

———. *Wonder Woman.* Issue 23, New York: DC Comics, October 2008.

———. *Wonder Woman.* Issue 24, New York: DC Comics, November 2008.

———. *Wonder Woman.* Issue 25, New York: DC Comics, December 2008.

Sims, Yvonne D. *Women of Blaxploitation: How the Black Action Film Heroine Changed American Popular Culture.* North Carolina: McFarland, 2006.

Steinem, Gloria. *Wonder Woman.* USA: Holt, Rinehart and Winston, 1972.

———. "Introduction." in Walker, Rebecca, ed. *To Be Real: Telling the Truth and Changing the Face of Feminism.* New York: Anchor Books, Doubleday, 1995.

Strickland, Carol. "Truly, Modly, Deeply: The Diana Prince Era Issues 179–204." *Fanzing: The DC Comics Fan Site.* Issue 37, August 2001. http://www.fanzing.com/mag/fanzing37/feature7.shtml

Sturm, James. *The Fantastic Four Unstable Molecules: The True Story of Comics' Greatest Foursome.* New York: Marvel Comics, 2005.

Tasker, Yvonne. *Spectacular Bodies: Gender, Genre, and the Action Cinema.* London/New York: Routledge, 1993.

Taylor, Charles. "Mrs. Peel, We're Needed." *Salon.* August 17, 1998. Accessed online: http://www.salon.com/ent/movies/reviews/1998/08/17review.html

Terry, Paul. "There's Only One Sydney Bristow." *Alias: The Official Magazine.* Issue 17, pp. 10–15, September/October 2006.

———. "This One Has a Kick . . . Interview with Shauna Duggins." *Alias: The Official Magazine.* Issue 17, pp. 70–5, September/October 2006.

Timmons, Anne. Interview with author. June 2, 2008.

Thomas, Rob, ed. *Neptune Noir: Unauthorized Investigations into Veronica Mars.* Dallas, TX: Smart Pop Books/Benbella, 2006.

Travers, Peter. "*D.E.B.S.* Review." *Rolling Stone.* Issue 971, p. 79, New York, April 7, 2005.

Various. *Catwoman: Nine Lives of a Femme Fatale.* New York: DC Comics, 2004.

Various. *Superman: Daily Planet.* New York: DC Comics, 2006.

Vaz, Mark Cotta. *Alias Declassified: The Official Companion.* New York: Bantam Books, 2002.

Walker, Rebecca, ed. *To Be Real: Telling the Truth and Changing the Face of Feminism.* New York: Anchor Books, Doubleday, 1995.

Warner, Maria. *From the Beast to the Blonde: On Fairy Tales and Their Tellers.* New York: Farrar, Strauss and Giroux, 1994.

Warn, Sarah. *"D.E.B.S.* the Movie: Will the Lesbians Stay in the Picture?" *After Ellen.* June 2003. Accessed online: http://www.afterellen.com/archive/ellen/Movies/debs/picture.html

——. *"Buffy* to Show First Lesbian Sex Scene on Network TV." *After Ellen.* April 2003. Accessed online: http://www.afterellen.com/archive/ellen/TV/buffy-sex.html

Weinberg, Samantha. "Between the Covers: How I Became Miss Money-penny." *Times Online.* April 7, 2008. Accessed online: http://entertainment. timesonline.co.uk/tol/arts_and_entertainment/specials/for_your_eyes_only/article3684723.ece?print=yes&randnum=1210704618575

Weisman, Kevin and Yelleth, Glenn, eds. *Alias Assumed: Sex, Lies, and SD-6.* Dallas, TX: Smart Pop/Benbella, 2005.

Westbrook, Kate. *The Moneypenny Diaries: Guardian Angel.* Great Britain: John Murray, 2006.

——. *The Moneypenny Diaries: Secret Servant.* Great Britain: John Murray, 2006.

——. *The Moneypenny Diaries: Final Fling.* Great Britain: John Murray, 2008.

Whedon, Joss. *Fray.* Oregon: Dark Horse Books, 2003.

——. "Ace of Case." in *Entertainment Weekly.* Posted online October 7, 2005. Issues 844–5, October 14, 2005. http://www.ew.com/ew/article/0,,1114734,00.html.

——. "10 Questions for Joss Whedon." *The New York Times.* May 16, 2003.

Wilcox, Rhonda and Lavery, David, eds. *Fighting the Forces: What's at Stake in Buffy the Vampire Slayer.* Maryland: Rowman & Littlefield, 2002.

Wilcox, Rhonda. *Why Buffy Matters.* London/New York: I.B.Tauris, 2005.

Williams, J. P. "All's Fair in Love and Journalism: Female Rivalry in *Superman.*" *Journal of Popular Culture.* Vol. 24, No. 2, p. 103–12, fall 1990.

Willingham, Bill. *Robin.* Issue 126, New York: DC Comics, July 2004.

——. *Robin.* Issue 127. New York: DC Comics, August 2004.

——. *Robin.* Issue 128. New York: DC Comics, September 2004.

Wood, Susan. "The Poison Maiden and the Great Bitch: Female Stereotypes in Marvel Superhero Comics." San Bernardino, CA: The Borgo Press, 1989.

Woolf, Virginia. *A Room of One's Own.* USA: Harcourt Brace Jovanovich, 1989.

Wright, Leigh Adams. "Only Ourselves to Blame." in Weisman, Kevin and Yeffeth, Glenn, eds. *Alias Assumed: Sex, Lies, and SD-6*. Dallas, TX: Smart Pop/Benbella, 2005.

Filmography

(Specific television episodes are cited within chapter endnotes)

A Chinese Ghost Story. Director Siu-Tung Ching. Starring Leslie Cheung, Joey Wang, and Wu Ma. 1987.

The Adventures of Superman. Producer Whitney Ellsworth. Starring George Reeves, Phyllis Coates, Noel Neill, and Jack Larsen. 1952–8.

Aeon Flux (TV). Series created by Peter Chung. Starring Denise Poirier. 1991.

Aeon Flux (Movie). Director Karyn Kusama. Starring Charlize Theron, Frances McDormand, and Sophie Okonedo. 2005.

Alias. Series created by J. J. Abrams. Starring Jennifer Garner. 2001–6.

Aliens. Director James Cameron. Starring Sigourney Weaver, Michael Biehn, Jenette Goldstein, and Carrie Henn. 1986. (Special Edition DVD 1999).

"Aliens Unleashed." Featurette. *Aliens*. Collector's Edition DVD. 20th Century Fox. Released: January 6, 2004.

Angel. Series created by Joss Whedon. Starring David Boreanaz, Alexis Denisof, Charisma Carpenter, J. August Richards, Amy Acker, Andy Hallett, James Marsters, Stephanie Romanov, Julie Benz, and Mercedes McNab. 1999–2004.

The Avengers. Series created by Sydney Newman and Leonard White. Starring Patrick Macnee, Honor Blackman, Diana Rigg, and Linda Thorson. 1961–9.

Barbarella. Director Roger Vadim. Starring Jane Fonda. 1968.

Battlestar Galactica. Series created by Glen A. Larson. Starring Lorne Greene, Jane Seymour, Richard Hatch, Laurette Sprang, and Herbert Jefferson. 1978–9.

Battlestar Galactica. Series created by Ronald D. Moore. Starring Mary McDonnell, Katee Sackoff, Edward James Olmos, Tricia Helfer, and Grace Park. 2004–9.

"Beauty, Brawn, and Bulletproof Bracelets: A Wonder Woman Retrospective." Featurette included on *Wonder Woman* DVD. Released June 29, 2004.

"Biography Julie Newmar: The Cat's Meow." Writer Gidion Phillips, director Jeanne Begley. Original air date: September 6, 2000.

The Bionic Woman. Starring Lindsay Wagner and Richard Anderson.1976–8.

Birds of Prey. Series created by Laeta Kalogridis. Starring Dina Meyer, Ashley Scott, Shemar Moore, and Rachel Skarsten. 2002–3.

"Bond Girls Are Forever." Documentary. Writer John Watkin and Mayam d'Abo, director John Watkin. 2002. Updated version included as a special feature on the *Casino Royale* DVD. *Casino Royale.* Director Martin Campbell, writer Neal Purvis, Robert Wade, and Paul Haggis. Starring Daniel Craig and Eva Green. DVD. 2-Disc Widescreen Edition. Sony Pictures. Released: March 13, 2007.

Buffy, the Vampire Slayer. Series created by Joss Whedon. Starring Sarah Michelle Gellar, Alyson Hannigan, Anthony Head, James Marsters, Nicholas Brendon, Emma Caulfield, and Michelle Trachtenberg. 1997–2003.

Catwoman. Director Pitof. Starring Halle Berry. 2004.

Coffy. Director Jack Hill. Starring Pam Grier. 1973.

Conan the Barbarian. Director John Milius, writer John Milius and Oliver Stone. Starring Arnold Schwarzenegger and Sandahl Bergman. 1982. Collector's Edition DVD. Commentary with John Milius and Arnold Schwarzenegger. Universal Studios. Released: May 30, 2000.

Dark Angel. Series created by James Cameron and Charles Eglee. Starring Jessica Alba and Valarie Rae Miller. 2000–2.

D.E.B.S. Director Angela Robinson. Starring Jordana Brewster, Meagan Good, Devon Aoki, Jill Ritchie, and Sara Foster. 2004.

Die Another Day. Director Lee Tamahori. Starring Halle Berry. 2002.

The Doll Squad. Director Ted V. Mikels. Starring Francine York and Tura Satana. 1973.

Double Dare. Director Amanda Micheli. Starring Zoë Bell and Jeannie Epper. 2005.

Elektra. Director Rob Bowman. Starring Jennifer Garner and Kirsten Prout. 2005.

"Elektra Incarnations." Featurette. *Elektra.* Director's Cut—Two-Disc Collector's Edition. 20th Century Fox. Released: October 18, 2005.

Eureka. Series created by Andrew Cosby and Jaime Paglia. Starring Colin Ferguson, Salli Richardson, and Jordan Hinson. 2006–?.

Faster, Pussycat! Kill! Kill! Director Russ Meyer. Starring Tura Satana, Haji, and Lori Williams. 1965.

Firefly. Series created by Joss Whedon. Starring Nathan Fillion, Gina Torres, Jewel Staite, Summer Glau, Alan Tudyk, Morena Baccarin, Adam Baldwin, and Sean Maher. 2002–3.

Foxy Brown. Director Jack Hill. Starring Pam Grier. 1974.

Friday Foster. Director Arthur Marks. Starring Pam Grier. 1975.

Get Christie Love. Starring Teresa Graves. 1974–5.

Goldfinger. Director Guy Hamilton. Starring Sean Connery and Honor Blackman. 1964.

Grindhouse: Planet Terror. Director Robert Rodriguez. Starring Rose McGowan and Freddy Rodriguez. 2007.

Grindhouse: Death Proof. Director Quentin Tarantino. Starring Zoë Bell and Rosario Dawson. 2007.

The Heroic Trio. Director Johnny To. Starring Michelle Yeoh, Anita Mui, and Maggie Cheung. 1993.

Heroes. Series created by Tim Kring. Starring Hayden Panettiere, Jack Coleman, Sendhil Ramamurthy, Masi Oka, Ali Larter, Greg Grunberg, Zachary Quinto, Milo Ventimiglia, Adrian Pasdar, James Kyson Lee, Leonard Roberts, Kristen Bell, and Dana Davis. 2006–?.

Honey West. Series created by Aaron Spelling. Starring Anne Francis. 1964–5.

"Investigation: The History of Aeon Flux." Featurette. *Aeon Flux: The Complete Animated Collection.* Paramount/MTV. Released: November 22, 2005.

Kill Bill: Vol. 1 and 2. Director Quentin Tarantino. Starring Uma Thurman, Lucy Liu, Vivica Fox, and Daryl Hannah. 2003/2004.

Lady Snowblood. Director Toshiya Fujita. Starring Meiko Kaji. 1973.

La Femme Nikita. Director Luc Besson. Starring Anne Parillaud. 1990.

La Femme Nikita. Starring Peta Wilson. 1997–2001.

Lara Croft: Tomb Raider. Director Simon West. Starring Angelina Jolie. 2001.

Leon, The Professional. Director Luc Besson. Starring Natalie Portman and Jean Reno. 1994.

The Long Kiss Goodnight. Director Renny Harlin. Starring Geena Davis and Samuel Jackson. 1996.

The Matrix. Director Andy Wachowski and Larry Wachowski. Starring Keanu Reeves and Carrie-Anne Moss. 1999.

Modesty Blaise. Director Joseph Losey. Starring Monica Vitti, Terence Stamp, and Dirk Bogarde. 1966.

My Name Is Modesty: A Modesty Blaise Adventure. Director Scott Spiegel. Starring Alexandra Staten. 2003.

"Mythology vs. Xena." Featurette. *Xena Warrior Princess.* 10th Anniversary DVD Collection. DVD. Starz/Anchor Bay. Released: July 26, 2005.

Night of the Comet. Director Thom Eberhardt. Starring Catherine Mary Stewart and Kelli Maroney. 1984.

On Her Majesty's Secret Service. Director Peter R. Hunt. Starring Diana Rigg, George Lazenby, and Telly Savalas. 1969.

Powerpuff Girls. Series created by Craig McCracken. Starring Tara Strong, Cathy Cavadini, and Elizabeth Daily. 1998–2004.

Red Sonja. Director Robert Fleischer. Starring Brigitte Nielsen and Arnold Schwarzeneggar.1985.

"Relentless: The Making of *Elektra*, Part 1." Production Documentary. *Elektra.* Director's Cut—Two-Disc Collector's Edition. 20th Century Fox. Released: October 18, 2005.

"Revolutionizing a Classic: From Comic Book to Television - The Evolution of Wonder Woman from Page to Screen." Featurette included on *Wonder Woman* DVD. Released: March 1, 2005.

Sarah Connor Chronicles. Series created by Josh Friedman. Starring Lena Heady, Summer Glau, Thomas Dekker, and Richard T. Jones. 2008–?.

Sarah Jane Adventures. Series created by Russell T. Davies and Julie Gardner. Starring Elisabeth Sladen, Yasmin Paige, Tommy Knight, and Daniel Anthony. 2007–?.

Secrets of Isis, The. Series created by Filmation. Starring JoAnna Cameron and Brian Cutler.1975–6.

"Seeing Double." Featurette. *Xena Warrior Princess.* 10th Anniversary DVD Collection. DVD. Starz/Anchor Bay. Released: July 26, 2005.

Serenity. Director Joss Whedon. Starring Nathan Fillion, Gina Torres, Jewel Staite, Summer Glau, Alan Tudyk, Morena Baccarin, Adam Baldwin, and Sean Maher. 2005.

Showgirls. Director Paul Verhoeven, writer Joe Eszterhas. Starring Gina Gershon and Elizabeth Berkley. 1995. VIP Limited Edition DVD. Released: July 27, 2004. Commentary by David Schmader.

Smallville. Series created by Alfred Gough and Miles Millar. Starring Tom Wells, Alison Mack, and Erica Durance. 2001–?.

Spider-Man. Director Sam Raimi. Starring Toby McGuire and Kirsten Dunst. 2002.

Spider-Man 2. Director Sam Raimi. Starring Toby McGuire and Kirsten Dunst. 2004.

Star Trek (T.O.S.). Series created by Gene Roddenberry. Starring William Shatner, Leonard Nimoy, DeForest Kelly, Nichelle Nichols, and George Takei. 1966–9.

Star Wars: A New Hope. Director George Lucas. Starring Mark Hamill, Harrison Ford, and Carrie Fisher. 1977.

Star Wars: The Empire Strikes Back. Director Irvin Kershner. Starring Mark Hamill, Harrison Ford, and Carrie Fisher. 1980.

Star Wars: Return of the Jedi. Director Richard Marquand. Starring Mark Hamill, Harrison Ford, and Carrie Fisher. 1983.

The Complete Superman Cartoons—Diamond Anniversary Edition. Director Fleischer Studios. DVD. Image Entertainment. Released: August 1, 2000.

Supergirl. Director Jeannot Szwarc. Starring Helen Slater and Faye Dunaway. 1984. DVD. European Theatrical Version. Commentary by Jeannot Szwarc and Scott Bosco. Warner Home Video. Released: November 28, 2006.

"Superior Firepower 57 Years Later: Continuing the Story." Featurette. *Aliens.* Collector's Edition DVD. 20th Century Fox. Released: January 6, 2004.

Superman: The Movie. Director Richard Donner. Starring Margot Kidder and Christopher Reeve. 1978.

Superman II. Director Richard Lester. Starring Margot Kidder and Christopher Reeve. 1980.

Superman II: The Richard Donner Cut. Director Richard Donner. Starring Margot Kidder and Christopher Reeve. 2006.

Superman Returns. Director Bryan Singer. Starring Brandon Routh, Kate Bosworth, and Kevin Spacey. 2006.

"Taking Flight: The Development of Superman." Featurette. Director Michael Thau, writer Jonathon Gaines. *The Complete Superman Collection.* Warner Home Video. Released: May 1, 2001.

Terminator. Director James Cameron. Starring Linda Hamilton, Arnold Schwarzenegger, and Michael Biehn. 1984.

Terminator 2: Judgment Day. Director James Cameron. Starring Linda Hamilton, Arnold Schwarzenegger, and Edward Furlong. 1991. *T2* Extreme DVD (Special Edition DVD). Artisan Home Entertainment. Released: June 3, 2003.

Tin Man. Director Nick Willing. Starring Zooey Deschanel, Kathleen Robertson, Neal McDonough, Alan Cumming, and Raoul Trujillo. 2007.

Trekkies. Director Roger Nygard. Starring Denise Crosby. 1997.

"Two Orphans: Sigourney Weaver and Carrie Henn." Featurette. *Aliens.* Collector's Edition DVD. 20th Century Fox. Released: January 6, 2004.

"Ultimate Super Heroes, Villains, and Vixens." Documentary. Writer Gary Simonson and Steven Smith. Prometheus Entertainment, Fox Television Studios and Bravo. Aired on Bravo May 27, 2005.

Veronica Mars. Series created by Rob Thomas. Starring Kristen Bell and Enrico Colantoni. 2004–7.

Wonder Woman. Series created by Douglas S. Cramer. Starring Lynda Carter. 1976–9.

"Xena's Hong Kong Origins." Featurette. *Xena Warrior Princess.* 10th Anniversary DVD Collection. DVD. Starz/Anchor Bay. Released: July 26, 2005.

Xena, Warrior Princess. Series created by Rob Talpert. Starring Lucy Lawless and Renee O'Connor. 1995–2001.

The X-Files. Series created by Chris Carter. Starring Gillian Anderson and David Duchovny. 1993–2002.

The X-Files: Fight the Future. Director Rob Bowman. Starring Gillian Anderson and David Duchovny. 1998.

The X-Men. Director Bryan Singer. Starring Patrick Stewart, Ian McKellan, Famke Janssen, and Hugh Jackman. 2000.

X-Men 2. Director Bryan Singer. Starring Patrick Stewart, Ian McKellan, and Famke Janssen. 2003.

The X-Men: The Last Stand. Starring Patrick Stewart, Ian McKellan, Famke Janssen, and Halle Berry. 2006.

Internet Sources

After Ellen http://www.afterellen.com/

All Things Philosophical on Buffy the Vampire Slayer and Angel: The Series http://www.atpobtvs.com

The Amazon Connection
  http://folk.uio.no/thomas/lists/amazon-connection.html

Avengers Illustrated http://wingedavenger.theavengers.tv/sitemap.htm

Bitch magazine http://bitchmagazine.org/

Cult Sirens http://www.cultsirens.com/

Don Markstein's Toonpedia http://www.toonopedia.com/

Friends of Lulu http://friends-lulu.org/

The Geena Davis Institute on Gender in Media
http://www.thegeenadavisinstitute.org/

Girl Wonder http://girl-wonder.org/index.php

Heroine Content http://www.heroinecontent.net/

Ink-stained Amazon http://www.ink-stainedamazon.com/blog/isablog.html

Modesty Blaise Entry http://www.toonopedia.com/modesty.htm

Modesty Blaise Page http://www.cs.umu.se/~kenth/modesty.html

Original Avengers http://www.originalavengers.com/home.html

Power Up http://www.power-up.net

Prism Comics http://prismcomics.org/

Redboots http://www.redboots.net/

Retro Crush http://retrocrush.buzznet.com/

Sequential Tart http://www.sequentialtart.com/

Slayage http://slayageonline.com/

Tart City http://www.tartcity.com/modesty.html

The Avengers Forever http://theavengers.tv/forever/

The Complete Modesty Blaise Dossier
http://www3.sympatico.ca/jim.pattison/modesty/

The Lost Characters of Frank Hampson
http://www.frankhampson.co.uk/modesty.php

The Modesty Blaise Book Covers http://modestyblaise.greboguru.org/all/all.htm

The Modesty Blaise Companion
http://www.modestyblaisecompanion.com/index.htm

Whedonesque http://whedonesque.com/

Whoosh! http://www.whoosh.org/

Women in Media and News http://www.wimnonline.org/

Women in Refrigerators http://www.unheardtaunts.com/wir/

War, Women, and Opportunity http://www.loc.gov/exhibits/wcf/wcf0001.html

Author Recommendations

The following recommendations may or may not be deemed "feminist"—I leave that to the reader's interpretation. But to me, whether they are good, bad, feminist, or intriguing but problematic, they represent some of the more interesting representations of female heroes in modern mythology. Some were explored in the book, some weren't, but I leave them here for your consideration.

Books/Comics

L. Frank Baum, *The Wizard of Oz*

Marion Zimmer Bradley, *The Mists of Avalon*

Chris Claremont, *The Uncanny X-Men: The Dark Phoenix Saga, The Uncanny X-Men: From the Ashes*

Peter O'Donnell, *Modesty Blaise* (strip run, as well as novels)

Linda Fite and Marie Severin, *The Claws of the Cat*

Ian Fleming, *The Spy Who Loved Me*

Astrid Lindgren, *Pippi Longstocking*

Alan Moore, *Promethea*

Charles Moulton, *Wonder Woman*

Trina Robbins, *Wonder Woman: The Once and Future Story*

Trina Robbins and Anne Timmons, *Go Girl!*

Greg Rucka, *Elektra/Wolverine: Redeemer, Queen & Country, Whiteout, Wonder Woman: The Hiketeia*

Gail Simone, *Birds of Prey, Wonder Woman*

James Sturm, *Unstable Molecules*

Kate Westbrook, *The Moneypenny Diaries*

Joss Whedon, *Fray*

Movies

Aeon Flux (2005)

Aliens (1986)

Coffy (1973)

Conan the Barbarian (1982)

D.E.B.S. (2003/2004)

The Doll Squad (1973)

Double Dare (2004)

Faster, Pussycat! Kill! Kill! (1965)

Get Christie Love (1974)

Grindhouse (2007)

Kill Bill, Vols. 1 and 2 (2003/2004)

Night of the Comet (1984)

Superman II: The Richard Donner Cut (2006)

Terminator: T2 Judgment Day (1991)

TV Shows

Alias (2001–6)

The Avengers (1961–9)

Bionic Woman (1976–8)

Buffy, the Vampire Slayer (1997–2002)

Dark Angel (2002–4)

Firefly (2002–3)

Futurama (1999–2003; 2008–?)

Heroes (2006–?)

Honey West (1965–6)

Sarah Conner Chronicles (2007–?)

Sarah Jane Adventures (2007–?)

The X-Files (1993–2002)

Veronica Mars (2004–7)

Wonder Woman (1976–9)

Xena, Warrior Princess (1995–2001)

Internet Resources

The Amazon Connection: a guide to online resources about Amazons in ancient and modern myth.
http://folk.uio.no/thomas/lists/amazon-connection.html

Bitch magazine: media commentary from a feminist perspective.
http://bitchmagazine.org/

Friends of Lulu: national organization whose main purpose is to promote and encourage female readership and participation in the comic book industry.
http://friends-lulu.org/

The Geena Davis Institute on Gender in Media: a nonprofit organization that researches and brings awareness to gender in children's entertainment.
http://www.thegeenadavisinstitute.org/

Girl Wonder: a collection of sites dedicated to female characters and creators in mainstream comics.
http://girl-wonder.org/index.php

Heroine Content: investigates depictions of gender and race in the female hero.
http://www.heroinecontent.net/

Ink-stained Amazon: feminist commentary, analysis, and critique of popular culture.
http://www.ink-stainedamazon.com/blog/isablog.html

Prism Comics: a nonprofit organization that supports lesbian, gay, bisexual, and transgendered (LGBT) comics, creators, and readers.
http://prismcomics.org/

Redboots: a Superman and Lois and Clark reference site.
http://www.redboots.net/

Sequential Tart: a webzine about the comics industry.
http://www.sequentialtart.com/

Slayage: the Online International Journal of Buffy Studies.
http://slayageonline.com/

Whedonesque: a Joss Whedon weblog.
http://whedonesque.com/

Whoosh!: birthplace of Xena Studies.
http://www.whoosh.org/

Women in Media and News: a media analysis, education, and advocacy group that works to increase women's presence and power in the public debate.
http://www.wimnonline.org/

Women in Refrigerators: a list originally compiled by Gail Simone of superheroines who had been grossly treated in mainstream comics.
http://www.unheardtaunts.com/wir/

Events

Comic Arts Conference: a conference designed to bring together comics scholars, practitioners, critics, and historians who want to be involved in the dynamic process of evolving an aesthetic and a criticism of the comics art form.
http://fac.hsu.edu/duncanr/cac_page.htm

San Diego Comic Con International.
http://www.comic-con.org/

Slayage Conference on the Whedonverses.
http://slayageonline.com/SC3/index.htm

WisCon: the first and foremost feminist science fiction convention in the world, held yearly in Wisconsin.
http://www.wiscon.info/

WW Day: an annual charity benefit for domestic violence shelters and celebratory event held in Portland, Oregon, and organized by writer Andy Mangels, who is also the curator of the online Wonder Woman Museum.
http://www.wonderwomanmuseum.com/WWDay2/WWDay2.html

Index